Rather Outspoken

MY LIFE IN THE NEWS

DAN RATHER

with

DIGBY DIEHL

GRAND CENTRAL
PUBLISHING

NEW YORK   BOSTON

Grand Central Publishing
Hachette Book Group
237 Park Avenue
New York, NY 10017

www.HachetteBookGroup.com

Printed in the United States of America

RRD-C

First Edition: May 2012

10   9   8   7   6   5   4   3   2   1

Grand Central Publishing is a division of Hachette Book Group, Inc.
The Grand Central Publishing name and logo is a trademark of Hachette Book Group, Inc.

The Hachette Speakers Bureau provides a wide range of authors for speaking events. To find out more, go to www.hachettespeakersbureau.com or call (866) 376-6591.

The publisher is not responsible for websites (or their content) that are not owned by the publisher.

Library of Congress Cataloging-in-Publication Data
Rather, Dan.
    Rather outspoken : my life in the news / Dan Rather. — 1st ed.
        p. cm.
    ISBN 978-1-4555-0241-7 (regular edition) — ISBN 978-1-4555-1346-8 (large print edition)
1. Rather, Dan.   2. Television journalists—United States—Biography.   I. Title.
PN4874.R28A3 2012
070.92—dc23
    [B]
                        2011052227

Dedication

How do you thank a lifetime of kindness, generosity and love in the dedication to a book? Well, I don't think you can. But I want to try.

To the Princess of Pin Oak Creek, fighting heart Jeannie Grace Goebel Rather—now my wife of 55 years. To her, a good-hearted woman in love with a too often wrongheaded man, this book is owed—as is just about every good and decent thing I have ever done in my adult life.

The pride of Winchester, Texas, she is both the prettiest and smartest girl ever to come out of at least that part of the state. Born at home there where the hardwood meets the pine along the banks of the Colorado River, her early school years were in a little one-room schoolhouse. She is the only woman I know who began in a one-room country school and grew up to conquer Washington, London and New York—not to mention Houston, Dallas and New Orleans. And she did it while being an ideal wife (far better than I deserved) and the mother of two wonderful, well-adjusted children. All the while she also determinedly pursued her childhood dream of being an accomplished artist. She became one—a painter whose works have sold in galleries in New York, Los Angeles and elsewhere.

She is descended from Lone Star pioneer women who helped stave off Indian raids and then beat out cabin fires with their husbands' bloody shirts. She came not from wealth or privilege—her family had little land and was not of the archetypical cattle-herding sort. She learned early how to pick cotton, how to milk a cow and how to wring a chicken's neck for Sunday dinner.

Jean is in some ways a walking contradiction: patent leather outside but rawhide underneath. If you want to see her eyes narrow and the veins in her neck pulse, just try threatening her children or grandchildren. Or her home and hearth in any way. (She'll give me hell in private when she thinks I've done wrong, but doesn't take kindly to anyone treating her man unfairly.)

Gentle and kind by nature, in every storm of life she is oak and iron. Or, to paraphrase what the late Eric Sevareid once said in another context, she's the kind of woman you wouldn't be afraid to have your back on a tiger hunt. I still marvel at how lucky I am.

Contents

Rather Outspoken

PROLOGUE

Alone

Come to the edge, he said.
They said: We are afraid.
Come to the edge, he said.
They came.
He pushed them ... and they flew.
APOLLINAIRE

It's a Friday evening in New York in the early spring of 2006. I'm in my combined *60 Minutes* and *60 Minutes II* office at 555 West 57th, across the street from the old renovated milk barn that has been CBS News world headquarters for many years. Out the window is a glorious view of the Hudson River, the view stretching across the river and into the trees and rocks of New Jersey.

There's nobody else around. It is quiet as a tomb, and my mind begins to wander: a kaleidoscope of thoughts. There are smiles, worries and concerns, and flashes of the past. I've been a professional journalist, a reporter, for 60 years, 44 of them at CBS News, 24 of them as anchor and managing editor of the *CBS Evening News*—the network's flagship broadcast. They called it "being the face and the voice" of CBS's storied

News Division. With the exception of Britain's BBC, it was the best known and most honored broadcast news operation in the world.

But that's all in the past. As "the face and voice of CBS News," Edward R. Murrow is long gone. So is Walter Cronkite. And so am I. This was supposed to be a new beginning for me, but it is feeling very much like the beginning of the end. At least at CBS.

I almost desperately don't want it to be. I am still hoping against hope that somehow, someway, things will work out and I can stay. In denial? Well, I don't think so. But time and the tides are running in that direction.

An old friend who, like me, grew up working in the oilfields and refineries of the Texas Gulf Coast as the son of an oilfield hand had called a short while earlier. He's been retired for a few years and called just to touch base, tell a few jokes and in general be support-ive and encouraging.

"Rags," he finally said, using my father's nickname that had been passed on to me in my youth. "You don't want to face it, I know. But you're finished there. They have decided to scapegoat you, throw you to the wolves and be rid of you. They're doing it to save themselves. It ain't fair or right, but it's what is. And the sooner you recognize it and deal with it, the better off you're going to be."

He went on to say some overcomplimentary things about "what a great reporter you've been...best of your time and one of the best ever...who's given CBS News some of the best years they've ever had," and so on. That kind of thing. But by this time, I had tuned him pretty much out. My mind was racing and wandering.

To hell with this, I was thinking. He's a friend, naturally he's going to say those things. He means well, and I appreciate it. More than he can know. He's trying to be helpful. But I know my weaknesses and strengths. This includes knowing, really knowing down deep, that I had wanted since childhood to do extended great reporting, work that might stand with the best of my time, if not the best ever. And I had not achieved that. Not nearly. Not yet. This is not false humility. It's not humility of any kind. It's how I genuinely feel.

What I felt at this moment was that in the dream of doing the kind of reporting that I like best and believe I do best—big breaking news, international stories including covering war zones and deep-digging investigative journalism—CBS News was the best place to be. By far. I loved the place, loved the people and loved what CBS represented: an institution—not just a great corporation, but an institution important to the country and to the cause of press freedom everywhere.

That last part may strike some people as overstated. It never struck me that way. About that, I was a true believer.

I also loved the history and tradition of the place, which I knew well. There may well have been (probably have been) better, much better CBS News correspondents than I over the years, but there's never been one who knew the history of the place better. I also loved the lore, the mythology and high sense of mission exuded by the CBS I had known. I loved it all when I was a young reporter just breaking in with the network. And I loved it even more now that I was an older man. I was now 74, and age had given me an even greater appreciation of how lucky I was to have spent most of my career at CBS.

But age also had given me perspective. Try as I had, and I had tried hard—I gave it everything I knew how—I knew within myself that the dream of doing sustained great work, work that would be recognized as truly important and a service to my country, was not completed.

Sure, I've had my good days—big interviews, world-class exclusive stories, breaking news and long, good reporting runs on big stories and the like. But I also know how often I've failed, haven't been as good as I could have, should have been. And a body, a lifetime, of great journalistic work? No, not yet. I'm working on it though, still striving, still trying, still determined, still chasing the childhood dream. And I want to do it here at CBS News—my home for most of my professional life.

"Never, never, ever give up," I was thinking as my old Texas friend's voice tailed off. (My father had quoted Winston Churchill's famous line so often that it had become rote to me long ago.)

And besides, I was thinking, I know this business and I know these people, the people of CBS News. And the people at the top of CBS corporate. We have, almost literally, been to hell and back together over the years, through good times and bad, through sunshine and storms. I trust them and they trust me. This trust has been tested time and again. It's been forged to strong steel in hot fires, past and present, over nearly half a century. We'll find a way to work it out. If nothing else, we will just will it to happen.

Was it hubris? Naïveté? Did I have my head in the sand? Looking back on it, maybe some or all of that. But I didn't think so at the time.

What I did think, what I knew, was that I was feeling deeply troubled. Among the things troubling me most (and there were a lot of things) was that some longtime colleagues at CBS had turned against me. Some of these people I had considered to be friends. Some were people whom I had hired, mentored, promoted and/or helped in various ways professionally. Fair to say that some of them had helped me along the way, too. Helped a lot. Couldn't have, wouldn't have done it without their help.

On the other hand, some good friends were standing tall and standing by me. And there were other people whom I didn't know well who did the same. I shouldn't have been surprised. It's an old story: When the heat's on and you need someone to stand with you, those who you most expect will don't, and those who you least expect do. But surprised I was, by those who did and by those who didn't.

The worst were those who, after pretending to be friends for all those years, stealthily snuck around giving anonymous newspaper quotes and otherwise scheming to put the dirk in deep when I was down and hurting.

One of them, a veteran news executive who was one of the most publicly lauded men in the craft and for whom I had worked since first coming to CBS, made a series of secret telephone calls to newspaper writers lambasting me personally and professionally—all under the cover of "don't use my name," of course.

But, hey, I said to myself, this is the big time; you've been privileged to play the game at the top for a long while. These are the major leagues: Envy, cowardice and betrayal are part of life. Stuff happens, and people will always surprise you; take it for what you can learn from it and take it like a man, like a pro. And just keep on keeping on. Which is what I was trying to do.

They pushed me out, but before I knew it, I was flying again.

CHAPTER 1

Abu Ghraib

Why was I out at CBS? Because I reported a true story. The story I reported in September 2004 of President George W. Bush's dereliction of duty during Vietnam is true, and neither Bush himself nor anyone close to him—no family member, no confidante, no political ally—has ever denied it. I remain proud of reporting that truth, and proud of the many people who were part of that report.

Looking back and reflecting on it, if shining a light on Bush's unexplained absence during his stint in the Texas Air National Guard was the story that got me pushed out of CBS, the first strong indication of trouble had come four months earlier, over a story I reported on *60 Minutes II* in April 2004. As a journalist, my core principle—my duty—has always been to get to the truth. This, however, was a story nobody wanted to be true: the story of how some American military personnel were humiliating, abusing and torturing Iraqi detainees at Abu Ghraib prison.

The duties of a journalist, however, do not stop with uncovering the truth. Absent compelling reasons of national security—which is very different from political embarrassment (at least it should be)—journalists also have a responsibility to inform the public about the truths they discover. And my determination to fulfill this obligation about Abu Ghraib became a very big problem (and, I suspect, a political embarrassment) for the management of CBS and for its corporate parent, Viacom.

At the height of the Iraq war, I was a frequent flyer to Baghdad. From the war's beginning in March 2003 to March 2004, I'd been there at least four times. On one of the early visits, I learned that the prison known as Abu Ghraib had been taken over by the U.S. Army. Refurbished and redubbed the Baghdad Central Correctional Facility, by the fall of 2003 it was being used to house those we had taken prisoner. The inmates were a mixed lot—some common criminals, some folks who were just in the wrong place at the wrong time and some considered to be "high value" prisoners suspected of leading the insurgency or participating in terrorist activities.

The name change didn't alter its reputation. Whatever you called it, Abu Ghraib was notorious. Under Saddam Hussein, it had been feared by all as a chamber of horrors, a gulag, if you will. Prisoners were maimed, raped and tortured. Many were also murdered, or at least presumed murdered. After being incarcerated there, they had vanished without a trace. The prison was trashed and looted by the Iraqis themselves during our invasion; Americans who had seen the interior immediately after our soldiers took Baghdad reported gruesome scenes of bodies mauled by dogs and electrodes coming out of the walls. Eventually, we would recover videotape shot by U.S. troops on the day they entered the prison. The tape showed squalor, filth and an incredibly unsafe area for American soldiers to be living, but this is where they were housed while they worked to rebuild and reclaim the facility for use by the U.S. military.

I had a more personal connection to Abu Ghraib as well. During the Gulf War in the early 1990s, Saddam's forces had captured one of our CBS correspondents, an outstanding journalist named Bob Simon. Bob and I have been friends and colleagues for more than 35 years. He is one of the best, most experienced foreign correspondents of his generation. A graduate of Brandeis University, he is brilliant, analytical and a swift, sure writer. And he has guts. His bravery is legendary among his peers. He could have held his own with the Murrow Boys of World War II. Bob and I had been in many of the same bad datelines and tight places—often at the same time—over the years: Vietnam, Lebanon, Gaza, the West Bank, Baghdad and others. He is, as many of the best foreign correspondents are, a bit of a loner, but every inch a gentleman and a scholar. He's generous, compassionate and friendly, loyal and protective of those who work with him and for him (especially camera crews, technicians and producers in the field). But he leans toward being taciturn, doesn't always talk a lot and stays to himself and within himself—more than most people in television news.

Bob was held prisoner for 40 days, and for part of that time he was in Abu Ghraib. We feared greatly for his safety. All of us at CBS worked every contact we had around the world to get him released. I was one of several who spoke with former secretary of state Henry Kissinger, asking him to intercede. Whatever else you may think of Kissinger, his involvement finally set Bob free.

On several of my trips to Baghdad, I had asked about the "new, improved" Abu Ghraib, and it always seemed curious to me that everyone made an extraordinary effort to be unresponsive, if not downright evasive. It was as if they wanted to keep what was going on there a secret. I found this odd, since it was being touted as a showplace of a modern correctional facility as part of its image makeover. Brigadier General Janis Karpinski, who oversaw Abu Ghraib (as well as 14 other prisons and detention centers in Iraq), had given Secretary of Defense Donald Rumsfeld a photo-op tour of the facility in September 2003, pointing out the newly installed ceiling fans, toilets, showers and medical center. In October, she assured *60 Minutes* correspondent Steve Kroft that those interned in Abu Ghraib were receiving "the best care available." At about the same time, President Bush trumpeted to supporters at a Republican Party gala that Iraq was now "free of rape rooms and torture chambers." Two months later, General Karpinski told the *St. Petersburg Times* that "living conditions now are better in prison than at home. At one point we were concerned they [the prisoners] wouldn't want to leave."

Given all the hoopla, I found it peculiar that when I asked to visit the prison, I was told in no uncertain terms to forget about it. I made a mental note but wasn't able to follow up at the time. Then, in late 2003, an Iraqi I had known for more than a decade approached me. "Mr. Rather," he said, "you really ought to do something about Abu Ghraib. Bad things are going on there." I made another mental note, but time pressures forced me to put the matter aside.

There is a time-honored saying in management: "When you start an enterprise, pick eagles. Then teach them to fly in formation." At 60 Minutes II, Mary Mapes was one of our very best eagles. She was head of the unit under me and was ever so capable in multiple roles—lead reporter, writer, investigator, producer. She had a great nose for a story and was outstanding under the pressure of writing against deadline. Working with her was another eagle, an associate producer named Dana Roberson. At CBS then and at HDNet now, one of Dana's jobs when she's not on deadline is to make phone calls to develop and culti-vate long-term sources. That means staying in touch with people who have helped you in the past, just in case they come across something again. Anyone who's worked with me will tell you that I'm a telephone person (as contrasted with an e-mail person, which I surely am not). It may be old-fashioned, but I'm a believer in working your Rolodex and getting in touch with people by phone. "Hi, Dan Rather here. Just checking in. Anything going on I should know about?"

Over the years, I had cultivated a network of contacts about Iraq, both here in the States and in the Middle East. Dana and Mary had, of course, developed their own. One of Dana's contacts was a well-connected source in the U.S.-led Iraq operation with whom she had built up an excellent rapport.

Early in 2004 he called to tell her he had something that could become "the mother of all stories." He laid out the story of a number of U.S. soldiers who had been arrested and charged with prisoner abuse. That past January there had been a bland press release from Central Command (CENTCOM) announcing that an official investigation was under way, but Dana's source suggested that it had mushroomed into something much larger. After hearing what he had to say, Mary, Dana and I all realized it was likely that there was an even more explosive story behind these allegations. There was strong evidence that the acts of abuse that these enlisted men and noncommissioned officers were accused of committing had been undertaken in response to orders from higher up the chain of command. In other words, the U.S. Department of Defense was encouraging the mistreatment and perhaps torturing of prisoners.

Dana's persistence with her sources had led to a tip on a major story. This is the way good reporters work, and Dana was good. She had just proven it once again. Mary and Dana flew out to meet with our source, who confirmed what he had said on the phone. Not only was there widespread prisoner abuse at Abu Ghraib, but there were photographs. Lots of photographs. He couldn't actually give them the pictures, nor could he specifically name names. What he did do, however, was give Mary and Dana a nugget of information that led to some clues about how to dig deeper into the story. He hinted that they should look into the rotation of units that had been assigned to Abu Ghraib. He indicated that the soldiers who had been arrested all belonged to the same unit. Their unit had now been rotated stateside, but the soldiers facing charges had been left behind in Baghdad.

After Dana and Mary brought this new information to me, we started pursuing it relentlessly. Mary began contacting her own sources. Dana started reaching out to more of her contacts. I spread out with mine. Early in March 2004, I actually went to Abu Ghraib, at least to the exterior. It was an incredible scene at the gate—hundreds, maybe thousands of people were outside, desperately holding up photos and clamoring for information about loved ones who had been incarcerated. I spoke with some of them, but my request for an interview with General Karpinski was stonewalled by her office, and no, I couldn't get a tour of the prison, either. Now my journalistic antennae were really starting to twitch.

The clues from the source were helpful, which didn't mean it was easy. Roger Charles, our military consultant, was involved in the investigation from the beginning. As a retired U.S. Marine colonel, Roger knew the ins and outs of tracking unit movement in any branch of the armed forces. In the beginning it was like looking for a needle in a haystack, but by tracking the assignments of various units that had recently served at the prison, we were able to start eliminating some units and targeting others.

We started with a huge circle of possibilities and began to draw the circle tighter and tighter. Mary, Dana and Roger stalked the Internet; if a given unit was within the time frame and area of assignment, they looked up everybody whose name they could find, tracked them down and asked them about arrests or abuse or any soldiers from the unit who had not come home with the rest of their team.

At first, progress was agonizingly slow. There were many dead ends, but we were able to glean just enough bits of information to keep us going. We were a long way from having the whole story, but we were getting more and more signs that there *was* a story, and a big one.

In addition to knowing how to track particular units, Roger Charles had great ideas about how to reach out to their individual members. Almost every unit that had come home from Iraq had its own website, a place where friends could post comments—a place where we could troll for names to contact about possible arrests, etc. Eventually this technique allowed Roger, Mary and Dana to narrow the search down to a single unit. The times and dates all matched up—it absolutely had to be the one. And they kept getting a sort of backhanded confirmation that they were right—whenever they called to various members of the unit, they were hung up on, led astray, lied to or cussed out. For a reporter, that's always a sign that you're on the right track. A few people fessed up that some soldiers had not come home with the rest of the unit because there had been a "problem."

As Mary reported in her excellent book *Truth and Duty,* our first big break came in late March after she put the word out on a website called Soldiers for the Truth (which has now become Stand for the Troops, sftt.org), looking for anyone willing to come forward with more information. Established by Colonel David Hackworth, Soldiers for the Truth was a resource for men and women on active duty in the armed services. Still is. Its primary mission is to ensure that troops get high-quality combat gear, such as body armor and helmets, but it also functions as a powerful, instantaneous information exchange.

Roger Charles had suggested this approach as a way to reach out to family members of soldiers in the unit. We were looking for someone—anyone—willing to speak with us. At the time, we had no names of individuals, only the name of the unit. What we did know is that we couldn't go through official military channels. That would only alert them that we were working on the story, which would cause them to choke off any further access to information.

Within a day, a man named Bill Lawson responded to Mary's query. His nephew, Staff Sergeant Ivan "Chip" Frederick, an Army reservist, had been a guard at Abu Ghraib. In January 2004, he'd been one of the first to be interrogated as part of the Army's official investigation. In March, the rest of his unit had returned to the States, but Frederick was still in Baghdad, pretty much under house arrest, awaiting court martial on multiple counts of prisoner abuse. Lawson was afraid that the Army was gearing up to let the little guys at Abu Ghraib—the enlisted men and noncoms who served as MPs—take the fall for abuse that the higher-ups had not only condoned but encouraged or even requested... soldiers like his nephew Chip.

Lawson had found his way to Hackworth's website because he'd been casting an ever-wider net in his effort to reach out to anyone he thought might help. He had been trying desperately to publicize Chip's plight by getting someone's attention in government, both in the military and in Congress. He wrote to countless congressmen and Army officials. He had even contacted Bill O'Reilly and the Red Cross, but apparently no one had responded.

Mary, Dana and I went into overdrive. There wasn't a moment to lose. Through Lawson, a telephone interview with Chip Frederick was quickly arranged. Although he was being detained in Baghdad, he still was afforded the privilege of speaking with family at home. Family, of course, did not include CBS News. If the military got wind that he was talking to us, he'd be put in lockdown.

To help maintain the cover, we set up the call from Chip Frederick not to New York, but to my home in Austin, Texas. Cameras were arranged. Mary and I juggled our schedules to get there; I spoke with Frederick by phone on March 25. He admitted his participation in the abuse. Perhaps more important, he also laid out a shocking and chaotic scenario of conditions within the prison. Security was lax; he'd been shot at within the confines of Abu Ghraib, and the rounds had come from *inside* a cell. The prison was overcrowded and understaffed. There were too many prisoners, too few guards. Perhaps worst of all, there was little if any direction from the top. "We had no support, no training whatsoever," Frederick told me. "I kept asking my chain of command for certain things, like rules and regulations, and it just wasn't happening." He indicated that he had not seen a copy of the Geneva Convention until *after* he'd been charged with prisoner abuse.

Frederick volunteered that the Army was not the only American presence in Abu Ghraib. Representatives of OGAs (other governmental agencies), as well as civilian defense contractors were present, and these individuals, not soldiers, had taken the lead in prisoner interrogation. "We had military intelligence, we had all kinds of other governmental agencies, FBI, CIA...that I didn't even know or recognize," he said. Frederick also told me that he and others had been explicitly encouraged, particularly by those in the OGAs, to go beyond what was customarily expected of prison guards and had even been commended by military intelligence for their help in "softening up" prisoners in advance of their interrogation. "We've had a very high rate with our style of getting them to break," he told me with a hint of pride.

Frederick indicated that at least one prisoner had died during questioning. He believed that the man had been beaten while under interrogation by men from an OGA—CIA operatives, Frederick thought. Fearing a riot, guards had smuggled the corpse out of Abu Ghraib on a gurney, an IV placed in the lifeless arm, to mislead other prisoners into believing he was still alive. For an extra dose of "reality," they had administered heart compressions—CPR—to the dead man until they were out of the compound.

When he said this, the horrified look on Mary's face said it all. The look on my face said nothing whatsoever. It couldn't—I was on camera, and I had to rein in my dismay. It was by no means easy, but I had to maintain my poker face. Because this would likely be his last chance to speak publicly about what had happened without military censorship, I had to continue to draw information out of Chip Frederick—without letting on that this was huge.

But huge it was, and once the interview was concluded, Mary and I retreated to a nearby restaurant to talk it over. Rosie's Tamale House, on the outskirts of Austin, is one of my favorite haunts. Before getting a table, we headed down Highway 71 to the closest gas-and-shop for some beer—after that interview, both of us wanted something a little stronger than our usual iced sun tea and Diet Dr Pepper. (Rosie's doesn't serve alcohol, but you're allowed to bring your own—at least, if you know her well.)

Once inside the family-friendly retreat that is Rosie's, both of us exhaled deeply. We were a bit shell-shocked by Frederick's revelations. Over a cold beer—or two—and a hot tamale—or two—we tried to make sense of it.

"So it's true," I said. "I wish it were not, but it is. And it's a lot worse than we thought. This is one helluva story."

Mary stared into the bubbles in her beer. "Yeah."

"This one will be trouble with a capital 'T,'" I continued. "A lot of people are not going to believe this, and many of them who do won't really want to hear it."

"Soooo…" Mary left the word hanging in the air, putting it on me to finish the sentence. She was trying to gauge whether I was willing to go forward, knowing the major blowback that was sure to follow if we did.

"So…So this is what we in journalism are supposed to do," I said simply.

Mary just nodded. I doubt whether my response surprised her in the slightest. "If it were easy," I continued, "everyone would be doing it. You and I both know that none of us do it often enough."

"Gut check," she replied softly.

Gut check indeed. We both knew that nobody handles a story like this and comes out unscathed. The gut check comes in when you ask yourself whether you're willing to pay the price for uncovering the truth. I heard the refrain in my brain: "Do this kind of work and there's always a price to be paid. Except you can't know—until the story is out there—what the price will be."

I'd had any number of conversations like this over the years, going all the way back to my days as a reporter just starting out in Huntsville, Texas. Sometimes these conversations were with myself; most times they were with colleagues. They were always over stories that mattered, stories where the choices I made changed the outcome and also changed me, both as a journalist and as a human being. The first was a racially charged high-profile murder case. The second was coverage of Martin Luther King and the early stages of the civil rights movement. And, much later, there was Watergate.

All of these gut check debates had ended the same way: What mattered was getting to the truth, or as close to the truth as humanly possible. The public's right to know—*our* right to know—what was being done in our name, in our country's name, was paramount.

Despite the fallout that was bound to come from running the story, we knew we had to go forward. It was just too important. There was surely a terrifying risk that going public might mean that Americans captured or kidnapped would be treated differently. There was the same risk in *not* going forward with the story. Hostile forces aware of the ongoing abuse would feel justified in using the same techniques on Americans they took as prisoners.

Going public was the only way to make the abuses stop. It was time for us to sit down again with Jeff Fager, the executive producer of *60 Minutes II*. Jeff had been kept informed on what we were finding out as we were going along, but now we were facing some weighty issues with major implications.

Fager is a Colgate graduate and the son of a Boston physician. He had started out in radio and worked his way up into network television. He is of medium height and weight with dark hair, sturdy of build—typical of the college skier he had been. His sense of humor and easy, regular laugh gives the impression that he might have been as interested in fraternity parties as he was class during college. Whether that's true or not, I knew him to be a good guy with whom to have a beer, a guy who knew how to have a good time. He can be, often is, a charmer. I also knew Jeff to be quick-smart and a very good producer of news stories. He's not the best writer—often the mark of a really good producer—but whatever he lacked as a writer, he made up for in his nose for a good story, his drive to get it and his knowledge of how to put it together.

Jeff was a friend and protégé of CBS News president Andrew Heyward. The two had worked together at WCBS, our New York O&O. (An O&O is a local television station that is owned and operated by the network, as opposed to an affiliate, which is independently owned.) I had given Heyward his first opening in the News Division, bringing him in as a producer shortly after I became anchor of the *CBS Evening News*. Heyward then brought Jeff on board. Heyward helped and looked after Fager, but Fager was not dependent on him. Jeff made and earned most of his own breaks. Having Heyward in his corner certainly didn't hurt, but that alone would not have gotten Jeff to *60 Minutes* as a producer, which he eventually became. And he was a good one, in a very competitive environment.

Andrew Heyward became a star producer at *Evening News* and eventually was nominated to become executive producer. At the time I had, by contract, consultation and veto power over who would hold that position. Regarding Andrew, I was in complete agreement. I was totally comfortable with him. By this time I had worked with him for a number of years, both when he was a producer for the *Evening News* and later when he became the first executive producer of *48 Hours* (which I had helped to create). He had done outstanding work (which didn't exactly make me look bad, since I had hired him); I thought he deserved the spot.

Not everyone shared my high opinion of him. There were those within the company who considered Andrew a classic overambitious climber, a "too much, too fast" Harvard man with an Ivy League entitlement complex who somehow believed he deserved to move ahead quickly, whatever his personal merits. They also said he was a child of television—which was not intended as a compliment. Andrew had come into television right out of college, with no experience as a reporter in print or anywhere else. Several others had expressed the opinion that he had no real loyalties except to himself.

But I was having none of that. I had hired him, he had proved himself repeatedly and I believed in him, not only as a professional, but as a person. Not only had I no reason to doubt him in any way, professionally or personally, I had every reason to trust him and believe in him. Heyward was unquestionably bright, if not brilliant. He was experienced, and I thought he had proved himself to be loyal—always a prime requisite with me. I had no qualms about Andrew.

Was I influenced by the fact that he often praised me, my talent and my work ethic to others? In retrospect, maybe. It's no secret that news anchors like to hear these things perhaps more than most people, television anchoring being an egocentric line of work, to say the least. But I believed then and believe now that Heyward meant those things when he said them. I also thought, then and now, that he was appreciative of the break I gave him in first getting him to CBS News.

He was a Phi Beta Kappa graduate of Harvard. Sometimes graduates of places like Sam Houston State Teachers College (as I am) don't mesh with the top graduates of schools such as Harvard. When this happens, it probably has as much to do with feelings of inferiority on the part of the little school graduate as it does with any feelings of superiority that are sometimes harbored by Ivy Leaguers. But there was none of that between us. Heyward and I meshed well. We always had. I had no doubts about him and, as far as I knew, he had none about me. We were about 20 years apart in age, but in my view we were two pros with respect for each other and a job to do.

And Andrew did his new job, as executive producer of the *Evening News*, well from the beginning. There was one surprise: He wanted to bring in his old compadre Jeff Fager, who was then at *60 Minutes*, as his second-in-command—our senior producer. This meant, in effect, vaulting Fager over several hardworking people already on the *Evening News* team—qualified, diligent producers who had stood in line for a long time, waiting their turn. I had nothing against Fager; I didn't know him well at the time. I did know that he got high marks from his peers at *60 Minutes*, but the leapfrogging factor concerned me.

Andrew argued hard for him, pointing out that fresh talent from outside *Evening News* could be a good—even necessary—thing, and that he would work especially diligently to have the rest of the staff understand. I was not completely convinced. I was by no means confident that Jeff would be good for the program, or that the remainder of the staff would "understand." But Andrew leaned hard on our personal relationship to persuade me. "You're looking to me to deliver for you, Dan, and to do that I need someone who I can count on to deliver for me—and us," he argued. "And Jeff Fager is that person. Give him a chance. You'll like him and what he does."

And I did. I liked Jeff, and I liked his work. He and Andrew were a good fit; they worked together hand-in-glove fashion. It turned out to be good for them, good for me and good for the newscast. We three worked together well as a team.

Then Heyward was moved up to become president of CBS News, a sudden promotion that was a triumph of the old school tie. A Harvard pal of his was a member of the top management team brought in to run CBS when the network was sold to a new corporation (Westinghouse), and he gave a boost to his old friend. When that happened, Heyward wanted Fager to succeed him as executive producer of the *Evening News*.

He did. For Jeff, however, the *Evening News* was a stepping-stone. When *60 Minutes II* was created in 2000, he wanted to become its executive producer. Badly. With Heyward and me both in his corner, Fager got the *60 Minutes II* top job. He did it well. I was the lead correspondent for the weekly program, in addition to continuing my daily duties as the longtime anchor of the *Evening News*. And we were now— Mary Mapes and I—in Fager's office. It was time to have a real honesty hour about Abu Ghraib.

"We know it's terrible," I said. "Mary, Dana and I don't know the full extent of it yet, but we have almost enough to go with."

The major issue was the photographs. We all wanted them and talked about how we might get them. As I recall, Fager said that we needed the images to be able to air the piece. Chip Frederick said he did not have them, but he knew they existed and he knew what they contained, because they were the basis of the abuse charges against him. CENTCOM's official investigation, led by Major General Antonio Taguba, had been ordered after one of Frederick's fellow MPs had turned in a disc containing the photos to the Army's CID.

Within the Army, CID had responsibility for investigating potential criminal activity; its Iraq headquarters were actually at Abu Ghraib. Thanks to digital technology, however, multiple copies of the photos were already in circulation far beyond the CID. Guards in the prison had passed them around among themselves and had even uploaded them to send home.

Mary and Dana worked the phones trying to get the photographs. Eventually their sources passed them on to other sources. On April 9, we received about a dozen images. It took a real act of will to open the envelope. The photos were as graphic as they were heartbreaking. We looked them over in stunned silence. A hooded detainee stood on a box, electrical wires attached to his hands. There was an additional wire snaking up under his gown, which apparently had been hooked to his penis. Some had been piled, naked, into a human pyramid and photographed from the rear. Others had been posed in simulated sex acts as guards pointed to their private parts and grinned at the camera.

We showed Jeff Fager the photos, expecting to get the green light to air the piece, but apparently he still needed more. Fager seemed edgy, testy and out of sorts. He seemed aggressive and challenging. He expressed no appreciation for what we'd done, which we all found to be out of character. It was my belief that he was reacting to pressure from Andrew Heyward. There was now no doubt whatsoever that we had everything necessary to put the story on the air. We had hard evidence: eyewitness testimony, secondhand testimony and photographs we knew to be authentic. We had a world-class all-media scoop; as far as I knew, no one else even had a sniff of it.

And management treated us as if we had just dragged a dead rat into the newsroom.

At CBS News, time was when getting the worldwide exclusive on an explosive story like Abu Ghraib would have been occasion for congratulations and great praise from top executives, both of the News Division and the network itself. Those times were long gone. From the days of Edward R. Murrow through civil rights, through Vietnam, through Watergate and into the 1980s, reporting the truth, regardless of who was trying to cover it up—or perhaps *because* of who was trying to cover it up—was a virtue unto itself and needed no further justification.

This fundamental doctrine was handed down from CBS patriarch William S. Paley himself. At Paley's memorial service in 1990, it was said of him that "as caring as Bill was of his friends, he did not allow that commitment to infringe on his love affair with CBS. While I knew him, he was impervious to the many appeals that reached him to intervene with CBS News. Bill took the position that the CBS News team was beyond his reach, because it was simply the best and the most dedicated group of journalists that had ever been assembled."

The eulogist was Henry Kissinger. Bill Paley simply believed that the news was the news and that reporting it was a public service—even during the early 1960s, when we started kicking up a lot of dust with our coverage of the civil rights movement. We were called "outside agitators"; we were called the "Colored Broadcasting System." Even some of our own southern affiliates tried to avoid carrying the national newscast, because what we were showing was too inflammatory and too controversial—and it made white people look bad.

Paley, however, wasn't having any of it. To him it smacked of politicization of the news. The fact that our southern stations were squeamish (or worse) about airing footage of blacks being attacked with fire hoses and billy clubs was no reason for self-censorship. At the time, Paley *was* CBS, and he ran the network as a benevolent dictatorship. When these affiliates started pushing, he pushed back, despite his awareness that powerful forces in Washington were applying pressure as well. Southern senators who were upset with our coverage were threatening to go for our jugular—which for a media enterprise is almost always accessed through the wallet.

Now, however, instead of kudos from corporate, I got the very strong sense from both Fager and Heyward that they really didn't want to run the story. The excuses were essentially a retread of the same old argument: The story was too inflammatory, too controversial—and it made Viacom/CBS look bad. I also got the feeling they were responding to heavy outside pressure, pressure that came from inside Black Rock (CBS corporate headquarters) and possibly from inside the Beltway.

The relationship between government and the media—and the large corporations that own the media—will always be complex, in part because media giants will always need something from government: license renewals, permission to expand, etc. For a very long time, national networks such as CBS were allowed to own and operate a maximum of six stations—own and operate them, as opposed to being affiliated by contract with local stations. The limit on O&Os was the Federal Communications Commission's way of ensuring that no individual corporation could monopolize the country's airwaves. Naturally, the networks claimed their six in the nation's biggest markets—New York, LA, Chicago, etc.—but the networks always wanted more, much more.

And beginning in the 1980s, they got it. Through campaign contributions and heavy lobbying, big media corporations succeeded in getting the FCC to loosen the restraints. The FCC is made up of political appointees, who generally do whatever the party in power wants them to do. First the maximum rose from six into the teens. Then, as corporations got bigger and their political influence grew, that was expanded to 20 and more, and then revised upward from there. Once the floodgates opened, these changes resulted in enormous new profits for the networks, not just for CBS/Viacom, but for the others as well.

Big media is big business. Virtually all major networks are now owned by large conglomerates whose reach extends beyond communications into many other industries as well. General Electric, which owns NBC, MSNBC and CNBC (among many other news and entertainment properties), is in addition a big defense contractor and a major provider of commercial lending, both of which are heavily dependent on positive relationships in Washington. Disney, which owns ABC and ESPN, also owns amusement parks, resorts and a variety of other businesses, both at home and abroad, that can be hindered—or stimulated—by action in Washington, either through legislation or government regulation.

Government needs media as well. They use us to publicize some activities; by the same token, they would much prefer it if we ignore others. This symbiotic relationship between media and government does not serve the public well. When I say that big business is in bed with big government, it is for their mutual benefit, not for the benefit of the public interest. At the time Abu Ghraib was breaking, CBS and its parent company Viacom were already in hot water with the FCC for Janet Jackson's "wardrobe malfunction" during the Super Bowl half-time show. From a corporate standpoint, we were vulnerable.

And corporate, apparently, was now running the show. I was never told outright not to run the piece. Instead, the News Division executives kept moving the goalposts, as it were, adding more prerequisites before they would permit it to air. There had already been any number of obstacles placed in our way, and we had overcome each and every one of them. Now Mary and I were told that we needed to get the Army's reaction. Jeff Fager delivered the message, but I believed that on a story of this magnitude, the order would have originated with Andrew Heyward. We couldn't run the piece without offering the Army the opportunity to give its version of the story.

I had learned from hard experience that this was a bad idea. It would give both the Pentagon and the executive branch the opportunity to throw up delay after delay, sprinkle disinformation, send us on wild goose chases and prepare a massive pushback on our sources in order to get them to change their stories. In my opinion, the Department of Defense had already been deliberately stonewalling and hiding this story for a long while. Cooling our heels while waiting for a response from the Army would provide the people most responsible for this nightmarish abuse a way to conceal the truth before we got the chance to tell it.

It looked—and smelled—like the red herring that it was. Somewhere, I suspected, Edward R. Murrow was shaking his head in sorrow and dismay.

I was angry, and I let management know it. "This is CBS News, and this is what makes us CBS News," I declared. "You asked us for pictures. We got them. You asked us for proof. We have it," I continued emphatically. "There is no 'Army version.' This IS what happened! Yes, it's going to cause controversy. Yes, there will be hell to pay. But we should be proud of that. We are CBS News. This is what we do."

None of that seemed to get through. Nevertheless, Mary Mapes dutifully contacted the military once again, asking them to give us someone to comment on the story, which we'd tentatively scheduled for the April 14 broadcast. The first thing they wanted to know in the Pentagon Public Affairs Office was whether we had the pictures, and they were so very sorry to hear that we did. Despite the volatile potential of the revelations, however, Public Affairs didn't think they could dig up a VIP to comment in time for the April 14 airdate.

Much to my consternation, Jeff Fager made the judgment call to hold the piece for another week. He insisted that we needed someone from the Pentagon to answer questions about Abu Ghraib, on air and on the record. I had the feeling that Fager was again following a directive from above, one that came from at least the Heyward level, if not higher.

If I was angry before, I was livid now. Mary says I was angrier than she had ever heard me, or as she put it, "snarling, foot-stomping mad." And rightly so, I believe. I was convinced that CBS would never run the story. Mary did her best to scrape me off the ceiling and started jumping through the required hoops to get a comment from the Pentagon.

She and Dana also got hold of information from the Taguba report, the official Army investigation into the abuses at Abu Ghraib. General Antonio Taguba's findings corroborated what Chip Frederick had told us—that MPs had been "actively requested" to "set physical and mental conditions for favorable interrogation of witnesses." Although that firmed up our story even further, things were now starting to get squirrelly. Our original sources were becoming restive, and rightly so. They'd stuck their necks out, and as far as they could tell, we'd done exactly nothing with their information. What were we waiting for? People like Bill Lawson accused us of having cold feet.

How could I argue when I felt the same way? It seemed more and more like management just wanted to get our dead rat out of the newsroom and bury it in an unmarked grave. I had never seen so much meddling by upper-echelon management in a particular story. Both News Div president Andrew Heyward and senior VP Betsy West were uncharacteristically involved in the process. To her credit, West had favored running the story as soon as she first reviewed fully what we had.

Poor Jeff Fager was caught in the middle. It seemed that one side of him was a real newsman, but the other side felt compelled to play the corporate game. His initial instincts had been much in line with ours: that we should get the story, run the story, take the heat and keep going. That said, Jeff was very ambitious about climbing the ladder in the News Division. I'm certain he was already eyeing his next rung, and he was aiming high. Fager hoped to take over as producer of *60 Minutes*—the post Don Hewitt had held since the show's inception in 1968. Hewitt obviously wasn't going to be there forever, and Jeff saw an opportunity to put himself at the front of the line whenever the time came for Hewitt to step down. Heyward saw it the same way. (Hewitt never really liked Heyward, and the feeling was mutual.) For that to happen, however, Jeff had to play ball with corporate. As a result, he seemed to me to be hopelessly conflicted, almost schizophrenic. For Jeff Fager, run it or not run it, Abu Ghraib could become a lose-lose situation.

It was about this time that I got a phone call at home, one that gave me a huge clue about why News Division executives were micromanaging the story and dragging their feet. The caller was Richard Myers, as in four-star general Richard Myers, chairman of the Joint Chiefs of Staff. To me, the call from Myers was a sign that major players both in Washington and within CBS were involved. I knew him to be every inch an officer and a gentleman. He was unusually knowledgeable and supportive of the role of the press in a democratic society. He appreciated what we did, and unlike many of his top brass counterparts, he was at ease around journalists. We were not particularly close, but occasionally, when he was in New York, we lunched. I liked and admired him, and still do.

At the time, Myers said, our forces in Iraq were having it particularly tough in Fallujah. The town could go either way; American lives on the front lines were hanging in the balance. Consequently, he told me, running the story would be a disservice to the country.

Over the years I have spent a lot of time with American servicemen and -women in areas of conflict all over the world. I have the utmost respect for them and would never knowingly make their job any harder

than it already is, let alone deliberately put them in harm's way. I had
been to Fallujah several times and knew that fierce battles were indeed
taking place there, but what Myers was saying struck me as odd. I gave
him the benefit of the doubt and believed him to be sincere. Nevertheless, it seemed to me that what was happening in Fallujah had nothing
whatsoever to do with the incendiary and, frankly, un-American behavior we had uncovered at Abu Ghraib.

Myers did not ask me to flat out kill the story; he asked instead for a
lengthy delay—three months—long enough to give the Pentagon time
to figure out how to deal with it. I told General Myers the truth—that I
was compassionate about the situation, but that I was first and foremost
a journalist.

As soon as I rang off, Mary and I talked about my conversation with
Myers. She did not share my opinion of the general's honorable intentions.

"You don't think it has anything to do with troop safety?" I asked.

"Just the opposite," she said. "Dan, if you need convincing, go have
a conversation with Roger Charles. As a retired Marine officer, he
believes deeply that running the story is profoundly important in keeping our troops safe. He does not want our own troops treated this way—
or worse—if they are captured.

"The Pentagon seems to think they can keep this a secret. They
can't," Mary continued. "We've been told by veterans and current military alike that the word about this kind of abuse always gets out. And
in the case of Abu Ghraib, it's *already* out. Since we've been working
on this story, Roger, Dana and I have spoken with many people, both
inside and outside the military, who know this has been going on. The
people of Iraq know it's been going on. The only people without a clue
are our American citizens at home. And they deserve to know. They
have a right to know."

Even though Myers had asked me to hold the story, he knew enough
about the news business to be aware that the choice to air or not air
the piece was not my call. The decision to take a story to air must first
come from the executive producer, in this case the oh-so-conflicted Jeff
Fager, after which it must be approved by the head of the News Divi-

sion, Andrew Heyward. I suspected that Myers had called Andrew Heyward before he'd called me.

Perhaps not coincidentally, the Pentagon Public Affairs Office still hadn't come forth with anyone we could speak with for the piece. Especially after the phone call from Myers, it certainly seemed possible if not likely that they were stalling so they could go public with the story themselves. Fager deferred the story once more, while Mary and Dana begged their sources to hang in there for yet another week. They were unhappy, and they gave us an ultimatum: Run the piece or we're taking our pictures elsewhere.

In this case, "elsewhere" had a formidable name and a formidable reputation: Seymour Hersh.

When I took this to Fager and Heyward, their jaws dropped—in unison. Somehow they hadn't reckoned with the possibility that another journalist might eventually catch wind of our story, and of course Hersh was far more than just another journalist. Sy Hersh is one of the greatest investigative reporters of our time. With Hersh onto the story, our dead rat had just become radioactive.

Shortly thereafter, Jeff Fager took an irate call from an apoplectic Department of Defense public affairs officer named Lawrence Di Rita. At the top of his lungs, Di Rita angrily accused us of giving our pictures to Sy Hersh.

This was, I thought, as dimwitted as it was rash. Why would we give away our scoop to another journalist? By April 2004, we were already well into the age of digital cameras and cell phones that could take pictures. There are a lot of smart people in the Pentagon. Did it not occur to anyone at DOD that other copies of the photos were out there?

As far as CBS was concerned, however, this had suddenly become a powder keg, a calamity in the making whose implications went far beyond the embarrassment of getting beaten to our own scoop. Not only did Sy Hersh have our story, he also knew that we'd had the story and that we'd been sitting on it for three weeks, in cahoots with the Pentagon. If he came out first, it would be a major black eye for the integrity and credibility of CBS News. Worst of all, the claim that CBS had sat on the story would, as our legendary producer Lane Venardos used to say, have the added advantage of being true.

You should have seen Andrew Heyward squirm—he understood at once that whatever the bigwigs at the network, at corporate and in DC might have wanted, they weren't getting it now. Spiking the piece was off the table entirely. We had no choice but to air the story, and to air it *before* Sy Hersh humiliated CBS News in print in the *New Yorker.*

Once the Army realized that it was all going to hit the fan, and that the fan was already spinning, they arranged for me to interview Brigadier General Mark Kimmitt, deputy director of coalition operations in Baghdad. Having delayed the story at the behest of the Pentagon while waiting for someone in the military to comment, we felt it was important to come clean about having done so, especially with Sy Hersh breathing down our necks. Kimmitt acquitted himself quite well on camera, but he stuck closely to the official explanation, chalking up the abuse to a few bad apples.

Management had been backed into running the story, but that didn't mean they were happy about it. After committing to run the piece, they made every effort to make sure nobody paid any attention to it. They eliminated any advance on-air promotion. This was highly irregular— the normal lead-up for an important story like this was to beat the drums and get the word out. There would be rounds of press interviews; we would have anchors talking about it on the morning and midday news programs; there would be promos for the affiliates. For the Abu Ghraib story, however, it was made clear that there was to be almost none of that.

We ran it on April 28 in as watered-down a version as possible. Orders from Andrew Heyward were to run it once, period. I do not believe he made that decision in a vacuum. I think he was reacting to what he believed Viacom head Sumner Redstone and CBS CEO Les Moonves wanted. Whether they had expressly directed that or not, I do not know.

Although the story was obviously still unfolding, we were forbidden by Heyward to do any significant follow-up, which is virtually unheard-of for a story of this magnitude. If the *New York Times* had broken the story, there would have been follow-ups for weeks. Sy Hersh's piece ran in the May 10 issue of the *New Yorker*. (Although the cover is dated May 10, the magazine became publicly available on April 30, two days after we aired.) Hersh then wrote a follow-up for each of the next two issues. Sadly, he wrote a third in 2007, detailing the scapegoating of General Taguba by Rumsfeld and the Pentagon.

Bill Lawson, Mary Mapes's original source, had talked with us because he was afraid that the Army was going to stick it to the little guys and leave them with the blame. His fear has proven to be well founded. The only individuals found guilty on charges in connection with Abu Ghraib were enlisted personnel and noncoms, none above the rank of sergeant. Those convicted included Lawson's nephew Chip, who served three years in Leavenworth for his part in the abuse.

Then as now, one must conclude that shielding the higher-ups was deliberate. When he was given the assignment to investigate abuse at Abu Ghraib, General Taguba was ordered to limit his inquiry to the MPs alone, even though he quickly realized that responsibility for the problem went much farther up the chain of command. "Somebody was giving them guidance, but I was legally prevented from further investigation into higher authority," he told Sy Hersh in 2007. "I was limited to a box."

In May 2004, as the scandal made headlines, the top echelons of the White House and the Defense Department struggled to maintain "plausible deniability." On May 2, Joint Chiefs of Staff chairman Richard Myers told the CBS program *Face the Nation* that he had not yet read General Taguba's report. I know Myers to be a truth teller, so I cut him a lot of slack. Nevertheless, that statement defied logic. If he hadn't already read Taguba's report, he'd surely been told of its contents. Otherwise, on what basis would he have asked me in April to delay running the piece? Taguba had submitted his report on February 26, more than two months earlier. He had ensured that it was widely distributed; more than a dozen copies were transmitted to various recipients at the Pentagon and at CENTCOM in Florida.

Even before the report was complete, however, information about the photographs had been forwarded to the Pentagon, and Myers admitted having been briefed on the problem. In sworn testimony on May 7 before Congress, Myers said, "I've been receiving regular updates since the situation developed in January, and have been involved in corrective actions and personally recommended specific steps." He confirmed that descriptions of simulated sex acts and abuse depicted in the photos had been given "to me and the Secretary [Rumsfeld] up through the chain of command" in January, within days of the original complaint. He testified to this just five days after telling *Face the Nation* that he had not yet read General Taguba's report. I had to admit that Mary's skepticism about Myers had some basis. He also said, "When I spoke to Dan Rather, with whom I already had a professional association, concerning the *60 Minutes* story, I did so after talking to General Abizaid [then head of CENTCOM]. And I did so out of concern for the lives of our troops."

That same day, Defense Secretary Donald Rumsfeld also appeared before the Senate Armed Services Committee. "I wish we had known more sooner and been able to tell you more sooner, but we didn't," he testified. Myers, of course, had testified that Rumsfeld had been in the loop since January. For his part, Rumsfeld seemed at least as upset that the photos had found their way to CBS as anything else. He railed against "people running around with digital cameras and taking these unbelievable photographs and passing them off against the law to the media, to our surprise, when they had not even arrived in the Pentagon."

In the same hearing, Rumsfeld also outed Sergeant Joseph Darby, the man who had originally turned in the disk of photos to CID and who had been promised anonymity in return for coming forward. As Justine Sharrock reported for *Mother Jones*, Darby was sitting in the Abu Ghraib mess hall and the TV was tuned to Senate hearings on CNN when Rumsfeld dropped his name. Darby was rushed home; officers met his plane and whisked him and his family into the military equivalent of the witness protection program, where they remained with 24/7 security for six months. Darby says that he was never formally thanked by the Army, but he *did* get a personal letter from Rumsfeld—

asking him to stop talking about how he'd been unveiled as the whistle-blower.

Perhaps not surprisingly, on May 24 Rumsfeld banned the personal use of cameras by the U.S. military in Iraq.

Brigadier General Janis Karpinski had been relieved of command at Abu Ghraib shortly before our piece aired. She was replaced by Major General Geoffrey Miller. General Miller had previously been responsible for running military detention facilities Camp X-Ray, Camp Delta and Camp Echo at Guantánamo Bay. Before assuming command of Abu Ghraib, Miller had made a prior visit to the facility in August 2003. His mission on that trip was to outline procedures for extracting more intel out of Iraqi detainees. In September he submitted a report that recommended what was later termed "Gitmo-izing" interrogation procedures at Abu Ghraib. Specific proposals included allowing military intelligence officials to have command over prisons and prison guards, as well as having guards be "actively engaged in setting the conditions for successful exploitation of the internees."

Chip Frederick had told us in dreadful detail how that directive was carried out. The term "enhanced interrogation" was about to enter the American lexicon.

Like Myers and Rumsfeld, General Miller testified before the Senate Armed Services Committee in May 2004. (He did, however, refuse to testify at the trials of some of the enlistees charged with abuse, invoking the military equivalent of the Fifth Amendment to avoid self-incrimination.) During his Senate testimony, he indicated that although he'd filed a report about his visit to Abu Ghraib in 2003, he had not briefed Secretary Rumsfeld or his aides about the trip. In a statement to attorneys three months later, however, Miller said something very different. He indicated that upon his return to the United States from Baghdad, he had indeed given a briefing to DOD deputy secretary Paul Wolfowitz and undersecretary of defense for intelligence Steve Cambone about his visit to the prison, together with his recommendations.

You'd like to think that the first prerequisite of plausible deniability would be plausibility, but then again, 2004 was an election year.

Looking back, the only ones who really paid for Abu Ghraib were the enlisted personnel, who were following orders, and General Taguba, who brought the problem to light.

Several other officers were demoted, pushed out of the military and/ or reprimanded, but none of them did time. General Ricardo Sanchez, who oversaw ground troops in Iraq, was among those asked to resign. This struck me as curious, since he appeared to have had little if anything to do with the actions of the OGA operatives, or with the private contractors who bullied with impunity at Abu Ghraib. Indeed, Sanchez maintained that he and others in the military had argued vociferously against the use of any kind of torture, and that those arguments fell on deaf ears at the top of the highly political Pentagon leadership.

Brigadier General Janis Karpinski had been busted down to colonel before being forced to resign from the Army. It's not difficult to believe that she might have been scapegoated, but officially her disciplinary action was unrelated to Abu Ghraib. She had allegedly been arrested in 2002 at Florida's MacDill Air Force Base for shoplifting cosmetics, a charge Karpinski has repeatedly denied—both the shoplifting and the arrest.

In 2004, she said that she had seen a letter from Rumsfeld green-lighting Guantánamo-style interrogation techniques for Abu Ghraib, then under her command. In 2009 she appeared on CBS's *Early Show* to talk about who paid the price for Abu Ghraib and why. "These soldiers didn't design these techniques on their own," she told Harry Smith. "We were following orders. We were bringing this to our chain of command, and they were saying whatever the military intelligence tells you to do out there, you are authorized to do.

"The line is clear," she continued. "It went from Washington, DC, from the very top of the administration with their legal opinions, through Bagram to Guantánamo Bay and then to Iraq via the commander from Guantánamo Bay, Cuba." She did not name him in that interview, but this would be Major General Geoffrey Miller.

Karpinski confirmed what Bill Lawson, Chip Frederick's uncle, had feared at the outset—that lower-level personnel were being scapegoated by those in the Pentagon and in the administration. "'Scapegoat' is the perfect word, and it's an understatement," she said.

* * *

It is a disgrace that those truly responsible for Abu Ghraib have never been held accountable. The whole episode left a bad taste in my mouth, not only because it was clear that people at the top got off scot-free, but also because of how the story had been handled at CBS. Although we did wind up breaking an all-world exclusive on an important story, I had the uneasy sense that CBS News was no longer CBS News as I had known it.

It was troubling to me that there had been a decided absence of executive backbone throughout our investigation. It was impossible to avoid the conclusion that, but for the looming specter of Seymour Hersh, the story of Abu Ghraib would never have seen the light of day at CBS. Sy Hersh got onto it because of our reticence. One of our sources, in frustration and fear that CBS News didn't have the courage to break the story, had revealed to him that we were working on it, and then gave him the proof that he needed to go with it.

The possibility that the financial and political interests of CBS corporate almost buried a story as compelling as Abu Ghraib was most unsettling. Little did I know that it was only going to get worse from there. Much worse.

CHAPTER 2

George Bush and the Texas Air National Guard

It was long said of me that I had the CBS Eye tattooed somewhere on my ass. And there was more than a shred of truth behind the jest. I did indeed think of myself as a team player, loyal to CBS News, and loyal above all to its long and honorable tradition of honest reporting. The Bush/Guard episode confirmed the suspicion I had developed in the wake of the struggle to air our story on Abu Ghraib—that CBS News had abandoned the principles on which it was founded. It showed that I was loyal to something that no longer existed, at least not at CBS.

The person most responsible was Viacom owner Sumner Redstone, with his personal political bias and his need for Washington help to feed his insatiable lust for profit. Redstone's CBS corporate headman, president and chief executive officer Les Moonves, and CBS News Division president Andrew Heyward worked to fulfill Redstone's desires—whether those desires were directly expressed or not. They, I believe, at least some of the time, did so against what they knew to be their own better instincts and judgment. They may have done it unhappily, but they did it. I believe they did it as part of their determination to survive and move up in the corporate world.

I realize that revisiting this painful period may be seen as dangerously close to the category of "So What?" It's old news. Who cares what an ex-president did 40 years ago?

I do.

For a journalist, the truth always matters, and that should be reason enough. The arrogant hypocrisy of it makes this story much more disturbing. A young man born of privilege whose family secured him a spot in the National Guard to avoid military service in Vietnam, and who then walked away for more than a year from even that safe level of obligation, eventually became the commander in chief who ordered tens of thousands of our young men and women, including those in the National Guard, into harm's way in Iraq and Afghanistan. This same young man who gamed the system to evade going to Vietnam became a president who did nothing to prevent, halt or disavow the distorted character assassination of his opponent, John Kerry, a decorated Vietnam veteran, by his own supporters.

There is an additional and very important reason as well: The legacy of what happened to our story on George Bush and his career in the Texas Air National Guard lives on to contaminate both our politics and our journalism today. There is a through-line, a long and slimy filament that connects the "murder" of Vince Foster to Swift Boat Veterans for Truth and to the discrediting of the Killian memos. That same dirty thread stretches all the way to the selectively edited ACORN "documentary" and the birther movement.

The Internet has played a larger and larger role in all of these incidents. Efforts by fringe groups to smear and discredit via innuendo and outright falsehood generate their own counterfeit credibility by endless online repetition, creating a digital echo chamber that reverberates through the partisan grapevine until someone in the legitimate media is foolish enough to pay attention. The ginned-up controversy over President Obama's birth certificate followed this pattern. Birthers stated and restated their accusations online with a frequency bordering on obsession, if not outright perseveration. Their charges were picked up and repeated by anti-Obama media outlets until the story became not just the birth certificate itself, but how much attention it was getting in the press. It was the faux news story that refused to die. Even after President Obama released his long-form birth certificate, there remain websites with "irrefutable proof" that it is a forgery. These same websites continuing their assault on President Obama's birth certificate were in the vanguard of the efforts to invalidate our reporting on President Bush's disappearance from the Texas Air National Guard. The "proof" they offer about the birth certificate is based on typeface and proportional spacing and has a great deal in common with their attacks on our report.

Ironically enough, it's probably fair to say that *60 Minutes II* was still on the air in September 2004 because of our story on Abu Ghraib four months earlier. We'd been bounced around the schedule from one weekday to another; once they start messing with the time slot, it's a sign that the show is on the bubble. CBS president Les Moonves is first and foremost an entertainment guy. For him, news is an also-ran, especially in prime time. It all had to do with ratings, the bottom line and his personal ambitions. In his view, having a news program in prime time took a coveted slot away from a sitcom or reality show that could generate more revenue. There already had been talk of dropping *60 Minutes II* that spring, when the fall schedule was rolled out. It didn't happen because News Division head Andrew Heyward convinced Moonves and other network executives that it would be a publicity black eye for CBS if they canceled us so soon after reporting the Abu Ghraib story. It would look too much like cause and effect. We made the cut and we became *60 Minutes Wednesday,* but our position on the schedule was tenuous.

The prospect of doing a piece on George W. Bush's highly irregular military career was something that producer Mary Mapes had first mentioned to me in 2000. It was always more than just a story about how a congressman's son had leapfrogged over hundreds of other young men to land a commission in the "champagne unit" of the Texas Air National Guard and avoid serving in Vietnam. It was also a story about the mystery surrounding what Bush did and did not do while serving his country, and where and how long he had done it. And it was a story about whether his service record had been selectively expunged to remove portions that could prove embarrassing to someone running for public office. It was a story about whether the man who wanted to and ultimately did become the commander in chief of our forces served his country honorably when it was his turn to stand and deliver.

Other news organizations, including the *Boston Globe*, the *Washington Post* and the *Guardian* in the UK, had looked into it before Bush became president, but the story never got much traction anywhere else. Inexplicably, it got far less media attention than Al Gore's "invention" of the Internet. I didn't follow up then—to my discredit—but in the middle of 2004, with George Bush running for reelection, serious questions about whether he had fulfilled his service obligations came to the forefront once more. These questions were magnified by the campaign mounted by Swift Boat Veterans for Truth to impugn the service record of John Kerry, Bush's opponent. The Swift Boaters alleged that one or more of Kerry's medals, including three Purple Hearts, a Bronze Star and a Silver Star, were undeserved.

Their assault on Kerry's wartime heroism continued to gather steam throughout the summer as Mary dug into Bush's National Guard records. In her book *Truth and Duty*, she has written a comprehensive and meticulous account of how she gathered information for the segment that aired on *60 Minutes Wednesday* on September 8, 2004. My purpose here is not to reexamine this episode in the degree of detail that she took many chapters to provide. What I will do is reaffirm and reinforce the essential veracity of our reporting and describe the craven manner in which CBS pulled the rug out from under all of us, as well as the reasoning behind their actions.

I am very aware that reopening this old wound may be met with wide skepticism and even some snorts of derision. In what has become the prevailing public view, I lost this round, big time. I have little expectation that I can win over those who are absolutely certain that CBS—and specifically Mary Mapes and I—screwed up royally. We stand accused and convicted of sloppy and irresponsible journalism—or worse. Many believe we deliberately broadcast a story knowing it was based on phony documents. Some allege that we falsified these documents ourselves.

All I ask is a chance to set the record straight and to present what I hope is a convincing argument that a lot of what you know, or think you know, is wrong.

With that in mind, it behooves me to acknowledge that we did indeed make mistakes in reporting the story. Should we have done more extensive vetting of the documents before we put them on the air? Yes. None of us adequately understood the implications of faxing with respect to document analysis. Ideally we should have brought more than one analyst to New York to examine the documents in person. More important, what we later uncovered after we were already under heavy criticism would have enabled us to demonstrate beyond all doubt that the attacks on them were a sham. Should we have held the segment to air at a later date? Perhaps, but we were told that was not an option. Was it an error in judgment to include the Killian memos in the piece? Knowing what we know now, we probably should have focused less on the documents themselves, more on the facts they contain and more on how well they fit within the context of what we already knew to be true. Do any of these issues invalidate the story itself? Absolutely not.

As Mary was looking into Bush's military career, we talked about reaching out to Ben Barnes. Barnes is a colorful fellow, and I'd known him for a long time, ever since he was an up-and-coming young Texas state legislator in the 1960s. He became the Lone Star State's youngest speaker of the house at age 26. By 1969, he was Texas's lieutenant governor, which meant he was in position to be a gatekeeper, if you will, for who got into the Texas Air National Guard and who did not. Mary started working on Ben to get him to tell what happened. To say that he was reluctant to tell what happened is an understatement, but Mary is a real reporter, an indefatigable reporter—the kind you make movies about. Just as the Republicans officially nominated George Bush in the first days of September, she called to tell me that Barnes had agreed to an on-camera interview. Like so many other people, Ben had found it tiresome to keep saying no to Mary. Eventually he realized that it was easier to say yes, just to stop her from calling all the time. Nevertheless, he remained skittish about it.

As soon as coverage of the Republican convention wrapped, I headed to Florida. Frances, a major hurricane, was brewing off the coast. Before I left, I called Ben Barnes to firm up his consent. Barnes was a Kerry supporter, and the swift-boating smear operation was a burr under his saddle. He was very aware that it was hurting Kerry badly. Worse yet, it was based in Texas. "I'm not happy about doing this," he told me, "but I think it's time." In 1999, Barnes had already sworn under oath that he had recommended Bush for a spot in the Guard. That was in a deposition, however; saying so on national television was another matter.

Meanwhile, Mary continued nailing down other parts of the story. Through the Texas grapevine she had made contact with a former lieutenant colonel in the Guard named Bill Burkett. Now a rancher in West Texas, in February 2004, Burkett had asserted that he had witnessed the selective editing of Bush's National Guard file in 1997. He was not exactly a neutral source; his dislike of Bush was well known. Burkett claimed to be in possession of documents that would, he said, blow the lid off the secrecy about Bush's record of service. After some considerable cajoling, on September 2 he gave Mary two documents allegedly written by Lieutenant Colonel Jerry B. Killian, who had been Bush's commanding officer. He would eventually give us four more.

Although Mary was urging me to come to Texas ASAP to do interviews, Andrew Heyward wanted me to stay in Florida with Hurricane Frances. I told him what Mary said she had, and what its implications were. I also told him we had to be very careful with the story, because it had thermonuclear potential. I reiterated to Andrew that it was essential for him to stay on top of the story as it developed.

"You work the hurricane until it moves on," he told me. "Then go meet up with Mary. I'm taking charge, I'll oversee this." On Sunday Frances began to weaken, and I drove fast and furious around fallen trees and downed power lines to get to Miami International. I barely made the flight to Dallas. I left Florida in need of a hot shower and a decent meal. Lots of reports at the time said I looked tired. Staying on top of a breaking news story means working odd hours, catching quick snacks on the fly, staying up late and getting up early. More than anything I was short of sleep, but this kind of fatigue went with the territory. I'd been short of sleep for much of the last 30 years. When I arrived in Texas, Mary laughed at my bedraggled appearance and told me I looked like I had just been through a hurricane—which was, of course, absolutely accurate.

Mary met me at the terminal and showed me the Killian memos

that Burkett had given her. She then took me through the key facts she had confirmed:

• In the waning days of May 1968, just 12 days before graduating from Yale, at which time his student deferment would have expired, George W. Bush applied to become a pilot trainee in the Texas Air National Guard. Ben Barnes had received a phone call from Bush family friend Sidney Adger and had subsequently put in a call to Brigadier General James Rose, Commander of the Texas Air National Guard. With the influence of his father, George H. W. Bush, then a congressman, Bush was accepted into the Guard's champagne unit.

• Despite Bush's lack of any aviation or ROTC experience, and despite his bare minimum scores on the pilot aptitude tests, General Rose immediately put him into flight school. He then made Bush a second lieutenant after only six weeks of basic training.

• Beginning in 1970, Bush's initial performance as an F-102 pilot was commendable—and well documented. Starting early in 1972, however, there were problems. Flight logs show that on two separate occasions, he needed more than two passes to land his F-102, even though by this time he had logged more than 200 hours in that aircraft. He stopped flying the F-102 and resumed flying a T-33 training jet, the same aircraft from which he'd graduated a few years before. He then was assigned to put in additional time in a flight simulator.

• In April 1972, he stopped flying altogether. At that point he still had two full years remaining on his obligation to serve as a pilot.

• On May 15, 1972, Bush left Ellington Air Force Base and the 147th Fighter Interceptor Group in Houston and went to Alabama with Jimmy and Linda Allison to work on Winton Blount's senatorial campaign. Jimmy Allison owned the newspaper in Midland, Texas, and at the time was a close confidante of George H. W. Bush.

• Mary had just spoken with Linda Allison. Although she declined to be interviewed on camera, she said that she and her husband Jimmy (since deceased) had been asked by Bush's father to take young George to Alabama because he was "getting in trouble and embarrassing the family." After about a month, she had asked Jimmy what exactly Bush was doing for the Blount campaign, since she never saw him do anything. And in all the time he was there, she never saw him in uniform.

• After leaving Ellington for Alabama, as far as the Guard was concerned, George Bush pretty much went off the grid for a year. In an annual evaluation, Bush's two immediate superiors stated that Bush "had not been observed" in Texas during the period of report, beginning May 1972 and ending in April 1973.

• He was not observed in Alabama, either. On September 15, 1972, Bush was ordered to report for training with the 187th Tactical Recon Group at Dannelly Field in Montgomery, Alabama. Neither his commanding officers nor any fellow Guardsmen remembered seeing him there. In February 2004, the *Washington Post* had tried and failed to find anyone in the 187th who remembered seeing him. Eventually John "Bill" Calhoun, a former Guardsman, came forward and vouched for having seen Lieutenant Bush at Dannelly about eight or ten times between May and October 1972. This gave him an instant credibility problem, since Bush was not supposed to report to Dannelly until September.

• In 1972, Bush failed to take the physical exam required of all Guard pilots, a serious violation. The question of his failure to do so had come up several times during Bush's political career, and over the years Bush spokesmen had offered various mutually exclusive explanations for it. One explanation had been that Bush's family doctor was unavailable, but physical exams for all pilots must be given by Air Force flight surgeons (who were available to Bush both in Texas and in Alabama). A second explanation was that the F-102 had been decommissioned; that did not occur, however, until 1974. Most recently, in February 2004, Bush's spokesman Dan Bartlett said that Bush didn't take the physical because he saw no reason to do so, since his unit at Dannelly didn't fly the same aircraft.

• In the wake of his failure to take a physical, a flight inquiry board should have been convened. There is no record that such a review board ever met.

• On September 29, Bush was officially grounded by Major General Francis Greenlief, chief of the National Guard Bureau, for failing to take his physical. Bush was ordered to acknowledge in writing that he'd been grounded. There is no such acknowledgment.

• On June 29, 1973, Bush's commanding officers in Houston were ordered to get additional information from the 187th in Alabama, so that Bush could be evaluated.

• Bush was honorably discharged in October 1973, eight months before his term officially was to expire.

These facts were just the top of a very large pile. Mary kept a thick notebook of all the documents, interviews and contacts she had amassed. There was more than enough research to raise important questions about Bush's National Guard service *without* the documents from Burkett. Our main challenge was to be selective about what to put on the air. With the seeming support of our executive and senior producers, we came to believe that the Killian memos would be a good addition to a story that needed more than talking heads. They also jibed with what we could already prove. They were new news, assuming we could confirm that they were genuine, but going to the author was not possible, since Killian had passed away in 1984.

What new information did these documents contain? A memo dated May 4, 1972, directed Bush to take his physical examination no later than May 14. That deadline was just one day before he "cleared this base [Ellington]," in the words of another superior officer, and left for Alabama. Another memo, dated August 1, 1972, said that Bush was being suspended because he had made "no attempt to meet his training certification or flight physical" and for "failure to perform to USAF/ TexANG standards." Since documents showed he'd been officially grounded shortly thereafter, the timing fit. In a third memo, dated

August 18, 1973, Killian indicated that Lieutenant Bush had not been in Texas during the rating period, that he was unable to get any information out of the 187th in Alabama, and that he was being pressured to "sugar coat" the problem. The memo bore the subject heading "CYA," and it was written by Killian for his own personal files as a way of protecting himself. Since we already knew that on June 29 Killian had been ordered to get additional information from Alabama, where Bush was to have been on duty, the timing fit in this instance as well.

The memos we received from Burkett underscored what we already had, but they were far from the only proof we had that Bush had gone missing for a year and had played fast and loose with his military obligations. Nevertheless, I knew that we needed to get someone reliable to vouch for the memos, in fact, multiple someones, if we were to use them on air. I asked Mary to get four independent experts to verify that they were genuine, but she was already on it. Mary had faxed the documents to New York and had asked Yvonne Miller, an associate producer, to start lining up experts to examine them.

Mary and I flew to Austin so I could interview Robert Strong, who had been in the Texas Air National Guard and who had known Jerry Killian. We showed him the documents. He felt very strongly that they were a good representation of Lieutenant Colonel Killian's attitude about military obligations. He also said that they reflected the opinions Killian had voiced to him about the part-time and privileged National Guard members he oversaw in his unit.

When the interview was over, we flew back to New York. I caught just a couple hours' sleep before coming in to anchor special-events coverage on President Clinton's heart bypass surgery. Mary logged about the same number of hours of sleep before going into the office, which on Labor Day was all but empty.

Josh Howard and Andrew Heyward were not present, even though Andrew had previously assured me that he would be personally involved, as he had been with Abu Ghraib. Josh was our new executive producer, and I would have liked to see Andrew looking over his shoulder, since this was Josh's first executive producer position. (Jeff Fager had ascended to the next rung and had been anointed as Don Hewitt's successor at *60 Minutes* Sunday.) As it was, neither Andrew nor Josh nor VP Betsy West was there at this crucial time. Despite the holiday, on a story with this much sensitivity and this much explosive potential, leadership in the News Division should have been in the office shepherding the story, debating approaches and helping with content decisions. In the days of Richard Salant and Fred Friendly, they would have been. I believe that if Andrew Heyward had done his job, if Betsy West had done her job, they would have made sure Mary had more help, but she was just swamped.

Yvonne Miller had sent the faxed copies of the Killian memos we'd received from Burkett to three independent document analysts: Marcel Matley, James Pierce and Emily Will, together with Killian signatures from Bush's official records. Mary had already handed off another set to a fourth analyst, Linda James. James indicated that she wanted to examine the originals before rendering an opinion. Emily Will had a problem from the outset. She doubted that they were genuine, she said, because according to official records Bush had been in Alabama at the time these memos were written—which, of course, was exactly the point. Jim Pierce had worked with the Los Angeles Police Department and had done document analysis for the FBI. He was unequivocal in his assessment that the memos we had received from Burkett were consistent with other official records in Killian's hand.

We flew Marcel Matley to New York to see the documents firsthand. Matley was considered something of a wise man in the field of document analysis. He had written a number of books on the subject and was regularly called to testify in court as an expert witness. We talked with him a great deal about the science and art of handwriting and document analysis. We knew that it was often used in court; we also knew that there were limitations on what the analysis could and could not confirm. Matley spent a great deal of time examining the signatures as well as the typeface. He looked for all kinds of specifics, what he called "consistent inconsistencies" and "inconsistent consistencies." Matley saw absolutely no reason to believe that what we had was not legitimate in terms of typeface, structure of the document and analysis of the signatures in comparison with other official documents already in our possession.

On Tuesday, September 7, Ben Barnes came in for his interview. With the cameras rolling, he said that he'd helped George Bush get into the Texas Air National Guard and that he'd done the same for other sons of privilege. He also talked about the personal remorse he felt at what he'd done and his realization over the years that what he'd done was wrong.

That same day, we came together to discuss the piece—Mary, Betsy West, Josh Howard, Andrew Heyward and me. We talked specifically about how the memos had been examined; everyone seemed satisfied that we had done due diligence in that regard.

It was time to ask the White House to comment. I was slated to go to Washington early on Wednesday morning, the day of the broadcast, to interview Dan Bartlett, White House communications director. The weather, however, looked bad for getting out of New York, and there was a chance that even if I got to DC, I wouldn't be able to get back. John Roberts, a CBS correspondent and a good friend of mine, did the Bartlett interview instead.

I was aware that Bartlett, along with Karen Hughes, had long been suspected in political circles as the pair who had allegedly sanitized Bush's National Guard record back in the late 1990s. From the beginning of Bush's political career, there had been a buzz in Texas about problems with Bush's record of service in the Guard. Bartlett and Hughes were consistently the point people authorized to discuss it with the media. Over time, the buzz got louder as to how Bartlett had "made his bones" by making the issue go away. It was Bartlett who had delivered several of the conflicting explanations for why Bush had not taken his physical, despite being ordered to do so. Nevertheless, if we were going to get a response from the White House, it had to come through him.

During the interview with Roberts, Bartlett glossed over questions about Bush's record while in the Guard and returned over and over to the idea that all this was old news, and to the fact that Bush had been honorably discharged. We had already faxed copies of our documents to the White House so they could have a look at them. At our request, Bartlett also showed them to President Bush and asked him to comment. His reply: "I have no recollection of any of this." Both Josh Howard and Andrew Heyward were ecstatic when they learned what the White House response had been, because it meant that they had denied nothing whatsoever.

As was the case with Abu Ghraib, the decision to air the segment on Bush and the Texas Air National Guard rested in the hands of the executives of the News Division. There has been a lot of hindsight discussion and second-guessing about why we did not defer the piece to a later airdate. That was not our decision to make, and we were told it was not possible. Because 60 Minutes II was to be preempted twice in various parts of the country over the next few weeks (once for Billy Graham and a second time for Dr. Phil), we would have had to hold it till October, and management deemed that too late to run it.

Josh Howard, our executive producer, said we had two choices: run the story on the 8th, or forget the story. Now or never. We even asked whether it could run on the Sunday 60 Minutes and were turned down. It was a matter of politics—internal CBS politics. Since I wasn't a regular correspondent on the Sunday show, they didn't want a segment of mine airing there. We had to make the piece work for the September 8 airdate.

Before any segment is broadcast, there is a final screening. Typically there is at least one lawyer from the CBS Corporate General Counsel's Office in attendance. This one had two. The screening was held at 3:30 in the afternoon; Betsy West, Mary Mapes and Josh Howard were there. Andrew Heyward got a private screening, after the others. I only know any of this secondhand, because I was not at the screening. In all my time at CBS, the correspondent had always had a chance to see his or her piece before it aired. Not only was I absent, I was not even notified that the screening was happening. I found out through a chance encounter with a tape editor as I was crossing 57th Street.

At that point I was crisscrossing 57th Street a lot, because I was shuttling back and forth between doing on-camera work and voice-overs for *60 Minutes II* and getting ready for the *Evening News*. There was a full-on frenzy of writing, editing and rewriting to get the Bush/Guard segment ready to air. Finally we were good to go, but only *after* Executive Producer Josh Howard, Vice President Betsy West, News Division president Andrew Heyward and the lawyers from corporate *all* signed off on the story. When I finally got a chance to speak with Josh, he neglected to mention that two portions of the segment had been edited down or out—probably at Andrew Heyward's direction. These were interviews that I thought were crucial to the story. With the benefit of hindsight, I believe that the key reason I was uninvited from the screening was that they knew I would object strongly to removing them.

One was the interview with handwriting analyst Marcel Matley, which was not eliminated outright but was much truncated. It was the only on-camera interview we had with an expert explaining why he was confident that Killian's signature was genuine, and he was the only document analyst who'd seen anything other than a faxed copy. In my opinion, the executives found him boring. In their view, his detailed explanations about why he believed in the documents slowed the story down.

The other was a conversation with David Hackworth, the highly decorated retired Army colonel who ran the website called Soldiers for the Truth. At this point, David Hackworth had less than a year to live. He was terminally ill with bladder cancer, a disease that may have resulted from his exposure to chemical defoliants in Vietnam.

At our request, Hackworth reviewed everything we had procured from Bush's official records. He was especially taken aback by the year-long gap in documentation. With the exception of seeing a dentist at Dannelly in Alabama in January 1973, there was no official record of Bush's having done anything with the Guard between May 1972 and May 1973.

Despite being debilitated by chemotherapy, Hackworth wanted to go on the record; for him, Bush's dereliction of duty was personal. Soldiers who had risked their lives in Vietnam had long known about Bush, he told me. "What we know," he said, "is that when his country needed him, our president walked away." On behalf of the grunts he had served with in Vietnam, as well as the grunts in Iraq and Afghanistan for whom he worked diligently to procure better lifesaving body armor, he deeply resented what Bush had done.

Hackworth had absolutely no doubt that Bush had gone AWOL, or worse. AWOL is defined as absence for 30 days or less, but Bush's absence had been far more lengthy. The question for Hackworth was whether George Bush had deserted. Desertion is defined as absence with a determined intent not to return. "Let me put it this way," he said. "I don't care if you're a buck private or a five-star general, nobody just disappears. No institution generates paperwork like the military. All duty is observed and evaluated. If he'd been doing drills, there would be a record. I think he deserted."

I didn't know about removals of the Hackworth and Matley interviews until after the show had already aired. At first I was incredulous: we had a hero, one of our country's most decorated senior officers, saying on camera that he thought his commander in chief was at least AWOL and probably a deserter—and that had been edited out? We had backed away from something as powerful as that? Josh Howard told Mary he thought Hackworth had come on too strong.

He pruned other portions of the script as well, cutting out sections that demonstrated how well the new information fit within the context of what we already knew. He also ordered the removal of a portion of the script referring to a statement by General Bobby Hodges, Killian's immediate commanding officer, saying that the Killian memos were consistent with what he'd heard Killian say about Lieutenant Bush at the time. Perhaps Josh didn't realize it, but with these deletions he eviscerated major underpinnings supporting the integrity of the piece. By the way it was edited, the impression left with the viewer was that everything we said rested on the Killian memos, not on the huge body of additional documentation we had amassed. I went from incredulous to angry when I realized that it had been deliberately done behind my back.

Soon enough, however, my anger no longer mattered. Shortly after the broadcast, someone called to tell me we were catching a lot of flack on the Internet. With a piece like that, I thought it was to be expected, but what was different in this case was the intensity of the vilification.

Bloggers on ultraconservative websites with names like Free Republic, Little Green Footballs, and Power Line were vociferously attacking our report, even before it finished airing, and they were focusing in particular on the Killian documents. The websites trumpeted their certainty that the Killian memos were counterfeit—and alleged that we had forged them ourselves.

One particularly detailed analysis was posted on Free Republic by a blogger calling himself Buckhead. With an apparently encyclopedic knowledge of the history of typography and of typeface minutia, Buckhead zeroed in on what he declared were obvious telltale inconsistencies in the Killian memos—the font was wrong; proportional spacing didn't exist yet; typewriters couldn't produce the superscript "th" back then. "I am saying these documents are forgeries run through a copier for 15 generations to make them look old," he wrote. "This should be pursued aggressively."

Buckhead had rendered his judgment about four hours after the broadcast ended. Moreover, what he ostensibly had scrutinized was a fleeting image on a television screen. Without actually having seen the documents themselves, Buckhead pronounced the memos to be phony. Other instant experts on other right-wing websites chimed in soon thereafter. To authenticate their accusations, they cited one another, and the reverberating noise in cyberspace picked up decibels with each bounce off the wall.

Although it is commonplace today, it bears mentioning that in September 2004, using the Internet as a political tool was in its infancy. We didn't realize it at the time, but what we were seeing was the beginning of a well-orchestrated Internet campaign, what has since become known as a blogswarm. And we were in the crosshairs. At the time, CBS News had no Internet presence of its own and was not accustomed to the new rules of engagement in cyberspace. The Internet attacks on our report snowballed overnight, so much so that by Thursday morning Josh Howard was completely unnerved.

He was not alone. Everyone at CBS was blindsided by what was happening. We had never been attacked this way before. CBS had no crisis management staff, no playbook for how to respond. We were overwhelmed.

The attacks didn't stop with the Internet, however. We were inundated with irate phone calls and deluged with vitriolic faxes. It was a tsunami of outrage. The fax machine right outside Mary's office was running constantly, spewing out hate mail, page after page after page. Fake! Fake! Fake! they screamed. And that was the best of it. Many were obscene. Some were threatening.

I was as astounded as I was outraged. "Mary—what the hell is going on here?" I asked as I watched the machine spitting venom as fast as it could.

"It's been doing that all day long," she said.

"There's a general fax line for CBS News, but this particular line is unlisted," I said. "How did anyone get the number?"

"One of the last times I used it was to send the Killian documents to the White House," she said. "Before the interview with Bartlett. Doesn't the outgoing fax number show up as a header on each page?"

Not surprisingly, the same allegations that were appearing on the Internet soon sprang up in right-wing media outlets. Creative Response Concepts, a conservative PR firm, sent out a media advisory on Thursday the 9th reading, "60 Minutes Documents on Bush Might Be Fake." CRC was headed by Greg Mueller, former communications director for Pat Buchanan, and by Mike Russell, former communications director for Pat Robertson. CRC clients included the Republican National Committee, as well as the National Republican Congressional and Senatorial committees. At the time, Mike Russell was also the media spokesman for Swift Boat Veterans for Truth. Their version of the story quickly aired on AM talk radio and, of course, Fox News.

By this time I had been employed by CBS for more than 40 years. During those four decades, the network had come under intense criticism on numerous occasions—for our civil rights reporting, for *The Selling of the Pentagon*, and for our Watergate coverage, to name just a few. I knew nothing about how to deal with an Internet-based attack— none of us did—but I did know how CBS News had always responded to assaults from the outside. During those crises, the News Division had instinctively closed ranks to present a unified front, both to the adversary and to the public. Richard Salant, who had been president of

CBS News during many of these attacks, put it succinctly in his memoirs: "The people in CBS News were, in their way, a tight and prickly extended family, which circled the wagons at any signal that News was, in its view, being threatened." In response to these new attacks from outside, I tried to keep that faith and circle my wagon, only to find out that there weren't any other CBS wagons circling with me.

I knew that the first 48 to 72 hours were critical, and that we had to hold ourselves together. If we believed in the story, and I unequivocally did, it was essential to fight the accusers ferociously, hand to hand in every trench. I was soon contacted by Gil Schwartz, CBS's corporate VP in charge of communications. It appeared at first blush that Gil's job was to craft that vigorous defense of our story, but I later concluded Gil's assignment was to keep CBS's Big Wagon—Leslie Moonves—as far removed from the circle as possible.

Shortly thereafter, someone in Gil's office asked me whether I would be willing to speak with a reporter from the *Washington Post*. I was happy to oblige. The interviewer asked what we had done to check out our sources on the story. I explained at some length, but then was amazed and disappointed when I saw that very little of what I'd said appeared in the *Post* the next morning. Instead, the story that ran on Friday, September 10th, took us apart. The piece reiterated everything the original attackers had claimed to be bogus about the Killian memos: The font was wrong; proportional spacing didn't exist yet; typewriters couldn't produce the superscript "th" back then... In short, the *Post* took at face value the allegations made by Buckhead and others in the blogswarm and then echoed them pretty much verbatim.

By rehashing the right wing's unsubstantiated allegations, the article in the *Post* stoked the fire of the controversy and validated the accusations made by the bloggers. This struck me as anything but objective journalism. It seemed to me to be downright incendiary. The piece in the *Post* detonated a series of virulent anti-CBS, anti-Rather, and anti-Mapes explosions coming not just from right-wing websites, but from legitimate media outlets as well.

The typeface smokescreen laid down by the bloggers paid off big time. By implication, they charged, because of the questions raised about the documents, everything else in the broadcast had to be false as well. In my estimation, the *Post* has a great deal to answer for. For the rest of the mainstream media, the *Post* story legitimized the blogo-sphere's accusations that the Killian memos were fraudulent.

From that point on, there was blood in the water—mine, Mary's and the News Division's. The long knives were out, and we were targets for every other news organization in the country. Ordinarily, with a story of this nature the rest of the press digs further into the story. Instead, they dug into us.

The ruckus over the Killian memos effectively diverted any and all further journalistic inquiry into Bush's activities; in close-up magic, they call it misdirection. While every other news outlet was preoc-cupied by the bloggers' sleight of hand about superscripts and pro-portional spacing, no other reporters picked up on the legitimate question of whether Lieutenant Bush had actually fulfilled his military obligations.

• No one tried to find an explanation for why he'd been bounced back into a T-33 training aircraft in spring of 1972, or why it had taken him two passes on two different occasions to land his F-102.

• No one asked President Bush to explain why he had refused a direct order to take the physical he was required to take to keep flying.

• No one asked whether his refusal had anything to do with the fact that the Department of Defense instituted random drug testing in April 1972.

• No one asked how he was able to just walk away from his aircraft and stop flying—after American taxpayers had invested upward of a million dollars in his training.

• No one looked into his missing year from mid-1972 to mid-1973, or the fact that he never reported to any Guard unit in Boston/Cambridge as he was obligated to do once he began graduate school, or how he got discharged early.

All further reportage about the story was solely about the Killian memos. The story, and the extreme reaction to it, had intimidated not just CBS, but the rest of the press as well. It was a journalistic meltdown of the first magnitude.

The *Post* story also meant that every phone in the News Division was ringing off the hook on Friday morning. Someone had to respond, and corporate believed that someone was me. What I heard time and time again was, "Dan, you care about the institution. You care about the legacy of Edward R. Murrow. You are the brand, the 'face' of CBS News, and you are the correspondent on this story. We want you to speak to every print organization that's made a request. We want you to speak to every radio organization. We want you all over TV. We need you to go balls out on our response on this."

Because I absolutely believed in the story, and because of that 40-year-old tattoo on my ass, I did. I spent an entire day at CBS News talking to other journalists. I assured one and all that we at CBS stood by our reporting—and by our reporters. I was so busy defending the story, my team and the network that I never noticed that I was circling my wagon all by myself. The leadership of the News Division had completely disappeared. Particularly conspicuous by his absence in the defense of our story was our president, Andrew Heyward, the man whose final approval had put the piece on the air.

With the benefit of hindsight, it is now clear to me that this was the beginning of the cocooning process by which the higher-ups hermetically sealed themselves off from the problem. It was particularly important to Leslie Moonves that he remain above the fray. Just over three months earlier, Viacom chair Sumner Redstone had named Moonves, CEO of CBS, and Tom Freston, CEO of MTV, as co-presidents and co–chief operating officers as part of what was billed as a Viacom corporate succession plan. Freston was as easygoing as Moonves was intense; small wonder they got along about as well as two tomcats in a gunnysack.

Which was exactly where Redstone had put them. Deliberately.

Redstone, then 81 years old, had yoked them together in a high-level rivalry—in every way a clash of the titans—to determine who would succeed him. Presumably, if Moonves was to get entangled in this Bush controversy, it would have jeopardized his chances of inheriting Redstone's mantle, provided Redstone ever let go of it.

Meanwhile, we started playing defense. Mary worked till she was truly cross-eyed to prove that every factoid that had been singled out by Buckhead and other bloggers, everything that had been parroted by the *Post*, was either untrue or unproven. In saying we were wrong, they were wrong on every count. Yes, you *could* make a superscript "th" on a typewriter back then. There were examples all over the newsroom. No, that font was most assuredly *not* computer-generated Times New Roman.

She did this virtually alone, because Mary had quickly become the office leper. Not only was she being demonized by outsiders, both online and in the mainstream press, she was taking a lot of heat internally as well. The chorus of boos within CBS was led by the *60 Minutes* Sunday contingent, which had its envies and jealousies of her going back to her story on Abu Ghraib, and to her story on Essie Mae Washington-Williams, Strom Thurmond's biracial daughter, before that.

By Sunday the 12th, I started to get all kinds of unsubtle hints that I should let Mary take the fall for what had happened. The pressure was coming from friend and foe alike. I found it necessary to reiterate that the tradition of CBS News had always been solidarity. We hold ourselves together while we're in the vortex, and we come out the other end together, just like any other fight you get into. You have to steel your will. Some well-meaning individuals even called my longtime friend and agent, Richard Leibner, asking him to intercede. They wanted him to put the bug in my ear to throw Mary overboard. Without apology then or now, my answer was, "Absolutely not. If you think I'm going to cut Mary loose or scapegoat her, you don't know me very well. Mary is a great reporter in the very best tradition of CBS News, a great producer, and not in my presence am I going to hear any talk of blaming her or cutting her loose. And by the way, if you think tossing Mary to the dogs is going to do anything other than increase their appetite, then you don't know much about how these things work."

Following the broadcast, the analysts came under almost as much scrutiny as the memos themselves. The issue was whether they could "authenticate" the documents. For a layman, "authenticate" means being able to verify that a given object is genuine. For an expert witness accustomed to testifying in court, however, the term "authenticate" has a precise and far more rigorous legal definition. For a document analyst, it denotes 100 percent certainty, based on being able to prove where and when the paper originated, what kind of ink was used, etc. Because Burkett had given us photocopies, our experts knew that they would not be able to fully "authenticate" the documents in this very specific legal sense of the word. We at CBS understood it as well.

In the blaze that arced the gap from the right-wing blogosphere to the mainstream media, however, we were all excoriated for this "failure to authenticate." Those who criticized us the most fiercely were, of course, using the word "authenticate" in the informal, everyday sense of the word—as if we had neglected to do any checking whatsoever. Lost in the ensuing firestorm was the fact that James Pierce never wavered in his opinion that the signatures were Killian's. Marcel Matley continued to reiterate his assessment that the typeface was consistent with what was available in the early 1970s and that all of the signatures, both in Bush's official records and in the Killian memos we received from Burkett, appeared to be by the same hand. And he stands by that analysis to this day.

Emily Will and Linda James, however, backpedaled furiously and insisted they had warned that the documents could be fake. Perhaps Emily Will should have revealed that she was not exactly nonpartisan. Her initial inclination to take Bush's records at face value and presume he was in Alabama when he said he was should have been a clue. Later records show that Emily Will is a Republican Party financial supporter. From an ethical standpoint, I believe that this was an assignment she should have declined.

Other typeface experts soon came out of the woodwork, including several who claimed they could produce exact replicas on their computers. It was not until months later that Dr. David Hailey, associate professor of Professional and Technical Communication at Utah State

University, confirmed and bolstered our initial findings with extensive and rigorous scientific analysis. After blowing up the documents to many times their original size—in his words, literally to the size of sofa cushions—he examined them in close detail. He prepared a 170-page report and summarized his finding as follows: "There can no longer be a question whether the memos were typed—they were typed."

Hailey found that what others had seen as proportional spacing was in fact fractions of carriage returns. He also looked at ink placement and saw idiosyncrasies and differences in wear on individual letters— especially on the "e" and "t," the most commonly used letters— something that is not possible on a computer. Through magnification, he discovered "signature interaction" between the pen stroke of the Killian signature and the typing—the pen sliding in and out of the vertical lines of typed capital letters, something only possible if there were impressions on the page from typing *before* the signature was made. He also identified characters in the documents that were not consistent with the Times New Roman typestyle. The Bush-supporting bloggers had relied on the false conclusion that the Killian documents were in Times New Roman, a typestyle not in existence during the Vietnam War. If a document is typed in a particular typestyle, *all* the characters have to match, and several of the characters in the Killian memos do not match Times New Roman.

In the days immediately following the broadcast, however, this ammunition was not available to us. As the controversy mushroomed, the Hard Right rallied Bush supporters to counter our version of events, and often to contradict themselves. General Bobby Hodges, who had initially corroborated the story to us in detail, now told ABC that we'd misled him and that he, too, thought the documents had been forged. Killian's son Gary assured the press that his late father would never have kept a CYA file, this despite having told us before the segment aired that he knew very little about his father's career in the National Guard.

On September 15, Mary accompanied 86-year-old Marian Carr Knox, who had been Killian's secretary, from Texas to New York to be interviewed about the memos. Neither Mary nor anyone on our team had found Mrs. Knox. The Associated Press had found her after our program aired. If we'd found her beforehand, we would have used her. "I know that I didn't type them," she told us. "However, the information in those is correct." She said that what was in them squared with what Killian thought of Lieutenant Bush. Killian and the other officers would "snicker about what [Bush] was getting away with." She clearly remembered the colonel being angry at Bush's refusal of a direct order to take his flight physical, and at his attitude of entitlement. She also acknowledged that Killian had started what she called a "cover-your-back" file dealing with problems such as these. That was the positive; the negative was that she said she had not typed the memos. What emerged in the press thereafter was only about the negative. There was nothing about Bush refusing a direct order and everything about Mrs. Knox saying that she didn't type them, so therefore, it was concluded, the memos weren't genuine.

At Andrew Heyward's direction, Mary set up a conference call with Bill Burkett. One huge question was how the memos had found their way to him. He had previously given us the name of George Conn as the source, but as Andrew began to question him more intently, he changed his story completely and now said that Conn had nothing to do with it. Betsy West, Mary, Heyward and I were all astonished when he said that a woman named Lucy Ramirez, whom he'd never mentioned before, had had a dark-skinned man deliver the papers to him at the Houston Livestock Show.

This came entirely out of the blue, and it was dreadful news. What Burkett probably did not realize was that when a source lies about anything, he completely loses all credibility. He handed potent new ammunition to those who were already screaming that the documents were false. He also handed Andrew Heyward a get-out-of-jail-free card for distancing himself and everyone above him from the crisis. After the call ended, Heyward directed Mary to get him on camera.

Shortly thereafter, Andrew Heyward ordered Mary to stop working on the story, even by phone, even from her own home. Professionally, she was placed under house arrest. Then CBS forbade *anyone* from working on the story in any way, shape or form, including me. In effect, we were ordered to surrender, and for the life of me I couldn't understand why.

I went to Heyward to complain. "This is madness," I told him. "We are under unrelenting attack on a story that you and I both know is true."

"That's not the point, Dan."

I tried to hide my amazement—unsuccessfully, I suspect. The president of CBS News was telling me directly that defending the truth didn't matter. "Why not?"

"Because the documents have been made the focal point."

"Andrew, anyone who has studied combat knows that you don't let the enemy choose the ground where the decisive battle is to be fought."

It didn't register. I might as well have been speaking Martian. "Dan, you don't understand. No more," he said flatly.

"Andrew, that's unacceptable."

And with that, I went back to my desk. I thought about it briefly and then headed back to his office. "Andrew, you've completely shut down CBS News from investigating this any further. To me that's just wrong. We can't just throw up our hands and surrender, above all on a story that we know to be true. I feel so strongly about this that I'm going to hire an investigator on my own, with money from my own pocket."

Andrew tried to keep a poker face, but his eyes registered alarm. I really knew I'd gotten his attention because he insisted there must surely be a clause in my contract that would prevent me from doing that. I had just lined up a former NYC homicide detective to begin my investigation when Heyward came back to me with a different proposal. CBS, he said, was going to hire its own outside investigative team. At first he indicated they were looking at Kroll Inc., a large and prestigious New York–based investigative firm, but he backed away from that quickly, saying that Kroll had wanted too much money. The company they turned to instead was SafirRosetti, a security firm that was run by Howard Safir.

I immediately expressed my skepticism. Even if they were competent, this hardly sounded to me like a disinterested outfit: Howard Safir had been Rudy Giuliani's police commissioner. Safir's firm jobbed out the assignment to a former FBI investigator named Erik Rigler. Word came back pretty quickly that Rigler had run up against stone walls everywhere. He never got any farther than Bill Burkett.

On September 18, a reporter for the *Los Angeles Times*, Peter Wallsten, broke what should have been a major development when he outed Buckhead as Harry MacDougald, an Atlanta attorney. In the wake of the Monica Lewinsky affair, Harry MacDougald had helped draft the motion to the Arkansas Supreme Court asking that former president Clinton be disbarred in his home state. But even this startling revelation—that Buckhead was not a typography expert but a conservative activist with strong ties to the Republican Party—did nothing to derail the "phony documents" juggernaut.

By this time, the story had taken on a life of its own. Instead of broadcasting the news, we had become the news, which is every journalist's worst nightmare.

The night before I was to interview Burkett, Andrew Heyward convened a meeting without my knowledge with some of his top staff and a few other colleagues in the New York broadcast center. A person who was in the room revealed to me several years later that Heyward told those in attendance that under no circumstances was I to learn what was discussed, or even that there had been a meeting at all.

The purpose of the clandestine gathering was to strategize and plan for the Burkett interview. I had been ordered to conduct the interview, but the purpose was not disclosed to me. I had been informed that the intention was to give Burkett a chance to explain himself and to give his side of the story. I was also told that it would be put on the air "at some length," but that was not the real agenda.

On September 18, I flew to Dallas to meet up with Mary and do the interview with Burkett. Betsy West was assigned to come with me, bringing a specific list of questions I was to ask. She didn't tell me at the time, but the list had come from Andrew Heyward. Earlier I had asked Heyward to go with me for the interview. He had refused. He was heavily into his distancing mode, but I wasn't smart enough to see it then. I still trusted him. As I later learned, he had given Betsy the job of making sure I got what management needed out of Burkett, which was for him to say that he had lied about the chain of custody of the documents, and to say it on camera. That's all they wanted out of him. I came to realize that it was never their intention to broadcast "at some length." Midway through, Betsy gave me a few extra questions. I knew these had come from Heyward as well, because she had just gotten off the phone with him. The questions turned the interview into a grueling interrogation, forcing Burkett to state over and over that he'd lied. The interview lasted the better part of three hours.

After finishing with Burkett, I went to see my daughter and grandson. While there, I was told to report to Andrew Heyward's office at 8:00 p.m. Sunday night. This was a first, the only time any CBS News president had ever given me a direct order. I was due back in New York at 9:00 a.m. the following morning, but I was told that was not soon enough. I flew back to New York for my command performance.

As I recall, when I arrived, Heyward told me that CBS was going to apologize for the documents and that they expected me to apologize personally as well.

"Are you going to retract the story?" I asked.

"No, but we're going to apologize."

"Well, what exactly are we apologizing about?"

It was a gentlemanly discussion, but I took the severity of it very seriously. Heyward then gave me another loyalty pep talk. "Dan, we need to stick together. You have always shown great allegiance to the institution, and this is about saving the institution. The company wants CBS News to come out of this as well as we can, and we want you to come out of this as well as you can, too. Surely you must regret what has happened."

"Of course I regret that we're under attack, and that it's giving us a mountain of bad publicity," I said. "That's why it's so important to defend the story."

"We're asking you to apologize. You need to do this for the good of CBS News, and for your own good."

Heyward also told me that the network was going to announce the establishment of an outside commission to investigate what happened. I told him immediately that this was a bad idea. We hadn't done it during the McCarthy era, during our civil rights broadcasts or after sustaining heavy criticism about either *The Selling of the Pentagon* or *The Uncounted Enemy*. *The Uncounted Enemy* was a documentary that aired at the beginning of 1982. It had been put together by Mike Wallace and George Crile, two excellent reporters, but it was revealed to have had some ethics and editing issues. At the time, CBS News conducted its own internal investigation of that case. While investigators said the reporting and editing *process* had serious flaws, the story was true. So CBS, top to bottom, stood by it and defended it—including defending it in court.

But that was then; Paley was in charge. This was now; Redstone was in charge. A lot had changed since then, Heyward told me; in today's climate, the outside review was necessary. He assured me that the commission would be truly independent and that the impartial individuals on it would be appointed by corporate.

After thinking about it overnight, I agreed to be the one to read the corporate speech of contrition, and also my own mea culpa. Andrew Heyward wrote it for me at my secretary's computer. On September 20, I delivered the official CBS apology, and a separate one of my own: "I made a mistake," I said. "I didn't ask enough of the right questions, and I trusted a source who changed his story. It turns out he misled us. There are no excuses...and I'm sorry for it." I didn't feel good about it going in, while I was reading it or after I'd finished. They used the interview with Bill Burkett in the same broadcast, cutting it down to just the snippets where he said that he lied.

On September 22, at 10:01 in the morning I was in a car being driven from a public appearance. I took a call from Andrew Heyward. "This is to inform you that we have appointed an independent commission. It's going to be led by Richard Thornburgh."

I slammed my fist down on the dashboard so hard I hurt my hand. I let out a string of expletives best left deleted. "Andrew," I said loudly, "this is insane!"

Richard Thornburgh had been the U.S. attorney general, first under Ronald Reagan and then under George H. W. Bush. He still had close ties to the Bush family. CBS had tapped Thornburgh, a Republican lawyer from Bush's cabinet, to investigate whether his own former boss and close personal friend had used undue influence to get his son into the Texas Air National Guard. It was the next best thing to asking Bush to investigate himself.

"Andrew, exactly what is independent and impartial about this?" I asked.

"Dan, you don't understand," he said coolly. "This is a masterstroke of genius. Dick Thornburgh has credibility with the Bush people and the right wing, and with everyone who is giving us a hard time."

Andrew was very calm—which I was not. "Of course he has credibility with them!" I shouted. "He *IS* them!"

"Dan, this is a courtesy call," he continued somewhat stiffly. "The announcement has just been made."

Named with Thornburgh was Louis Boccardi, the recently retired CEO of the Associated Press. Boccardi was indebted to the Bush family as well. As vice president, George H. W. Bush had been instrumental in securing the release of AP reporter Terry Anderson, who'd been held hostage by Hezbollah in Lebanon in the late 1980s and early 1990s. Two kangaroos had been issued black robes and installed in the Star Chamber. They were to render their verdict with all deliberate speed.

Shortly thereafter, Andrew Heyward made the pilgrimage to Washington and apologized to the White House. For good measure, the network spiked a *60 Minutes* Sunday story by Ed Bradley on how forged documents had been deployed by the Bush administration to make the case for going to war in Iraq.

Then, on September 24, Viacom chief Sumner Redstone issued the following statement:

> From a Viacom standpoint, the election of a Republican administration is a better deal. Because the Republican administration has stood for many things we believe in, deregulation and so on...I vote for Viacom. Viacom is my life, and I do believe that a Republican administration is better for media companies than a Democratic one.

When I heard that, I was hotter than the anvil of the Devil himself. After the establishment of the "independent" Thornburgh commission, however, I suppose I shouldn't have been surprised. Now, even the fig leaf of "independent" had been dropped. Viacom's naked partisanship was out in the open. At the time, Viacom had a number of matters before federal regulatory agencies. Although still rebounding from the $550,000 fine levied by the Federal Communications Commission over Janet Jackson's Super Bowl "wardrobe malfunction," the company was engaged in an aggressive lobbying effort targeted at key House Republicans and friends of George W. Bush to ensure the maintenance of loosened FCC regulations on media ownership, regulations that had a direct effect on Viacom's bottom line. This was corporatization of the news at its most blatant, and Sumner Redstone seemed to be boasting of it to the world.

It now seemed absolutely clear why we had been ordered to drop any further investigation into Bush's experience in the Texas Air National Guard. CBS News was messing up Viacom's game plan in Washington. Redstone's agenda for an ever-bigger Viacom was jeopardized by the emergence of truths about Bush's past. Moonves had to defer to Redstone if he wanted to inherit the throne. Had I known this, of course, I would have had nothing to do with the on-air apology or the punitive interview with Bill Burkett.

It's a shame that Leslie Moonves missed his moment to stand tall. At a time when he needed to put steel in his spine—to stand up to Redstone and Viacom on behalf of CBS, and in particular on behalf of CBS News—Moonves had Jell-O in his spine instead. It's too bad he didn't "man up," in contemporary parlance. Here was his chance to show leadership, to do what Bill Paley and Richard Salant and other leaders of CBS had done before. In my mind, history would have been quite different if Moonves and Heyward had had the guts CBS and particularly CBS News had been known for.

Since they did not, from then on there was little doubt that we were to be thrown under the bus—or perhaps thrown under the Big Wagon.

Election night 2004 ran long. I was on the air until about 6:00 a.m.

the next morning, until it became clear that George W. Bush had been
issued four more years. Not long after that, I took a call from Richard
Leibner. "I met with Moonves and Heyward," he said. "They want you
gone from the *Evening News* chair as quickly as they can get you out of
there. Their proposition is that it's better to go now, because if you wait
till the Thornburgh report comes out, it could be that they'd have to
ask you to leave because of it.

"I believe Moonves is under extraordinary heat from Sumner to have
you out the day before yesterday," he continued, "but I can work with
Moonves. He really does have your best interests at heart, Dan. He likes
you, and he's very sorry this has happened. If you agree to make the
announcement that you're stepping down, you'll segue into working on
60 Minutes Sunday and everything will be fine."

Although Richard was—and is—my friend and longtime agent, I
still had major concerns. The situation with CBS put him in a bit of
an awkward box, because he had to deal with Les Moonves on behalf
of several of his other clients. And, of course, I knew who the people
on the commission were, and that most of the work was being done
by Kirkpatrick & Lockhart, Dick Thornburgh's law firm. These were
people with no background in journalism whatsoever.

No way did I expect a fair shake from them.

But I did expect a fair shake from Les Moonves when he said I would
become a regular full correspondent on *60 Minutes*.

On November 23, I announced that I would be leaving the *CBS
Evening News* as of March 9, 2005, my 24th anniversary in the anchor
chair.

On January 10, the "independent" Thornburgh commission regur-
gitated its final report, all 224 pages of it. While the report boasted that
CBS News "did not have any input or influence with respect to the
findings of the Panel," the Thornburgh commission had engaged in
an ongoing dialogue with CBS News executives and had shared preliminary drafts with Heyward and Linda Mason, then vice president
for public affairs. I believe a later draft had been sent to Leslie Moonves
while he was in Mexico on his honeymoon with CBS *Early Show* news

anchor and *Big Brother* host Julie Chen before the final version was released. Now that's what I call independent.

The report faulted our "myopic zeal" to be the first to broadcast the story. Josh Howard and Betsy West were asked to resign. So were Esther Kartiganer, who gave the final okay to scripts, and Mary Murphy, senior producer. Both had worked under Howard. They all did resign, eventually, but only after they lawyered up. We later learned that each of them, despite being shoved out the door, received a generous six- or seven-figure settlement (Howard's is believed to have been more than $2 million.) These settlements in some cases came only after the employees threatened to sue. They also received generous severance pay.

All of that came with a gag order attached. Viacom had bought their silence. I have no hard feelings about these four good people doing this. I understand. I understand completely. Just as I hope they will understand why I felt I had to go the way I did. Better off in personal finances, I would not consider agreeing to remain silent forever, and could afford to do so without hardship. These pay-for-silence deals raise questions not about why they were accepted but about why they were offered.

Andrew Heyward, who had signed off on the segment and presumably had made the final decision as to when and with what content it was to go on the air, escaped, at least for the moment. Even then, however, I thought it was only a temporary reprieve. Heyward left the company nine months later. His departure came less than a week after his 55th birthday, the milestone he needed to reach to be eligible for early retirement benefits. I doubt that was a coincidence.

Mary Mapes was fired outright. Mary had testified extensively before the commission and had submitted lengthy documentation as well. What she called her "meshing document," based on the thick notebook she'd been developing since she started working on the segment, demonstrated how well the Killian memos fit within the framework of what we officially knew about Bush's Air National Guard service. Although the 224-page report ballooned to doorstop heft with the addition of more than 700 pages of appendices, Mary's meshing document was omitted.

Thornburgh's team found fault with the fact that we relied on the two document experts who believed that Killian's signature was genuine. That said, they never interviewed James Pierce, the one analyst who never wavered in his belief in the authenticity of the documents, nor did they seek out their own expert analysts.

The report also criticized the documents' lack of a "chain of custody," a bit of legalese that is miles beyond the journalistic norm. By this criterion, the editorial board of the *Washington Post* should have required Bob Woodward to divulge the identity of Deep Throat before publishing a word about the Watergate break-in. As James Goodale, former vice chairman and general counsel for the *New York Times*, pointed out, by this standard, the *New York Times* should never have published the Pentagon Papers. In a piece for the *New York Review of Books*, Goodale demolished the Thornburgh report:

> The panel was unable to decide whether the documents were authentic or not. It didn't hire its own experts. It didn't interview the principal expert for CBS. It all but ignored an important argument for authenticating the documents—"meshing." It did not allow cross-examination. It introduced a standard for document authentication very difficult for news organizations to meet—"chain of custody"—and lastly, it characterized parts of the broadcast as false, misleading, or both in a way that is close to nonsensical.

No one should have been surprised that the kangaroo court had rendered a kangaroo verdict. Astonishingly, CBS was amazed that it satisfied no one. Because the report did not conclude that we had forged the documents and did not find that my reporting was politically biased, it greatly angered the right-wing torch-and-pitchfork bearers who had started the controversy.

I've spent a lot of time trying to figure out how a match lit on the Internet so quickly became a conflagration. The most plausible explanation is that there were a whole lot of folks blowing on the flame. On September 15, White House press secretary Scott McClellan told a press briefing that the White House had released the Killian memos we had shown them to other news organizations, or as he put it, to "everybody else, so you could look at them yourselves." Presumably, at the time these news organizations would have included Jeff Gannon at Talon News, who attended the daily White House press briefing. Gannon was an odd member of the White House press corps who always seemed to have the inside story. On September 13, Gannon had identified Mary as the producer on the Bush/Guard segment. On September 17, he had interviewed Mary's estranged father, who accused his daughter and me of plotting this "ever since Bush was elected"—four years earlier, in 2000.

Gannon was unmasked five months later as a fake correspondent for a sham news agency. Talon News was in fact an appendage of GOPUSA, a conservative website, which went a long way toward explaining his "insider" information. It would be reasonable to theorize that copies of the documents went from the White House to Jeff Gannon to Harry "Buckhead" MacDougald before the segment aired.

At this point, the White House was in full reelection mode, and they knew it would be a tough fight. During Bush's 2000 campaign, White House communications director Dan Bartlett had been Director of Rapid Response. As such, his job was to fight back quickly and aggressively against damaging news stories about the candidate. With the Killian memos, we had in effect lobbed a hanging curveball into Bartlett's wheelhouse.

Bartlett had been with Bush since his days in the Texas governor's office. Among his other responsibilities, he had served as the governor's liaison to the Texas National Guard and held that position in the year Bush's files had allegedly been scrubbed. Before working with Bush, he'd worked at Karl Rove & Associates. Following his departure from the White House, Bartlett became CEO of Public Strategies, Inc., a PR firm specializing in crisis response.

He also became a political analyst for CBS News.

When the Thornburgh report was published, it was my wife who provided the perspective I needed to hear. "You got into a fight with the president of the United States," she told me. "During the heat of his reelection campaign. What did you think was going to happen?"

What happened was that we spoke truth to power. And power had bellowed back through every bullhorn it could command. At the time, it was loud enough to drown out the truth.

CHAPTER 3

Roots

I can't remember a time when I didn't want to be a reporter. My parents were avid newspaper readers. The news mattered; they had yeasty discussions about it over dinner. Even when I was very young—four or five years old—I remember seeing them not only reading the paper but being thoroughly engrossed in it. To them, journalists were important people. They had great respect for reporters, and they passed that respect on to me as a child.

That didn't mean they agreed with everything they read. My father often took issue with the editorials and expressed his displeasure by flinging the paper up against the wall. "Byrl!" he'd yell at my mother. "Drop the *Houston Press*!"

My mother, Veda Byrl Page Rather, had been through this exercise many times before. At the time, my hometown of Houston had three daily papers: the *Chronicle*, the *Post* and the *Press*, and in our house they came and went out of favor in rotation, depending on my father's most recent reaction to them. As I was growing up, we canceled each of them at least five times. That day's *Press* was just the latest in a series of papers to leave the table airborne.

"Irvin," Mother said, "we've already dropped the *Post* and the *Chronicle*." My father's name was Daniel Irvin Rather, but everyone called him either Irvin or Rags.

"In that case," he muttered, "get the *St. Louis Post-Dispatch*."

"But Irvin, it'll take two or three days to get here by post."

"That's all right...Goddammit, I'm finished with these!"

The wonder of it was that it wasn't just talk. My father didn't just read newspapers; he devoured them. Much to my mother's displeasure, he stockpiled the ones he hadn't had time to get through in one sitting. He barricaded his favorite chair with them, and the piles never seemed to get smaller. In a house that was anything but spacious, his stacks of old newspapers were a problem, but they were sacrosanct. He refused to let my mother get rid of them.

Our small house at 1432 Prince Street was located in what was known as the Heights Annex. The Heights itself was a neighborhood that had started out at the turn of the century with dreams of grandeur and fancy Victorian gingerbread houses. By the 1930s, both the dreams and the houses had faded. The Heights Annex was many rungs below faded. There was nothing grand about it, never had been. What we think of as standard improvements were few. The streets were still unpaved. The houses weren't shacks, but some weren't much more than that, either. There were many vacant lots—and some outhouses—in the neighborhood. Although burglary was rare, domestic violence and street fights were not.

As far as the rest of Houston was concerned, the Annex was the wrong side of the tracks. If you weren't from here, you didn't come here. And if you were from here, getting someplace else wasn't easy; the nearest bus and streetcar were miles away, as was the nearest grocery. We minimized trips to the market by keeping a cow and some chickens, and by growing vegetables on one of the empty lots.

My mother worked part-time as a waitress and also took in sewing. She did whatever she could to supplement the family income, but always had dinner on the table when my father got home from work. My father was the breadwinner and in every respect the head of the household. He was a pipeliner, which meant he was a specialty ditch-digger, digging trenches for the pipes that carried crude oil from the wellheads inland to the port area on the Gulf. It was tough, sweaty, manual labor, but in the Depression of the 1930s, it was steady work, and we knew that was a blessing. In the neighborhood, the fact that my father always had a job made him something of a local VIP.

Even as a small boy, I understood that there were many other families in the Annex who were not so fortunate. Most men had no regular employment; many were on the dole. Several evenings a week there would be a soft knock on our back door. Men presented themselves hat in hand, asking as politely as they knew how whether there might be anything left over from our supper. Their families huddled a few paces off to the side. After satisfying himself that the family was worthy, my father would allow my mother to wrap up something for them. If we didn't have enough to spare, he would call other neighbors on their behalf. The message to me was clear: we were not flush, but we were not in need, and it behooved us to share what we had with those who had less.

There was never a lot of money for extras in our family, but to my parents, newspapers were an essential, not a luxury. After my father's outburst, we *did* get the *St. Louis Post-Dispatch*. We were probably the only people in a 50-mile radius of Houston—and maybe the whole state of Texas—who did. Eventually, one year we ended up with the *Christian Science Monitor*, and that had to come all the way from Boston.

Looking back, our family's love of news influenced me greatly. I always knew I wanted to be a reporter; the biggest dream I dared hope for was to hire on with the *Houston Chronicle* when I grew up. In my child's brain, one step toward reaching that goal was to work on the school newspaper. But at William G. Love Elementary School, we didn't have a school paper, so I decided to start my own.

My mother always did anything she could to encourage me. She put her support behind my idea of a school newspaper and went to the school to see what could be done. She found a willing ally in Mrs. Simmons, Love's principal. With the help of my mother and Mrs. Taylor, my first-grade teacher, I put together my newspaper. Mrs. Simmons had it typed up and copied as a stencil and distributed to each grade. It was the beginning of my career in journalism; I think I was missing my two front teeth at the time.

There's an Indian saying in Texas: "From time to time in life, you

should sit tall on your horse and look back over the trails you have traveled." From this particular vantage point on my particular horse, it is
clear that one of the great godsends of my life has been a series of excellent teachers. The first of these were at Love Elementary.

At that time, it was a pluperfect example of what you hope an elementary school will be, and mind you, this was in the toughest white
neighborhood in town. It went from first through sixth grade; we had
no kindergarten. Mrs. Simmons, by force of her intellect and her diligence, made it a nearly ideal place to educate and encourage young students. She found a way to nurture not just my dreams, but the dreams
of each child in her care. She always let us know that we could do anything we wanted to do, if we were willing to be hardworking and persistent. Today we would say she empowered us.

Mrs. Simmons ruled William G. Love as a personal fiefdom. She
was given very little direction from the central school district, never
mind the school board. It was very much her school, and she hired
very good teachers who shared her vision. I can still name every one of
them. Each was excellent in her own way, and all of them were truly
memorable. Mrs. Taylor, very much the earth mother, took me through
first and second grade and then passed me on to Miss Spencer, who
was much more of a schoolmarm. Each of them recognized my interests and nourished my abilities. It was Miss Spencer who pushed me to
improve both my handwriting and my spelling, not just as academic
disciplines but as practical skills an aspiring reporter needed to have.
(I did improve under her instruction, but I remained a poor speller all
through school, and beyond.)

I must have been about seven or eight one summer when I met "the
lady at the park," at least that's what we called her. Looking back, I'm
sure she was some sort of social worker hired by the city, but she gathered me and my friends around her at the park and read to us, then
asked if we'd like to go to the library. She took us to the Heights Library,
not just once but several times thereafter. I loved it so much that at the
end of the summer she took me to the main library downtown, which
was a major expedition. The building looked like something out of the
Knights of the Round Table, and the inside was even more astonishing.

Who knew so many books even existed? That summer with the lady at the park made a lifelong reader out of me, and my Houston Heights Library card was one of my most cherished possessions.

At home, the newspaper was a constant presence, and the radio was always on in the evenings. My parents listened intently. Through the late 1930s they followed the militant resurgence of Germany with increasing alarm. After hearing about *Mein Kampf,* my parents—these two people who worked with their hands—got a copy and read it. They discussed the book and the ominous developments in Europe with Uncle John, my father's younger brother, sometimes late into the night. As a kid, I felt privileged to sit around the edges of their discussions, listening to them. There were plenty of people at the time who were impressed with what Hitler had accomplished and were either unaware of or untroubled by the darker side of Nazism. You'd hear it said often enough: "Hitler pulled Germany out of despair; maybe this guy is on to something." My father wasn't having any of it. "He's a dictator and a dangerous man," he declared.

When Neville Chamberlain allowed Hitler to take the Sudetenland from Czechoslovakia in 1938, I can remember my father and Uncle John discussing it. I sensed that they knew this was a decisive moment, and not because they believed for an instant that Chamberlain's sellout of the Czechs had brought "peace in our time." When the Nazis moved on Poland in September 1939, there were earnest conversations about what would happen next.

My parents had their radio favorites. They made a point to hear Edward R. Murrow, Eric Sevareid and Charles Collingwood during this period before the war, a period Winston Churchill would later call the "gathering storm." Although they also listened to broadcasters like H. V. Kaltenborn, Gabriel Heatter and Lowell Thomas, names that have now faded into the mist, their radio favorites were the reporters on CBS who became known as "the Murrow Boys."

All too soon, I was listening to far more radio than I could have ever wanted. I didn't have a choice. When I was ten, I got sick. It started simply enough: My feet hurt. For the longest time, I didn't mention it to anyone. In the Heights Annex, whenever you hurt, whatever was hurting, we all knew to suck it up and keep going. There wasn't a lot of coddling to be expected.

Except that it kept getting worse. The pain intensified as it moved up my legs to my ankles and knees, and then began affecting my wrists. I had frequent sore throats. I was losing weight. I had no appetite and no energy. Everything hurt. Doctors were puzzled for many months until Dr. R. Louis Cope diagnosed my illness as rheumatic fever. Dr. Cope said there was no drug he could give me for it.

Although Alexander Fleming had already discovered penicillin, it had not yet become part of a doctor's arsenal against infection. Worse yet, the long-term prognosis for survivors of rheumatic fever was potentially dire. Patients were at risk of developing carditis—inflammation of the heart muscle. Too often this was followed by congestive heart failure and lifetime disability, or death. Only by not overtaxing the heart could this fate be avoided.

"I want him in bed and I don't want him to move," Dr. Cope told my mother sternly.

This has to be one of the hardest things for any 10-year-old to hear, and it was harder still for me. I loved school and I loved sports, baseball and football most of all. I'd always been an active child. Up till then I had lived something of a Huck Finn existence. In summers my friend Georgie Hoyt and I had fashioned rafts to float along the Buffalo Bayou. When we weren't skinny-dipping or hunting armadillos, he played Davy Crockett to my Jim Bowie. Now in an instant, all that was gone. I became an invalid. I was to be bedridden. Bedridden seriously, as in using a bedpan.

"For how long?" we asked.

"For as long as it takes," Dr. Cope replied. And even he couldn't guarantee that I'd ever be truly well again.

During those first few weeks I was petrified, literally scared to move. I didn't understand carditis, but I surely understood what the future held for a kid from the Annex who was disabled. My mother monitored my heartbeat and reported to the doctor on a regular basis. It was many painful months before I showed any signs of improvement at all. Eventually I got permission from Dr. Cope to get up and use the bathroom, and I treated each trip like the great pajama safari that it was.

He did warn us that rheumatic fever had a tendency to recur, and so it was with me. I had two long bouts of it, one from age 10 to 11½, the second from age 12 to 13½. Essentially I spent almost all of junior high in bed. I was officially enrolled in Hamilton Middle School, but it was pretty much a wipeout for me, because I had to be homeschooled. That makes it sound far more structured than it was. No teacher came to the house; they would sporadically send home whatever material we were studying, and Mom kept me up to speed with the schoolwork. From time to time I submitted papers. In a sense, during these years I was pretty much self-taught. It was a long, depressing time. My friends sometimes came by to cheer me up, but too often their visits just hammered home the fact that I was an invalid.

My parents had never touched a book on psychology, but they knew a lot about love, and about the importance of family togetherness. My mother turned our home life upside down to accommodate my illness; she would have done the same for my brother, Don, or my sister, Patricia. To keep me included in the life of the family, she served our meals on trays, and most nights everyone ate in my bedroom with me. Before I got sick, all of us kids had slept in the back room together. Now, to give me something to look at, my mother completely rearranged the sleeping quarters in our tiny house. I was moved into my parents' room in the front, overlooking Prince Street. They squeezed into the back bedroom with my siblings. I can only imagine how cramped that was, but if my father ever complained, I didn't hear it. To give me something to listen to, they put the radio within easy reach.

So there I was, by myself with the radio. All day long. That's one reason why I like country music so much: Bob Wills and His Texas Playboys sang to me every day. Mostly, however, I had the Murrow Boys in my ear. I looked forward to Edward R. Murrow coming on the air: *"This* is London." He had a remarkable ability to place his listeners in the center of the action and to convey a sense of time and place with his words alone. As he spoke, it was easy for me to imagine myself looking up into the skies of Britain as the Luftwaffe came overhead. I listened to Charles Collingwood, he of the polished Oxford diction—even though I probably hadn't heard of Oxford, England, at that time. Believe me, in the Heights Annex, Oxford was as far away as the planet Neptune. In my mind, I can still hear Eric Sevareid's voice. I liked him, too, even though he kind of mumbled sometimes.

The Murrow Boys reported on both the battles and the politics of the Second World War. Murrow was in London during the Blitz; Sevareid was in Paris as the Germans marched in; and Collingwood was with the troops on the beaches of Normandy as the Allies came ashore. It was the beginning of my understanding of "boots on the ground" reporting—of the need to go where the news was being made.

I can trace my desire to be a reporter back to my parents' immersion in the news and to the many hours spent listening to some of the best journalists history has ever known. By the time I finished my last attack of rheumatic fever, I was very committed to news in the same way I can see my eldest grandson is dedicated to golf. I can see myself in him. By the time I was 13, becoming a reporter was my driving dream.

The question then became whether my body would ever measure up to my ambition. I was not prepared when Dr. Cope finally gave me permission to get out of bed for good. It was late in the school year in the eighth grade. During my long convalescence, all my muscles had atrophied, and I was extremely self-conscious—embarrassed, even—about how "different" I'd become. I was pasty white and feeble. I no longer fit in, and the Heights was always a place that had little sympathy for anyone with a disability. I was very weak, so weak that I lost confidence in myself. I wasn't able to keep up with Georgie and Homer and my other friends and feared that I never would. Mentally and physically, I was quite literally a shadow of the active boy I'd been before.

I'm not sure how, but my father knew this was a critical time for me. He arranged for me to take a summer job on a brush-cutting crew. The crew was organized by a neighbor who had a small surveying company, Jeff Stramler. His son Charlie had been a close friend of mine, but Charlie had died of leukemia a couple of years earlier. Officially they listed my age on the crew sheet as 16, but everyone knew I was only 14.

At first I was so frail that I had trouble doing the work, but no excuses were allowed. Hard as it was, the last thing I wanted to do was let my father down, and Charlie's dad in the bargain. My parents had instilled persistence in me; I was raised to never be a quitter. My father gave me quite a few lectures about how I had to keep up with the others on the crew—most of whom were rough-and-tumble grown men of less than upstanding character. He told me that I had to shoulder my fair share of the load; otherwise I'd be sent home. On the pipe-laying crew, my job was to help the surveyor to provide a clear line of sight for him to keep the pipe running straight. We took away any heavy brush, vines or even trees that might be in the way. I spent months living in small hotels before I came home at the end of my 14th summer.

I must have been quite a sight: this scrawny toothpick with a red bandana tied around my head, railroad engineer's cap perched on top, khaki work shirt buttoned to the neck, and a yard-long machete swinging in its holster from my belt. We worked through forests and snake-infested swamps all summer long. The work was all Indiana Jones and Paul Bunyan and no Edward R. Murrow, but I survived and eventually thrived. It was a lifesaving, life-changing experience for me, and a true turning point. As I got my strength back, my self-confidence returned as well.

Having skated through middle school, I looked forward to Reagan High School. We had some outstanding students, and the school had a pretty good overall reputation for discipline and academics. In far too many cases, however, the boys had to make one of three career choices: They went to the oilfields, they joined law enforcement or they went to jail. Many dropped out of school early.

I struggled with schoolwork at first, but it was again my good fortune to have an outstanding teacher. My particular angel in high school was Miss Wilkerson, who taught English. More important, at least from my point of view, she was also the adviser to the school paper, the *John Reagan High School News*. From the first, she recognized how important my dream of becoming a reporter was to me, and she mentored me all the way through to graduation.

Graduation...then what? My parents held dissimilar views on the subject. My father had started but did not finish the 10th grade. When he was a boy, it was expected that children would help support the family as soon as they were able. For him, the idea that I might make a living working in the oilfields was a viable possibility. He used to call newspapers "the poor man's university," and I suspect it was his belief that it was the only university I would ever get to see.

Not so my mother. She was a firm believer in the idea of bettering yourself, a process that began with getting as good an education as possible. She not only wanted me to graduate from high school, she was absolutely adamant about my going to college. She'd been whispering to me about it all through my childhood. She didn't have a clue about how she was going to make it happen; she just knew I was going. My father didn't approve as much as he acquiesced. Generally speaking he ruled the roost, but on this issue he did not cross her. He just didn't know how we were going to pay for it.

I had that all figured out. Football would be my ticket, or so I thought. Then as now, high school football was a religion in Texas. One thing that spurred me to regain my strength after having rheumatic fever was the desire to play, a desire that also kept me from dropping out of high school. And football at Reagan was a big deal, a *Friday Night Lights* big deal. We filled the stadium with upward of 20,000 enthusiastic fans every week.

Pretty much by force of will, I made myself into a reasonably good football player. I was no superstar, but by the time I was a senior, I was a starter. Miss Wilkerson didn't puncture my love of football, but she wanted me to stay focused on my desire to become a reporter. She knew I needed more schooling, and at the end of football season my senior year, I was sorely in need of a reality check. I was born in October, so I started school in February and graduated in January, which was common. In January 1950, right before the graduation ceremony, Miss Wilkerson called me in for a good talking-to. "Dan, you must go to college," she said. "Right now you're much too fixated on football. If football is your ticket to higher education, then so be it, but never forget that it's a means to an end. You weren't born to be a coach. Keep your eye on your true calling—your career as a journalist."

She backed up that advice with concrete support. That winter there was a conference of high school journalists. I don't know why she thought it was important, but Miss Wilkerson was determined that I attend. I had not planned to go, but she insisted. In fact, she loaned me her car as transportation. I was 18 years old and hadn't been driving all that long. I was so nervous all the way there and all the way back that I stopped at every light even before it turned red. I remember thinking to myself, "God, I can't have a wreck in Miss Wilkerson's car."

In February 1950, my mother proudly accompanied her newly minted high school graduate to Huntsville, Texas, to enroll me in Sam Houston State Teachers College (now Sam Houston State University). Even though the Rathers owned a car, we took a Greyhound bus to get there, which was a vote of no confidence in the ability of our 1938 Oldsmobile to survive the trip. She had pretty much all of the family savings in her purse: two war bonds that wouldn't cover the $38 tuition, and another $15 in cash that she'd scraped together to make up the difference.

A few weeks earlier, I had hitchhiked the 75 miles to Huntsville to talk with the football coach, a man named Puny Wilson. When I told him I was a football player, he was not immediately impressed, but finally mumbled that he'd be glad to have me come out for the team. What he meant was that I was welcome to come participate in spring football camp, but in my mind I inflated this to mean that I was all but guaranteed a football scholarship. Foolish? Yes. Delusional? That, too. But playing football was my only strategy for getting a college education. I had no plan B.

From the first day of spring camp, I was in over my head. I hung around practice like some unwanted dog. Coach Puny couldn't run me off, even when it started to become pretty clear I wasn't going to get the scholarship.

I was hanging on by my fingertips when the good professor Hugh Cunningham came to my rescue. Prof Cunningham taught journalism, and he was yet another wonderful teacher who showed up in my life exactly when I needed one.

I was at another turning point. Prof Cunningham was not much older than I was—he was probably 27 or 28 years old at the time. With only 900 students in the college, his department consisted of seven journalism majors—which made it possible for him to give each of us a lot of personal attention. In his words, he was turning out a "handcrafted product."

He came out to watch me at football practice one afternoon. I was an end, and we were running end sweeps. I was getting wiped out on every play. After practice he scraped my shattered ego off the gridiron and tried to talk some sense into me. "Son, you've got to get out of this," he said. "You're not a football player. You're never going to be a football player." The words stung, but he continued, and as he continued he offered hope and a lifeline. "It's not compatible with my making a reporter out of you. Let's grab some supper and talk about how you're going to become a great journalist."

He could see that for me, playing football was a dream that died hard. Moreover, he understood right away that it threatened to take my dreams of becoming a reporter down with it. And he knew that the threat was imminent: Without a football scholarship, I had no idea how I was going to eat or sleep with a roof over my head, much less stay in school. I was painfully close to dropping out, so he let me sleep on the couch in his front room for a bit until I could make arrangements at a boardinghouse. His wife, I'm sure, was less than delighted, but without his intervention I'd have been gone from Huntsville in a matter of days.

With that, Cunningham took me under his wing, just as he took every one of his "handcrafted" students. Knowing how badly I needed income to stay in school, he helped me cobble together an assortment of part-time jobs. I worked at a filling station, at the local equivalent of a Tastee-Freez stand and as the publicist for the sports department. None of these gigs paid very much, but taken together they were enough to keep me in school and in groceries.

Eventually he landed me a job at KSAM, the local radio station, where I was a virtual one-man band. I was a DJ; I did live broadcasts of gospel singing at night, which was sponsored by the local funeral home. Occasionally, I sang with them. Most important, I did play-by-play for sporting events. Basketball, baseball, track, and a whole lot of football—black high school football on Thursday, white high school football on Friday, college games on Saturday. Although I didn't fully realize it at the time, the skill of ad-libbing I developed during those many hours on the air would eventually prove invaluable.

What did Prof Cunningham see in me? I think more than anything else, he saw my determination. I think he said to himself, "This kid is raw. He doesn't write as well as he thinks he does, and he's got a lot to learn, but he has the will, and the force of his energy."

Prof Cunningham was also very practical. He was tough on me because he knew a whole lot about how tough it was out there in the real world of journalism. He also had no illusions about where Sam Houston stood in the academic pecking order. To put it bluntly in the vernacular of the day, it was a cow college. "Look, Dan," he said, "you're going to graduate from Sam Houston State Teachers College. No one is going to give you a break. You have it in you to be really good, but your biggest challenge is going to be whether you can make a living doing this. You're going to have a hard time getting a job, and you'll be competing with guys from Harvard and Stanford. They will be better educated than you. They'll probably write better than you do, too."

Based on that understanding, Prof Cunningham took it upon himself to level the playing field as much as he could. "Even though you have a certain number of journalism classes that are required by the curriculum for your major, what you do in them does not matter," he said simply. "Everything you need to know about journalism I'm going to teach you through the school newspaper. Your job is to take as many electives as you can. Take a full load, and extra classes in English and algebra."

What he was trying to do was make sure I got a broad liberal arts education. In that regard, he knew, there was only so much I'd be able to glean from my coursework at Sam Houston. In 1952, the *Encyclopaedia Britannica* published a series of 54 volumes that they called Great Books of the Western World. Put together by faculty at the University of Chicago, today it might be viewed by some as the Dead White Males collection. At the time, however, it was taken seriously as a survey of western civilization conveyed through original works of literature, history, philosophy, mathematics and the sciences.

Thanks to the lady at the park, I already loved to read, but I hadn't been exposed to anything like this ever before. I had never heard of Tolstoy. I had never read Euripides. Now Prof Cunningham wanted me to read all 54 volumes, from beginning to end. He felt that reading the classics would be one way for this kid from the sticks to stand toe to toe with the sons of privilege in the job market. I didn't read every volume of the Great Books all the way through, but I did read some parts in each one. I became familiar enough with them to at least recognize the names and some of the ideas—which was more or less what Prof Cunningham wanted.

Hugh Cunningham was a pivotal figure in my life in so many ways. I paid him back by getting him fired.

Not on purpose, of course. My time at Sam Houston coincided with the Korean War. As soon as it began, the college started losing students. Young men either were drafted or they transferred to schools with reserve units. Concerned by the attrition, the school quickly put together a reserve outfit, and all of us male students joined it. Except that it was kind of a bogus unit, because the school didn't have the money for real equipment. We didn't even have uniforms; we lined up wearing baseball caps.

My roommate at the time was a guy named Cecil "the Weeper" Tuck. Cecil was a good ole boy who had been introduced to alcohol at an early age. He was also prone to fits of melancholy—at the time, we were too young to think there might be a connection between one and the other. Like me, Cecil wrote for the campus newspaper, and the two of us took turns writing pieces mocking the school's hastily formed Army reserve unit as the sham that it was. We were pretty blunt about it, too. "If this is supposed to be training for the war, we'll all die in the first round" is a pretty fair example of what we were writing. This did not go down well with college administrators, who wanted desperately to retain their newly established campus reserve outfit. They pressed our faculty adviser—Cunningham—to "control" the mischief-makers, Cecil and me.

No dice. Prof Cunningham turned them down flat. "I'm training these people to be fiercely independent journalists," he said. "I can't train them to do that by censoring what they write in the paper."

The administration took a hard line. "You are the head of the Journalism Department, and we don't like what we're reading. Put a stop to it."

He refused. "The only way I can stop them from writing satire about the reserve program," he told them, "is to censor them. I'm not going to do that." In short order, Prof Cunningham was asked to leave.

Sam Houston's loss was eventually Florida's gain. After two years as the editor of the *Bryan Daily Eagle*, Hugh Cunningham was hired by the University of Florida to teach journalism. He became a revered, nigh on legendary figure on campus. In 2001, the University of Florida endowed a journalism chair in his name.

It was now 1953. My mentor was gone, but because I had taken extra coursework like Prof Cunningham told me to, I had enough units to graduate early. I was anxious to get out; despite my feelings about our rinky-dink reserves program, I wanted to go into the military. I knew that since I'd had rheumatic fever I was not eligible for the draft, but I also knew I was fully recovered and able-bodied. I'd played football; I'd worked several summers in the oilfields. I was ready to serve my country, and I wanted to go to Korea. I was actually worried that the war would end before I got there.

I graduated in the summer of 1953 and there was a formal commencement ceremony that both my parents attended. They stood on the grass of Pritchett Field, which was the football stadium. The school orchestra played the Sam Houston alma mater, the Sam Houston fight song, the national anthem, and "America the Beautiful." My parents were thrilled and very proud of me. My father had never been on a college campus, and when he saw my diploma, I can remember the look of astonishment—almost disbelief—on his face. And the pride.

I joined the Marines soon thereafter. Even though I enlisted in September, I could not be inducted right away, largely, as I understand it, because the war was winding down. I actually taught journalism at Sam Houston for the fall term until I shipped out to San Diego for boot camp in January of '54. The Corps had a strict list of debilitating diseases that you could not have ever had. When I enlisted, I simply didn't mention anything about the rheumatic fever. I got away with my deception for just a couple of months; when it was discovered, I was abruptly given a medical discharge—over my vociferous protest. Despite several weeks of cleaning latrines, I was terminated. I used my mustering-out pay to take a long bus trip in search of work. I traveled from San Diego to Los Angeles, San Francisco, Salt Lake City, Casper (Wyoming) and Denver, but there was a recession on and there was no work to be had.

I returned to Houston at the end of the summer to job hunt closer to home. I spent more months knocking on doors until I finally was given a tryout at the *Houston Chronicle*, writing obituaries. Despite Miss Spencer's best efforts in the third grade, however, I was still a poor speller. I spent a lot of time looking up words in the dictionary. My work ethic was solid—the city editor saw that I got there early, stayed late and worked hard, but it wasn't enough. Especially with obituaries, there should be no misspelled words. Because I was too slow, it wasn't working out; *I* wasn't working out. The editor took pity on me and sent me over to the Rice Hotel, where the *Chronicle's* radio station, KTRH, was headquartered. He thought they might have an opening. He knew I'd worked at KSAM in college, and he put in a good word for me.

In addition to my good fortune to have excellent teachers, there have been many times in my career when I received help at crucial moments from absolute strangers. The news director at KTRH was a cigarettes and whiskey lifetime newsman named Bob Hart. (Bob was by no means alone in this regard. In those days, reporters were notorious for their consumption of alcohol and cigarettes. The stereotype of the hard-drinking, nicotine-stained journalist was rooted in fact.)

At the time, radio news was changing from rip-and-read to actually covering local events, and Bob needed somebody to cover the courts, city hall and the police beat. "You know how to write a newscast?" he asked as I walked in.

"Yes sir, I do," I replied.

"Well, write one," he demanded, as he headed upstairs to the Press Club for his customary two-drink lunch. Hugh Cunningham had taught me well. I got the wires and the dispatch from the police station. I had the five-minute newscast written before he got back.

I got the job, and it was another turning point for me. I started at the princely sum of $45 a week, which was not good pay, but I didn't care. I had a full-time job in journalism; someone was paying me money to do what I loved.

I immediately discovered that KTRH was a world apart from KSAM. KSAM whispered over the Huntsville airwaves at 250 watts. KTRH boomed all over the Gulf Coast with 50,000. When I began, I was still rough around the edges, and it was station manager Bill Bryan who voluntarily took on the job of sanding them down. Bill was a smooth gentleman who had been an announcer for bandleader Kay Kyser. He was handsome and what we used to call a snappy dresser. I would come to work in a short-sleeved shirt, which was de rigueur for hot, muggy Houston, or so I thought. Not Bill. He led by example—his work attire was a suit, tie and long-sleeved shirt. He not only showed me how to dress, he instructed me in the niceties of personal grooming. When my full head of black hair was showing signs of a dandruff problem, he told me how to get rid of it.

This was radio, so why did I care? I cared because KTRH's secretary was a beautiful, vibrant young woman with a killer smile, and I desperately wanted to make a good impression on her. The spark was there right from the beginning—bingo bombshell holy smoke. She was smart, and that was one of the many attractions. She also had a figure that would make a bishop kick out a stained glass window—leggy, chesty, tiny waist, winning smile and sparkling eyes—just a beautiful girl. Her name was Jean Goebel, and I was crazy about her from the first moment I saw her. I'm still crazy about her. On our first date, I remember going to a Tex-Mex place with a small dance floor. Because I thought it was so special, I saved up to buy the first of many bottles of Lancers screw-top wine, which I thought was very sophisticated at that time. Jean was appropriately appreciative.

Jean Goebel became Jean Goebel Rather on April 21, 1957. The reason we chose that particular date is that it is also the anniversary of the Battle of San Jacinto, when in 1836 Texas finally was separated from Mexico. We were married in Jean's Lutheran church off the Gulf Freeway in Houston. Her family and my family both attended. Some of our friends attended, including Cecil "the Weeper" Tuck, I recall. My colleagues from KTRH were there, too. In fact, they held a small bachelor party for me, and many of us were still recovering the next day. For our honeymoon, Jean and I drove to Monterrey, Mexico, in a used 1954 Pontiac. I am afraid we hit one goat en route.

I stayed at KTRH for six years. Six years might strike some as a long time to stay at a radio station—too long, some might say. I would disagree. People then tended to stay at one job longer than they do now. More than that, however, I stayed because KTRH gave me a productive apprenticeship in broadcast journalism. While there I honed the skill of ad-libbing to the point where it became a genuine strength. I learned to take radio airtime and hold radio airtime indefinitely with ad-libbing. Meanwhile, however, Bill Bryan continued to nudge me along by reminding me that even though I was learning valuable skills, KTRH was never going to be a place where I would be recognized as a great reporter. Maybe, he prodded, I should think about moving on.

By now I had worked my way up to become director of news and community affairs. My salary had grown to about $9,200 a year, but this was hardly enough to raise a family on. Robin, our daughter, was born in 1958. I made extra money by doing football, basketball and baseball play-by-play, but we were still strapped.

Bob Levy, an acquaintance, told me about an opening at television station KHOU, which was the Houston CBS affiliate. Levy was a baseball nut and a phenomenal statistician. I met him at pregame workouts and batting practice when I was doing play-by-play for the local professional minor league Houston Buffs (as in Buffaloes, or Bison). One night, Levy told me, "Dan, television is the thing of the future; this is where the opportunities are. You would be good at it, and you really should give them a call."

I confess I was a little slow to appreciate the importance of TV, but KHOU was offering $10,200, and Jean and I were expecting another baby. I was offered a tryout with program director Calvin Jones. Cal had been hired away from KDKA in Pittsburgh—highly regarded as one of the best local news outfits in the business—to build the station into a competitor. At the time, KHOU was a distant third in the market.

Before my audition, he explained to me that eye contact was very important, and then he told me to do a 15-minute newscast. Because I already knew the day's news well and had done so much radio earlier that day, I didn't use a script. Jones was surprised, to say the least. "You never looked down!" he exclaimed. "I never saw anyone who could do that."

"You told me to look at the camera," I replied simply.

I started at KHOU in January 1960. It was another turning point, and once again I was the beneficiary of the kindness of strangers. Cal Jones became another one of my enthusiastic mentors. He had gotten into television relatively early and had already been in it for five or six years. Jones really taught me what I needed to know to be in TV, which was pretty much everything, since I was starting with a knowledge base of zero. Television lighting at the time was notoriously harsh, and I have always had a heavy beard. Cal taught me how to apply makeup and pressed powder to hide it from the camera. (Ironically, just a few months later presidential candidate Richard Nixon refused to put on makeup to hide his own heavy beard for his televised debate with John Kennedy. His visible five o'clock shadow and generally tired appearance was a major contributing factor to his loss that November.)

My title at KHOU was news director, but the joke was that I was simply the director of myself. The news department was me full-time, a part-time cameraman Bob Wolf and Bob Levy, who was working in the program department but helped out on an as-needed basis.

I had to shoot some of my own stories, so Cal, Levy and Wolf gave me a crash course in the operation of a Bell & Howell silent movie camera. I learned how to put the film in, how to shoot, how to take the camera apart and how to remove the film. Once it was out of the camera, the film had to be sent downtown to be processed.

Since this was almost all silent film, everything was scripted with voice-over, and I wrote my own script. On the left side of the page was the narration; on the right was a description of the film snippet that went with it. There were no film editors at the station. It was my job to select the snippets and physically splice them together. The splicer was a hand-run piece of equipment with glue in it. I put two pieces of film into it, pressed down and held it long enough to make sure the glue set. When it didn't, my skill at ad-libbing came in handy.

I did two 15-minute broadcasts, one at 6:00 p.m., right after Douglas Edwards with the network news, and the second at 10:00 p.m. When it came time for the broadcast, there was no studio cameraman. There was a camera in front of me and a person in the control room. I had a wire running up my sleeve with a button. I'd say, "The mayor had a news conference today, and this is what it looked like." With that, I'd push the button, and the man in the control room would roll the silent footage while I narrated over it. I had a second button in my other hand for commercials. Until I got up to speed, there were a few instances when I pushed the wrong button, which meant that the ads ran instead of the news piece that was supposed to be there. My learning curve went up pretty quickly, though—it had to.

During the day, I went out and covered the same beat I'd had at KTRH, except now I had a camera. I'd be out all day filming the stories before sending the footage to the processor. After that, it was a push to get it spliced and scripted and ready for airtime. Fairly soon it became obvious that getting the film processed was expensive, both in time and in dollars.

I went to our station manager, a proper Bostonian named James Richdale, and proposed the idea of buying a processor. He said we couldn't afford it. In the interim, we had hired cameraman Bob Wolf full-time. Somewhere between Wolf and Levy, we found an Army surplus processor that was about the size of a coffin. You put the film in one end and ran it through the chemicals inside. It came out the other end and into a dryer.

I went back to Richdale. "We can buy this processor for $1,500, and look what it will save us," I told him. The financial benefits were obvious, but Richdale was also practical. "Are you sure you can make it work?" he asked.

"Of course we can," I assured him, even though I had no idea whether that was true or not.

The processor arrived in pieces, and it took Levy, Wolf and me the better part of a weekend to put it together. After a couple of missteps, we got it working. Now I not only shot and spliced the film, I processed it, too.

At the radio station, I never had the sense that I was trying to squeeze a quart into a pint jar. But at the television station, I felt that way all the time. No doubt about it, it was a lot of work. I was responsible for creating the 6:00 p.m. and 10:00 p.m. newscasts in their entirety. I was not on the noon broadcast, but I was expected to contribute stories. I always had three radios on in the newsroom—the police radio, the sheriff's radio and the state police radio. Whenever I heard something, I would jump into our Nash Rambler station wagon to get to the scene. Diligence paid off; in a relatively short period of time, we took KHOU from third place to first in the ratings.

Cal Jones believed that the name of the game for building viewership was live coverage of local news, and in Houston, there was no bigger local news than a hurricane. Cal was from Pittsburgh, and despite his experience in TV, this was something he knew nothing about. Me, I'd been dealing with them all my life. I knew how dangerous they could be, and I already had some experience covering them. I was still at KTRH in 1957 when Hurricane Audrey came ashore in Louisiana, killing several hundred people. We stayed on the air all night long to cover the disaster.

In September 1961, the U.S. Weather Bureau began tracking a storm system that had crossed the Yucatán from the Caribbean into the Gulf. Even though it was still a long way off, I knew it could be a problem. Tropical storms feed off the warm waters of the Gulf and can quickly grow to monster size. On September 7, they named it Carla.

Despite it being Labor Day weekend, I talked Cal into sending me with a mobile unit to the nearby Galveston branch of the U.S. Weather Bureau to cover the hurricane. I wanted to go to Galveston because it had one of the first WSR-57 weather surveillance radars in the country. By nothing more than luck, Vaughn Rockney, a hurricane expert and the U.S. Weather Bureau's chief of observation, was visiting from Washington. With his blessing we put the image of Hurricane Carla on the air. It was already huge—400 miles across, with an eye that was 50 miles in diameter.

When Cal and I suggested that we superimpose the Galveston radar image of the storm over an area map, everyone in the studio back in Houston gasped. The map instantly slammed home the enormity of the threat that Hurricane Carla posed. By letting people see the mass of the storm in relation to the coastline, we invented modern hurricane coverage. It is commonplace now, but it had never been done before. On Sunday, Vaughn Rockney invoked his authority and ordered the evacuation of Galveston and nearby low-lying areas. About 500,000 people headed for higher ground, but my crew and I stayed behind. We were the only news team broadcasting live from Galveston when Carla hit.

Since that time, numerous overly dramatic myths and legends have sprung up about the coverage of Hurricane Carla, myths that seem to have grown with each retelling. For example, I *did* briefly tie myself to a tree out in the storm. Because Carla's winds were projected to reach 175 miles an hour, however, that effort was mostly just an experiment. We gave up on it quickly. The truth was dramatic enough. As Carla made landfall, we were marooned in the Galveston weather station. At one point an engineer had to climb the transmitter tower to restore the signal. The storm surge rose as high as the second floor (we were on the fifth); we subsisted on candy bars for several days.

Carla still holds the record as the most severe hurricane ever to make landfall in the United States; severity in this case being a *combination* of size and intensity. In the end, however, only 46 people died. Without the mandatory evacuation, it would have been worse, much worse. Our coverage was acknowledged to be instrumental in convincing people to flee ahead of the storm, and I was nicknamed "Hurricane Dan."

Shortly thereafter, I got a phone call from New York. CBS national was offering me a job. I turned them down.

CHAPTER 4

New York, Civil Rights...
and Dallas

Are you nuts?!"

Several of my pals at KHOU, including intrepid taxi driver/father of seven/fly-by-night cameraman Dick Perez, thought I was crazy to reject the CBS offer. Two months later, the network came back to me with a better deal—I was to come on board as a full correspondent, not a deskman/reporter—and I accepted.

I first walked into the CBS News building at 524 West 57th Street in Manhattan on the last day of February 1962. Before I entered, I stopped on the curb across the street, just to take in the scene. Not that the building itself was any kind of imposing edifice—in its former life it had been a dairy barn. Built as the Sheffield Farms dairy depot, until the late 1940s they were still milking cows there.

I didn't care. What I cared about was that after Bill Paley bought it in 1952, he had converted it into TV studios, an essential step in creating what many were now calling the Tiffany Network. And the Tiffany Network's crown jewel was CBS News. Standing on the curb that February morning, I wasn't looking at an old dairy barn. I was looking at the cathedral of electronic journalism. With no intent whatsoever to be sacrilegious, what the Vatican is to Catholics, the CBS News Broadcast Center was to me.

I stood across the street in a swirling emotional stew that was equal parts gratitude, humility and pride. I was keenly aware that I was standing on the shoulders of so many key people in my life, mentors and supporters who had propped me up and propelled me forward at crucial moments, because they loved me and believed in me: my parents; Mrs. Simmons, the principal at Love Elementary School; Miss Wilkerson at Reagan High School; Hugh Cunningham at Sam Houston; Cal Jones at KHOU; and of course my wife, Jean. Without them, I never would have found myself here. Now I was ready to work harder than I'd ever worked before—and I knew I'd have to. I was painfully aware that I'd have to raise my game, just to be good enough to make the grade. I was standing at the base of Mt. Everest—failure was not an option, not with a wife and two small children depending on me.

At the same time, I knew I'd been hired because people at CBS already believed I was good at this. More than that, I had a feeling in my gut that I was embarking on my life's work—the work I was meant to do. It wasn't exactly a calling; it was a sense of being part of something bigger than I was. I knew that as a CBS News correspondent, I would be doing important work, work that *mattered*. This was the job I'd been dreaming of since I was a boy stuck in bed with rheumatic fever, listening to the Murrow Boys on the radio during the war. Two decades later, some of the "Boys," including Charles Collingwood and Eric Sevareid, were still very much present, but Murrow was no longer with the network. In 1961 JFK had tapped Murrow to head the U.S. Information Agency. As I was not to learn until much later, Murrow had been having increasing problems with network corporate brass. He was discouraged and feeling that they no longer wanted him, and the brass encouraged that feeling. The cabinet-level job with the Kennedy administration was a respectable out for him. But I didn't know any of this at the time.

I quieted my butterflies, said a quick prayer and, not being a New Yorker, walked up half a block so I could cross at the light. It was a telltale sign, one of many, I'm sure, that loudly proclaimed that I was new in town. (New Yorkers, of course, are habitual jaywalkers; crossing anywhere but at the corner is common.) I entered the building and went straight to Ernie Leiser's office.

Ernie Leiser was my new boss and had been largely responsible for hiring me. Leiser had not been one of the Murrow Boys, but he was one helluva newsman. He had written for *Stars and Stripes* during World War II and was among the first journalists to enter Berlin. Rumor—strictly rumor—was that he might also have been involved with military intelligence. After the Hungarian Uprising of 1956, Leiser had earned a Peabody Award as the first reporter to smuggle footage out of Budapest, despite having been tossed in jail by the Communists. Now he'd made the transition from foreign correspondent to news executive. Hiring me was a bit of a risk for him; if I stumbled, he was on the line for it.

We chatted in his office, and the first thing he told me was that I was to do an on-camera audition. Screen test? Now? I'd already been hired. Usually auditions take place *before* you're on the payroll, not after. Besides, Ernie had hours of me on tape from Hurricane Carla. What more did he need? At least I knew enough to say nothing more than, "Yes, sir."

As Ernie walked me down the hallway to Makeup, we ran into Charles Collingwood, one of my boyhood idols. I was momentarily tongue-tied, not an ideal state for an on-air reporter.

A graduate of Cornell and a Rhodes Scholar at Oxford, Charles Collingwood was easily one of the most elegant men alive. That day he was wearing an impeccable bespoke Savile Row suit from Kilgour, French and Stanbury that probably set him back a month of my old salary—at a minimum. (My suit, on the other hand, had cost about $30, tops.) He shook my hand and introduced himself. I got the marbles out of my mouth well enough to hold up my end of how-do-you-do. Collingwood himself could not have been more gracious. "Let me know if there is anything I can do to help you," he said warmly. And he meant it—he went on to become yet another mentor, and a dear friend.

Charles was on his way to Makeup in preparation for reading a five-minute afternoon newsbreak. Actually, we were both headed in the same direction. For my screen test, I was to read the same newscast

Charles had just given. This prospect left me seized not by stage fright, exactly, but by something that surely seemed close enough to it. I felt like Ernie had just asked me to follow Horowitz at the piano and play the same Tchaikovsky concerto. I'd never had airtime jitters like this before, but then again, it had never mattered this much before, either.

Charles introduced me to Frances Arvold. Franny was a legend in her own right. She was the first woman member of the makeup artists union in New York, and she'd had to fight her way in to get there. Murrow himself had demanded that they let her take the test, but the good old boys in the union were determined to keep her out. They tried to rig her exam to guarantee failure. Her test was to get an actor ready in full Kabuki makeup. No problem. Franny knew her stuff—applying the flawless Kabuki whiteface, exaggerated black brows and deep red character lines and shadings didn't faze her in the slightest. Grudgingly, they had no choice but to let her in.

Franny dabbed Pan-Cake on us both. Like Charles, she did her best to put me at ease. He made sure I knew where the teleprompter would be and that I could make out the type—I didn't wear contacts back then. Collingwood read his newscast, and then I did my audition tape immediately thereafter. I might not have read it with as much feeling and polish as would have been ideal, but I did it flawlessly. No flubs. While I was reading, Charles stayed there in the shadows. "Come with me," he said after I finished. "I'll show you around."

The Charles Collingwood was showing me around! I guess that meant I passed. I was walking the corridors of CBS News with a legend, going past the doors of other legends. Within CBS News, Ed Murrow and the Murrow Boys were the equivalent of King Arthur and the Knights of the Round Table. When they began, the quality of their reporting and the immediacy of their voices was something entirely new, and it came at one of the critical times in the history of the world. Other networks would have other knights, but never like those of the Round Table.

On D-Day, Collingwood had come ashore on Utah Beach with a Navy underwater demolition team—on an LST laden with explosives—while the Germans were still shelling the beach. Before that, he'd distinguished himself reporting on the North Africa campaign, culminating with the recapture of Tunis in May 1943, racking up a Peabody Award in the process. He took me past the office of Richard C. Hottelet. In Berlin in March 1941, Dick Hottelet woke to a knock on his door early on a Saturday morning. He'd been expecting a plumber but was met instead by seven members of the Gestapo. He was arrested for espionage, interrogated, and held as their "guest" for almost five months before being released. At first light on D-Day, Hottelet was airborne in a B-26 over Utah Beach on a bombing run to soften up German bunkers, right before the Allies swarmed ashore. There's the office of Paris bureau chief David Schoenbrun. Schoenbrun covered the invasion of southern France in 1944 and was with the French Army when it captured Vienna, for which he was awarded the Croix de Guerre and the Légion d'Honneur. That's Walter Cronkite's office. During World War II, Cronkite had been part of the "Writing 69th," a group of journalists who flew with the Eighth Air Force on raids over Germany. He'd also participated in a glider assault with the 101st Airborne, the Screaming Eagles.

Cathedral of electronic journalism indeed. It was not lost on me that I was literally surrounded by journalists who had repeatedly gone to where the news was happening—often enough at their own peril—to get the story.

Eventually Collingwood had to excuse himself; other responsibilities beckoned. Before leaving he said, "Would you care to join me for a drink after work?" I told him I'd be honored. I stayed in the building long enough to say good night to Ernie Leiser and to watch Douglas Edwards do the *Evening News*, which was only 15 minutes long at the time. I met up with Charles at a place across the street, a somewhat notorious newsmen's hangout called the Slate. Of course he drank Scotch.

We were joined by Doug Edwards and Don Hewitt. Edwards had anchored the *Evening News* since the fledgling days of television, beginning in 1948. During the war, he had been a latecomer to Murrow's team, but was nevertheless a valued member. I had grown up with him on radio and television, and I respected and admired him. He was a pro and, as I learned after I came to CBS News, a genuinely good person.

In his trademark plaid jackets, Don Hewitt might have been mistaken for a horse tout. Having started as a copyboy for the *New York Herald Tribune*, he was now the producer of the *Evening News*. A year and a half earlier, Hewitt had directed the pivotal Nixon-Kennedy presidential debate, the one in which Nixon's refusal to let Franny Arvold apply TV makeup on him did much to put John Kennedy in the White House. That September 1960 televised debate is arguably the beginning of a heady 15-year period during which TV literally changed the course of American history.

Next morning I shined my new Florsheim wingtips and headed for my first real day on the job. I arrived early and was issued a cubbyhole office, about the size of a broom closet, and a fly swatter. Being from Texas, I didn't give the swatter a second thought, but it turned out to be more valuable than I'd anticipated. From time to time, echoes of the building's dairy past resurfaced, which is to say that periodically we would be besieged by huge infestations of flies. Because there had been cows in the building for such a long time, thousands of fly colonies had formed. For many years the flies resisted all efforts to get rid of them completely.

The flies were not the only echoes. The CBS News Broadcast Center was perched atop a labyrinthine warren of burrows and catacombs dating from the Roaring Twenties that extended all the way to the Hudson. During Prohibition, bootleggers and smugglers brought barges of whiskey up the river, then off-loaded their illicit cargo onto the banks and into the tunnels that led to the dairy. Once in the dairy, the whiskey was transferred into milk cans—the perfect camouflage—and then delivered to speakeasies all over town. After Prohibition ended, however, the passageways were never sealed off. Rats found their way into the labyrinth, and occasionally they found their way into CBS News. Years later, Eric Ober was president during a particularly heavy rat invasion. These were nasty, snarly XXL New York City river rats, big enough to mate with a possum. We had otherwise sophisticated women standing on chairs and screaming at the very sight of them, but corporate seemed a little slow to grasp the magnitude of the problem. It was only half in jest that I threatened to get an ocelot to keep in my office—which would be the down-home Texas solution to any rat problem—but at that point Ober called in the exterminators.

As I first settled in, Ernie Leiser told me I'd be in my cubbyhole for about six months. Management wanted me to get comfortable with the CBS way of doing things. It wasn't more than six weeks later, however, that I started getting the feeling that I was spinning my wheels. I wasn't nearly busy enough. I was used to going out daily and reporting from the field; now I was going stir-crazy.

Ernie's solution was not at all what I expected: He sent me back to Texas.

I'd hoped to be assigned to London, Paris or Berlin, but what CBS needed at the moment was more domestic beachheads in our major cities. I tried not to look crestfallen, but Ernie assured me this would be a great opportunity for me. My territory was huge: 23 states (including the most hurricane-prone ones along the Gulf), Mexico and Central America. Still, I was going back to Texas. When I told Jean, she was as pleased as I was disappointed—and then some.

I knew nothing about setting up a bureau, but I went to Dallas and started looking at office space. After I found a spot, I contacted the CBS real estate division and they gave me the go-ahead to sign the lease. I was now the Dallas bureau chief; chief of a bureau of one. When I found a story that I felt was worthy of being on the *Evening News*, I was to call a freelance cameraman who lived in Manhattan, Kansas—Wendell Hoffman.

Wendell was a 6 foot 4 inch lanky farm boy who had landed on the beaches of Normandy on D-Day. A graduate of the University of Nebraska, he was something of a Renaissance man, much more Jimmy Stewart than country bumpkin. He was also gutsy and very creative about finding ways to get a story. Five years earlier, Wendell had accompanied CBS producer Robert Taber to Cuba. The wild cover story they invented to mislead the regime of military strongman Fulgencio Batista was that they were Presbyterian clergymen traveling across the island to survey their missionary schools. After leaving Havana, however, Hoffman loaded his bulky Auricon camera, batteries and film onto a mule for the harrowing 600-mile five-day trek into the wildest reaches of the Sierra Maestra mountains. They went in search of some local troublemakers; whether they were bandits or revolutionaries depended on your point of view.

They found them, then spent several days filming and interviewing the dynamic leader and his ragtag band of followers. On the way back to Havana, Wendell buried his camera and batteries in the roadside brush to make it easier to smuggle his film back out of the country. That footage became *The Rebels of Sierra Maestra—Cuba's Jungle Fighters*, a CBS documentary that aired on May 19, 1957. The program gave U.S. viewers one of their first glimpses of a very young Fidel Castro and instantly gave lie to Batista's assertion that the Castro-led insurgency was a myth. Less than two years later, Castro ousted Batista and at age 32 became Cuba's prime minister.

Wendell was obviously another guy who'd pursue a story wherever it led him. He and I hit it off right away. He saw me for what I was: eager, ambitious, hardworking, kind of raw, but with potential. Not only did he help me look for stories, he also helped me hone my writing and my on-air presentation. "The biggest difference between where you are and where you want to be," he told me in his high-pitched nasal twang, "is the quality of your writing.

"I've been shooting film since *Movietone News*," he continued. "I can get us the pictures we need, but your writing is key to telling the story. Occasionally you have to write under pressure, but more often you have enough time to really craft a script. Use it. Think about opening lines, closing lines." That struck a chord with me, because in the brief time I was in New York, I'd looked at scripts. I was impressed by the beautiful scripts of Charles Kuralt, the youngest CBS News correspondent ever hired. Collingwood, of course, wrote as elegantly as he did everything else.

Wendell and I would trade story ideas back and forth. He was one of the savviest people I'd ever met on the subject of race, and on the importance of race in the American saga. It was Wendell Hoffman who first suggested to me that we should be following Dr. Martin Luther King.

In the summer of 1962 we went to Albany, Georgia, to cover what was called the "Albany Movement," one of the earliest sustained desegregation campaigns. Wendell and I arrived to take over for Atlanta bureau chief Hughes Rudd, who'd already been on the story for several weeks and had earned a break.

Albany was a crash course in battlefield journalism acquired on the fly. The most valuable lessons involved how to operate in an intense, hostile environment. I learned quickly—I had to. Put simply, we weren't wanted there, and everyone let us know we weren't wanted there. No matter where we went, we stuck out. Because we obviously were "not from here," I made it a point to look professional—dark suit, dark socks, trousers creased, shoes shined, white shirt, black silk tie à la James Bond. I wanted it to be readily apparent that I was a reporter and that I represented CBS News, the most distinguished and honored news organization in the country. I also upped the "yes ma'am/no ma'am; yes sir/no sir" content of my speech. That ritualized politeness was something every child learned in the South; it certainly had been thoroughly drummed into me as a boy. Wendell Hoffman thought I risked appearing too deferential, but in Albany, Georgia, it became the grease I relied on to slide through touchy situations when we found ourselves surrounded by angry white crowds. "I'm not being obsequious, Wendell," I told him. "I'm trying to get this job done and stay alive."

I'd been asked by Ernie Leiser to get as close to Dr. King as possible, and it was here in Albany that I met him for the first time. I was instantly impressed. As the center of the storm, he was grounded, secure in the knowledge that his cause was just. He was always thinking beyond that moment, that hour, that day, plotting out what the movement's next steps should be. No matter how much chaos swirled around him, Dr. King exuded an aura of calm. He also had tremendous focus, a precious ability to make you feel like you were the only person in the room. Overall he had a quality I came to know as "peace at the center," and I among many others respected him greatly for it.

His main adversary in town was the Albany police chief, Laurie

Pritchett. Pritchett was wily enough to cloak his efforts to foil the protesters in the guise of maintaining public order. Dodging and weaving, he deftly avoided direct confrontation with Dr. King himself.

King's efforts in Albany resulted in a standoff at best. In Dr. King's own assessment, "We got nothing." Nevertheless, I came away believing that the civil rights movement was on the verge of gaining traction and really gathering momentum. I told Ernie Leiser what I thought. "Get all over it," he told me. Leiser saw it not only as an important story, but also as a potential coup for the News Division; CBS had been the only national TV network reporting the story from Albany. By this time, Walter Cronkite had replaced Doug Edwards in the anchor chair for the *Evening News*; with expanded civil rights coverage, Ernie saw an opportunity to gain some ground on NBC, which at the time was on top of the ratings with Chet Huntley and David Brinkley. At my suggestion and urged on by Wendell Hoffman, we started crisscrossing the South in search of civil rights stories, covering protests and head-knockings in tank towns and backwater places like Yazoo City, Mississippi, and Plaquemines Parish, Louisiana.

Looking back, I was almost spectacularly unqualified to be covering what I was covering. As I was growing up, the Heights Annex was a segregated society, as was Houston, as was Texas, as was the rest of the South. As was, frankly, the rest of the country. Race, however, was not a topic we shied away from at home. I remember my parents discussing the 1936 Olympics. Held in Berlin, these were the so-called Nazi Olympics. Hitler had elaborately staged them to showcase the physical superiority of the Aryan master race, but the real Superman of the Games was a black American track star named Jesse Owens. To the chagrin of the Third Reich, Owens earned four gold medals in Berlin, more than any other athlete.

Upon his return to the States, Owens was given a ticker-tape parade up Fifth Avenue. When the parade ended, however, he was obliged to ride the freight elevator at the Waldorf-Astoria to the reception in his honor. At the time, African Americans were called "Negroes" in polite parlance; sadly, polite parlance was often hard to come by. "Nigger" and other derogatory epithets were at least as common and were uttered openly and without shame. Racism wasn't just common; it was the norm.

My parents were by no means integration activists, but they did have a sense of decency about how folks—of any race—should be treated. As a teenager, I had accompanied my father to a local Democratic Party precinct meeting to elect a slate of delegates to the county convention. It surely sounds odd today, but back then there were virtually no Republicans in Texas. The scars from the Civil War ran long and deep; being nominated as a Democrat was pretty much the same thing as being elected. My mother had sent me along to ride shotgun, as it were, because she thought there might be trouble. Her instincts were correct. Some black veterans newly returned from the war showed up, expecting to participate fully in the meeting, which was their right. As had been prearranged, however, the white men used to running things had already chosen an all-white slate of delegates. In essence, the fix was in—voting was a mere formality. Though they were few in number, the black vets loudly objected to the sham. When the chairman called for a vote, saying, "All those opposed to the nominations, stand," the black vets all stood up. My father rose to his feet with them.

The chairman gave my father a chance to back down, suggesting that perhaps he'd stood up at the wrong time. My father stood his ground, a trait that seems to go far back in the Rather DNA. He made it clear that there had been no mistake; he was siding with the veterans. The rest of the white men—men he'd known for years—looked at him as if he were Judas himself. I understood why my mother had asked me to go along. Things got testy at that point, but after some rough jostling and some name-calling, the meeting ended.

My father was very proud when I got the job with CBS in New York, but he did not live long enough to see me do much reporting. In May 1962, less than two months after I began at the network, a 16-year-old boy lost control of the concrete truck he was driving. Dad was on his way to work when the truck crossed the centerline and hit his car head-on. He died instantly. I think it was Uncle John who reached me in Dallas. I immediately asked how my father was, and Uncle John answered, "He has passed." My first reaction was disbelief: "How could this be?" I went into a deep depression and made immediate plans to fly to Houston to be with my mother. None of us could have expected this. I was touched that the men who worked on the pipeline with my father kept a vigil. They stayed the night with my father's casket. There could be no doubt of the nobility and decency of those laborers. All of us in the family were devastated, and it was especially devastating to me when my mother said through her tears: "You are the leader of the family now." My father's death affected me for a long time thereafter. For many years, I thought that I would die at the age my father died: 52 years old. I don't think my mother ever got over it. She died six years later, in 1968.

The Texas I grew up in was a segregated society, but Texas was not like Georgia or Alabama or Mississippi. Growing up, I had never seen a cross burned on anybody's lawn, or a Klan meeting. My first direct exposure to the Klan happened in south Georgia. Conventional journalistic wisdom of the time had it that covering Klan rallies wasn't worth the trouble. The Klan, it was said, had been thoroughly infiltrated by the FBI.

I wanted to see for myself. As soon as we pulled up, I knew that conventional wisdom had it all wrong—this rally was much too big. They couldn't all be informants.

Up until then I'd considered Klansmen as something cartoonish, almost humorous in their white satin hooded costumes. To me they were an anachronism, a bizarre remnant left over from a bygone era. Seeing them in person changed all that in a heartbeat. It was a surreal experience, absolutely revolting and repellent, but also mesmerizing. And, I realized, potentially very scary.

There were upward of 200 people there, and yes, they were all in hoods. An involuntary shiver went down my spine. Seeing them in person gave me an instant deeper understanding of the terror that the Klan represented. For this shoot, Wendell had picked up a local soundman named Leroy. "Is this dangerous?" I asked him as we parked.

"Make no mistake," Leroy replied in his honeyed Georgia drawl.

"These sum' bitches *will* kill you. They *want* to kill you, and they'll do it with great joy and happiness."

We were warned as soon as we got out of the car to get the hell out and don't you dare film anything. Behind the hoods, the eyes flashed nothing but hostility, and I immediately realized that Leroy was right. "If I had just a second alone with you in the dark," those eyes seemed to say, "I would cut out your heart and throw your liver to the dogs."

Soon we were surrounded by a menacing circle of hooded Klansmen. They bumped us and put their hands over the camera. They began murmuring, and then the shoving got stronger. We formed a wedge to break free of the circle. After that we stayed about 15 minutes on the outer edges of the rally before I gave Wendell the hand signal to get out. Although we actually did manage to shoot some footage clandestinely, there wasn't enough to make a decent segment for air.

We weren't beat up that night, but there was a real risk of it. By late September 1962 in Oxford, Mississippi, however, the stakes were much higher, and the risk was a lot more serious than just getting beat up. Wendell and I had headed for Oxford because James Meredith was about to enroll as the first black student at Ole Miss. Attorney General Robert Kennedy had deployed a phalanx of U.S. Marshals to ensure his matriculation. The entire city of Oxford was on edge. In anticipation of the confrontation, the town was swollen with outsiders, not just reporters but a lot of diehard sons of the old South, bent on stemming the tide of integration at any cost. In short, they were out for blood.

They got it. We had expected trouble; we just badly underestimated how much. What started as an Ole Miss football-style pep rally quickly turned ugly. Fifteen hours of rioting followed. Wendell and I had been joined by Laurens Pierce, another CBS photojournalist, and by my Houston friend Dick Perez, the erstwhile cabbie. Dick had simply shown up one day—unannounced and unpaid—to pitch in with civil rights coverage. In Oxford I was paying him out of my own pocket, but he was worth every penny, and I was very glad he was there.

Despite being on an American college campus, there was no doubt that we were in a war zone. Once it got dark, every time we turned on our battery-powered lighting, we made ourselves a target. Bullets flew in our direction. We spent much of that night crawling on our stomachs, alligator style, from one vantage point to another, trying to get good footage while under fire.

That was the difference between us and someone like Claude Sitton, who won a Pulitzer covering the civil rights movement for the *New York Times*. When we traveled on assignment, our cumbersome equipment made it virtually impossible to maintain a low profile. Because Claude traveled solo and carried little more than a reporter's notebook, he could pretty much blend in.

The first fatality on campus that night was French journalist Paul Guihard. Tragically, his last dispatch that day had been even truer than he knew: "The Civil War has never ended." Guihard was shot at point-blank range—in the back. I'd been speaking with him minutes before; he and I were the same age. There was one other death, a local white resident who'd come to the campus out of curiosity and was shot execution style, between the eyes. Countless more were injured. The next morning, spent shell casings littered the walkways. The problem was much bigger than the small group of marshals could handle. It took 3,000 federal troops in full riot gear to restore order.

I had come of age during the earliest stages of the cold war. After World War II and throughout the 1950s, we all took it as a given that the greatest potential threat to our country was coming from the Left, in particular from the Communist bloc. Castro's takeover of Cuba, of course, reinforced that belief. My first indication that there could be a threat from the Right—especially the Right within our own country—took place while I was still in Houston. While at KHOU, I tried and failed to get an interview with John Birch Society founder Robert Welch—and was reviled by him as a Bolshevik for my efforts. The right-wing riot at Oxford was further proof that threats could come from the extreme fringes of both sides of the political spectrum.

Most of the civil rights news at that time was coming from what we think of as the Deep South—Alabama, Mississippi, Georgia and South Carolina—none of them particularly convenient to the Dallas bureau, or to home. Jean and I had chosen a place on the outskirts of the city, halfway to Fort Worth. I was on the road a lot, sometimes coming home for little more than a catnap, a shower, and a change of clothes. Worse yet, often enough when I did come home, I was not alone. I'd have Wendell with me; we'd put him up in the guest bedroom before we set off again. Wendell and I would arrive with all his gear in a beat-up station wagon. Its suspension was pretty much gone, so the jarring metallic scrape of the tailpipe bottoming out on the pavement heralded our arrival and departure to the neighborhood. When we arrived at 2:00 a.m. and left before dawn, as was often the case, we set local tongues to wagging: "Who the hell are these people? The husband comes and goes in the middle of the night with that strange man in that huge station wagon dragging on the ground and who knows what's in there? They must be part of a crime syndicate. Mafia, obviously." And of course Jean was the one who had to deal with it, not me.

As tough as covering civil rights was on the home front, it was even tougher in the trenches. Above and beyond the dangers and problems of being on assignment, which were indeed considerable, we were having a lot of trouble getting our civil rights footage back to headquarters. We were repeatedly getting bushwhacked by our own affiliates. After we shot our piece, we generally took it to the closest local CBS affiliate; they were supposed to process it and send it to New York. Time after time, however, we found that our own local stations wouldn't cooperate. For many of them, CBS had become either the Colored Broadcasting System or the Communist Broadcasting System, or an unholy amalgam of both. "By giving so much airtime to those black agitators, those niggers, you're helping the Communists. We don't want anything to do with you" was a pretty fair summation of what we often heard.

What finally tore it was an experience in Jackson, Mississippi. Wendell and I brought in some film to be processed. We were on deadline. We waited and waited. Finally someone came out and said, "Unfortunately, we had a malfunction in the processor. All your film was ruined. So sorry." He didn't make even a token effort to sound sincere.

I got on the phone with Ernie Leiser. Noncooperation from the affiliates was bad enough; deliberate sabotage was another matter entirely. "This is well past the point of acceptability," I told him.

Ernie immediately went into problem-solving mode. "We need to get you a more convenient home base, and a place where you know you can get your film processed," he told me. "What about New Orleans?" New Orleans was the home of station WWL, which was owned by the Jesuits of Loyola University. Because WWL was very profitable for them, they wanted very much to keep their CBS affiliation, which meant they were willing to commit to processing our film and sending it on to New York.

"But we just got here!" Jean exclaimed when I told her that we would be moving from Dallas to the Big Easy. While Wendell and I were on assignment, she visited New Orleans to check it out. She found it strange and exotic, a good thing if you're on holiday, less so if you're trying to raise two young children pretty much single-handed. "I just can't do this," she told me when I returned home. "If I move there, I won't know a soul. You're on the road all the time, and I'll have no support system. I think it's better if I take the kids back to Houston."

"But we're married," I said. "That's not the way married people live."

"The way we live *now* is not the way married people live," she responded sharply.

Jean's arrow found its mark; there was nothing I could say. Looking at my calendar for 1962 and 1963, I was home for 31 days one year and 43 the next. I had become an absentee father and an absentee husband. One year I barely remembered to call Jean on her birthday. I think I dialed the number just a couple of minutes before midnight, and it did not help matters that I was calling from the newly opened Playboy Club in New Orleans. Not surprisingly, things were a little frosty in the Rather household for some time thereafter.

Even though I had to acknowledge the stress my schedule was placing on our family life, being home more and not working as hard wasn't really an option. Jean did extract a promise from me to make certain that what time I did spend at home was quality time. I promised to be genuinely present—physically, mentally and emotionally—for her and for the children when I was home, and it's a promise I have tried very hard to keep. When we moved the bureau to New Orleans, she packed up the house in Dallas and found a place in Houston near my mother and her parents.

Our civil rights reporting provoked a firestorm of responses, and the complaints went all the way to the top. CEO William Paley had to contend with irate southern senators who threatened our broadcast licenses, but in dealing with Washington, network president Frank Stanton was our ace in the hole. Stanton was very close to Vice President Lyndon Johnson. Many decades earlier, Stanton had put LBJ, at the time a raw young congressman, into the radio business and then into the television business. For several years, Johnson's television station was the only one on the air in Austin. It had a lock on the market because Stanton had showed Johnson the ropes with the FCC. As those media businesses boomed, they became the foundation of Johnson's personal fortune. Meanwhile, LBJ rose up the DC food chain. Before being tapped as Kennedy's vice president, Johnson had become arguably the most effective Senate majority leader in history. Now as VP, he still wielded enormous power and influence in the Senate, and behind the scenes was able to effectively neutralize the threats against CBS.

In addition to causing political problems, civil rights coverage was also a potential drain on the CBS bottom line. Companies that did a lot of business in the South were skittish about sponsoring anything that smacked of unrest or racial conflict. They warned the network that they might pull their advertising, and some made good on their threat. For a time, our own Atlanta affiliate made peace with its advertisers by refusing to air some of the *Evening News*, in order to avoid showing footage of sit-ins and other protests. Other affiliates threatened to jump ship and leave the network entirely.

Naturally this did not sit well with Paley, who believed in the integrity of the news. Despite the political problems and the threats of boycott, his commitment—and hence that of the network—to reporting on the civil rights movement never wavered. The news and its "public information service," as he saw it, are "necessary to the people of a democratic nation who are faced with the need to be informed on all important issues." Paley understood that by presenting the news seriously and honestly, CBS was fulfilling a major obligation that was part of its public trust. Besides, by any yardstick, the civil rights movement had now become a story that was too big to ignore.

Paley had the guts to back up his beliefs and now moved swiftly to deal with the insurrection among the affiliates. At his direction, Frank Stanton played hardball with the Atlanta station owner. He delivered an ultimatum: If he chose to continue to black out or censor the national newscast, he would find himself adrift without a network. Stanton would pull the plug and sign up a different local station as the CBS affiliate. What gave the threat real financial teeth was that CBS was the leading station in the Atlanta market. Once Atlanta agreed to air the *Evening News* uncut, their capitulation had the desired deterrent effect on the others.

Paley also received mailbags full of vitriolic letters written by angry viewers. There were allegations that we were taking the side of the black community, that we were all pink-tinged fellow travelers from New York and knew nothing of the South, and that I myself was a rabid Marxist revolutionary, just like Robert Welch had said I was. Back in Houston, a few people Jean would run into took it personally. Jean was put on the defensive for what I was reporting. "What the hell is your husband doing, giving free publicity to those niggers and riling up all those Yankees, just so they can come down here to cause trouble? And why is he lionizing that Communist, Martin Luther King?"

When I came home, Jean and I would talk about it. She'd ask me what Dr. King was like, and I'd tell her as best I could. Dr. King and I were cordial, but we maintained a carefully defined separation. That said, he always knew how to reach me if he needed to communicate. My code name for him was "Volunteer," and there were a few times when I received a message from a hotel clerk saying, "Mr. Volunteer called." I was closer to Medgar Evers, and our relationship was much less formal than the one I maintained with Dr. King. I considered Medgar a friend, and he eventually became one of my principal sources within the civil rights movement. I went places with him where most black people wouldn't set foot. I accompanied him to the polls to vote, and Wendell's camera was rolling when Medgar was told flat out that he could not cast a ballot—which was, of course, flagrantly against the law.

That image and so many others prompted people across the country to begin examining their own beliefs about desegregation and the civil rights movement. Television was hugely instrumental in changing public opinion, and with it the course of American history. It certainly was a vivid part of my evaluation of my own beliefs. Covering the civil rights movement was the making of me, both as a journalist and as a human being.

It was by extension the making of Jean as well, because she had to take care of the kids and run the home and defend what I was doing. It was a Herculean performance on her part. In a way, it prepared her for Watergate a decade later. With all the time I was away from home, I was relieved to know that Jean and the children were safe in Houston. Throughout the South during this period, there was open hostility not just toward blacks, but toward the press as well.

I have always felt a strong sense of responsibility for my crew. Whenever I picked up an extra cameraman, soundman or lighting man for a civil rights assignment, I was mindful that I was bringing him into harm's way. This was true even if he was from the local community. Some, like Leroy, the soundman who accompanied us to the Klan rally, were fully aware of the dangers, but others were not. One cameraman was pursued through town by thugs armed with wickedly sharp sawed-off pool cues. Realizing that these hooligans really meant to do him harm, he took refuge in a men's store. He tried to disappear into the inventory, suspending himself by his arms among the suits on the rack. The experience precipitated a coronary that left him incapacitated for several months.

When we were covering a story, I was on edge, all day, every day. Every sinew in my body was tight. Only when we were finally airborne on the way out of town did I feel like I could exhale. Fatigue started being a factor, however, and I began the habit of checking into a hotel, sometimes even during the day. Not every hotel would accept reporters, and even those that did weren't exactly warm and welcoming. We often had trouble getting served breakfast in the hotel dining room. We'd sit there for a half hour and be deliberately ignored.

If a situation looked particularly dicey, we would sleep in shifts. Wendell and I would sleep while the soundman kept watch. Then I'd get up and the soundman would bed down. I didn't wake Wendell; it was always more important for the cameraman to get more shut-eye. In these situations, the camera and the footage were far more important than the correspondent. Sometimes each of us would take turns sleeping in the car. There were a few places where I was worried enough to send the housekeeper downstairs with $20 to take another room in her own name—and that would be the room each of us would sleep in. Late at night, in case the wrong people came looking for you, you didn't want to be where they thought you were.

We developed standard tactics to protect ourselves while filming, including hand signals. I was like a baseball coach, flashing signs from third base. The cameraman was most at risk; with his eye glued to the eyepiece, he was pretty much blind. This meant that the correspondent was always to his right and shoulder-to-shoulder with him. The sound-man stuck to the cameraman's left shoulder and was responsible for protecting our left flank, as well as for watching the rear. Often enough we'd bring a lighting man with us, not necessarily because we needed one, but because we could use the extra set of eyes.

Because we were doing more civil rights coverage than the other networks, CBS, and by extension me and my crew, became a particular lightning rod. The phrase I heard most often from local citizens at this time was "We don't want trouble." But as they saw it, trouble seemed to arrive hand in hand with CBS News. We were pulling back the scab on a long-festering sore and putting it on TV every night. NBC and ABC were doing some coverage but not as much as we were, for reasons that are not clear to me.

We were threatened all the time. In one instance, we had just landed at an airport in Alabama and were at the rental car counter debating what model to select. The optimal vehicle was something big enough to hold all the gear but also nondescript—grey or black, never red or green. Off to the side, not spoken to me directly, but in a deliberately audible stage whisper, I heard, "It doesn't make any difference what kind of car he gets. We're gonna blow it up anyway."

It turned out to be an empty bluff, but I will go to my grave believing that some of my problems with what is commonly called the Right and the Hard Right started during this time. In my opinion, the malice that began during the civil rights movement was carried forward to Watergate, and then again to the coverage of George Bush and the Air National Guard.

I struggled to remain an honest broker of information, and where possible to report both sides of the story. Now, however, I saw brutality on a daily basis, and it was a shock from the very beginning. There certainly had been institutionalized racism in the Houston I grew up in; everything from movie theaters to water fountains to football teams was segregated. What I saw now, however, was much more than just racial prejudice. It was hate, and hate with an intensity and a virulence I'd never seen before. I saw not just Klan rallies but cross burnings, and people beating women and children. Time after time I said to myself, "I can't believe what I'm seeing, but I'm here to be an eyewitness, and to make the camera a witness."

None of the violence I'd seen to date prepared me for what took place next. Dr. King and his supporters had learned a lot from what happened—and did not happen—in Albany a year earlier. Albany had been the Petri dish. They realized that they could march and chant and sing till hell froze over, but it wouldn't make a dent unless they elicited an extreme response from the segregationists and the press was there to witness it, report it and show it on the air.

The civil rights movement needed to get America's attention in a dramatic fashion. They needed to get their story out—visually. And perhaps most of all, they needed to find a police chief who was so filled with racial hatred and was such a dumbass that he didn't care what the pictures looked like.

Welcome to Birmingham, Alabama.

Birmingham was by consensus the most segregated city in the South, and its white leadership wore that title as a badge of honor. In April 1963, when the Southern Christian Leadership Conference launched the Birmingham campaign, an important component was Project C. The "C" stood for "Confrontation." The plan was to protest segregation through sit-ins, kneel-ins, economic boycotts and other nonviolent actions, all concentrated in Birmingham's central business district, in hopes of sparking an overreaction from the authorities.

The movement found the perfect foil in Bull Connor, Birmingham's commissioner of public safety. Connor was already notorious for his rabid segregationist views and harsh tactics. In 1961, he had allowed KKK thugs to viciously beat a group of Freedom Riders arriving in town on a Greyhound bus. To give the Klan enough time to really inflict injury, he intentionally waited 15 minutes before sending in his officers to intervene. A year later, he closed down 60 city parks rather than comply with a court-mandated desegregation order.

Now in the spring of 1963, Connor responded to the demonstrations the way Dr. King expected he would and began arresting protesters in downtown Birmingham. King himself was arrested on Good Friday, April 12, and placed in solitary confinement. While there, he wrote his eloquent manifesto "Letter from Birmingham Jail." "For years now I have heard the word 'Wait!'" he wrote. "It rings in the ear of every Negro with a piercing familiarity. This 'wait' has almost always meant 'never'...

"Injustice anywhere is a threat to justice everywhere," he continued. "We are caught in an inescapable network of mutuality, tied in a single garment of destiny. Whatever affects one directly, affects all indirectly." Scribbled on toilet paper and in the margins of pages from the phone book, the letter was smuggled out. Excerpts soon began appearing in newspapers and journals across the country.

On May 2, organizers launched a second phase of the campaign, a controversial tactic that came to be known as the Children's Crusade. For the first time, the movement was deliberately putting kids aged 6 to 18 on the front lines. Like their parents, waves of children—kindergarteners and high schoolers alike—left the park across from the 16th Street Baptist Church, arm in arm and singing "We Shall Overcome." And like their elders, they, too, were thrown in jail. That day the Birmingham Police Department arrested almost a thousand children in a single three-hour period, overwhelming the city's justice system and filling the jails to overflowing.

Bull Connor was nothing if not predictable. The next day, when more children gathered at the park and started marching, he ordered the fire department to turn its high-pressure hoses on them. Up close, the jets of water would be forceful enough to flay flesh from bone; even at a somewhat greater distance, the water ripped clothing and sent children rolling down the street. Connor also set police dogs on protesters trying to take refuge in the 16th Street Baptist Church. Cameraman Laurens Pierce got it all on film for our reporting team.

Birmingham was the tipping point. Until Birmingham, we were mired in a sort of national denial. Even urban blacks in the North were unaware of how extreme conditions were in the South. No one wanted to acknowledge that things were as bad as they were, that separate-but-equal had always been a fraud, and that every day peaceful protesters were getting jailed and savagely beaten by the police and by white supremacists for doing nothing more than insisting on their civil rights and basic human dignity.

Now, however, TV cameras captured the brutal reality of it in a way that even the best newspaper reporting could not. The eyes of the entire country were now on Birmingham, because television made it impossible to look away.

King and other leaders of the movement kept up the demonstrations for another week. Business came to a standstill. Finally on May 10, both the city and the chamber of commerce had had enough. King announced an agreement to desegregate major public facilities, lunch counters and store dressing rooms. As of May 11, Bull Connor was out of a job.

This was another crucial moment in which television changed the course of our nation's history. Andrew Young, who would eventually become the mayor of Atlanta, told me directly that without TV, the civil rights movement might never have been as successful as soon as it was.

A month after Birmingham, Alabama governor George Wallace made his "Stand in the Schoolhouse Door," an attention-getting publicity stunt to block registration of black students at the University of Alabama. We were in Tuscaloosa covering that event when I got the call. Medgar Evers, my friend, had been shot to death on the steps to his front porch—shot in the back, in full view of his family. I and my crew quickly chartered a plane to Jackson, Mississippi, and got to the scene before any other members of the press arrived.

This was one of the instances when I did get a message from Mr. Volunteer. Dr. King wanted to know if the police had been involved in the assassination. There were no obvious signs that they had been, but at the time it was impossible to say one way or the other. I was the first to break the news of Evers's death. Less than six months later, I would be the first to break the news of another political assassination.

When it was announced that President Kennedy was to come to Texas in November 1963, I was assigned to coordinate CBS's coverage of the trip, because I knew Texas and because I had covered the Dallas desk. It was to be an all-hands-on-deck operation. Robert Pierpoint, our White House correspondent, would of course be traveling with the president. In addition, we brought in not just our crew from New Orleans, including reporters Lew Wood and Nelson Benton and cameramen Wendell Hoffman and Dick Perez, but camera crews and correspondents from all over the country. I was to be the field marshal, making assignments of who covered which venues and which events. Once I'd done that, my major duties were completed. There was never any expectation that I'd be on the air much, if at all.

This particular visit was seen as the unofficial kickoff to Kennedy's reelection campaign. Even though Texas was Lyndon Johnson's home state and still heavily Democratic, Kennedy had carried it in 1960 by a scant 2 percent. Now gearing up for 1964, JFK wanted to get to Texas early on, both to raise money and to make nice with all the local political powers, Governor John Connally in particular.

On the morning of November 22, 1963, Air Force One landed at Love Field. Because Kennedy was in campaign mode, once it was determined that the weather would cooperate, the bubble canopy of the presidential limousine was removed. Crowds in downtown Dallas, hoping for a glimpse of the president and first lady, lined the route to the Trade Mart, where JFK was to give a speech. In the motorcade, Governor Connally and his wife were riding with the Kennedys. Vice President Johnson was in another limousine, several cars behind. Following the president's Lincoln convertible was a truck carrying photographers from the various news services, including our own. At intervals along the motorcade route, I had stationed individuals holding bright yellow grapefruit bags. The bags were lightweight and distinctive; without screaming "CBS News," they were easy to spot. Our cameramen in the truck would toss their film cans to the grapefruit bag holders, who would then rush the footage back to KRLD, our Dallas affiliate, for processing.

I positioned myself at the last drop-off position, grapefruit bag in hand. I was just on the other side of what we have all come to know as the grassy knoll. I didn't hear a shot; I didn't witness the actual event. I was waiting for the motorcade when a squad car sped past me, followed in short order by the president's limousine, flying by at top speed. I didn't see the president in the car, and the camera truck was nowhere to be seen. I knew something was wrong, very wrong, but I didn't know exactly what had happened.

As I hightailed it back to KRLD, I sprinted past a scene of incredible chaos: people on the ground, fathers lying on top of their children, shielding them from some unseen but lethal danger. When I got to the station, the UPI wire was already reporting that shots had been fired and that the president had been wounded, perhaps seriously.

All my old instincts as a police reporter kicked in. I knew that if anyone had gotten hit, he or she would be taken to Parkland Hospital. I also knew that the phone lines into the hospital would get jammed up pretty quickly. I immediately started calling Parkland. I got a busy signal the first time but then got through to the switchboard operator. "Don't hang up on me," I said, "I'm a reporter. Is there anyone I can talk to?" She patched me through to a doctor.

I identified myself and asked what had happened. "The president has been killed," he told me before clicking off. I redialed the hospital and again reached the switchboard. The operator was by now much put-upon, but she connected me with a priest.

"Father, I'm Dan Rather with CBS News, and I'm trying to confirm whether the president has been shot."

"Yes," he replied. "The president has been shot and he is dead."

This was a hammer to the heart. Once I knew that the president was dead—and it happened in nanoseconds—I had the same gut-wrenching emotional reaction, the same sense of shock and disbelief that everyone else in America had. At the moment, however, I had to push that feeling aside. I couldn't give in to it, not then, and as it turned out, not for many days. To be able to continue to do my job, I had to check the flood of emotion before it overwhelmed me. It was a very conscious and deliberate choice, much like a doctor or medic must make, and in times such as these, it is absolutely necessary. Whether by instinct or by training, this is where steely professionalism has to kick in. You must become single-minded and focused on the work at hand. "I don't have time for any of that now," I told myself. "I'll grieve—later. Right now people are depending on me to take care of the story." It's something I've always been able to do. Years later, the same habit kicked in during our marathon coverage of 9/11.

The question now was what to do with the terrible knowledge I possessed. There had been no official announcement, but I had a doctor and a priest at Parkland Hospital saying that John Kennedy was dead. Eddie Barker, KRLD's news director, had been stationed at the Trade Mart. Eddie had an excellent source, a high-ranking Parkland Hospital official, who had corroborated what I had been told. If I were still working the Houston police beat at 61 Riesner Street for KHOU, this would have been more than enough confirmation. What we had was a dead man. But this was not just any dead man. This was the president of the United States.

I got on the phone with CBS radio in New York. A guy I knew well, Mort Dank, was on the other end of the line. Mort asked me what the situation was, and I told him the president was dead. The next thing I heard was Allan Jackson, our New York radio announcer, somberly intoning, "The president of the United States is dead," followed by the playing of "The Star Spangled Banner."

I was still on the phone with Mort. Dumbstruck, I said, "Wait a minute! I didn't say go with that!"

"Well," Mort replied, "you told me he was dead."

I had expected that Mort would pass the information up to someone in higher authority to clear it for broadcast before it went out over the airwaves. Now, of course, it was impossible to take it back, in effect to unring the bell. On the TV side, Barker's report and mine were mentioned, but Ernie Leiser made the decision to wait for official word before formally announcing the news on television. Finally Mac Kilduff, the White House assistant press secretary, made the announcement and confirmed the news.

CBS stayed on the air for the next four days straight, without commercial interruption, covering the assassination, the execution of Lee Harvey Oswald by Jack Ruby, and the presidential funeral. Although I'd gone to Dallas as the coverage coordinator, with the expectation that other correspondents would do most of the reporting, during those four days people saw a lot of me on the air. There was no time now to craft a masterful script in the manner of Kuralt or Collingwood; there was no time to craft a script at all. When it was airtime, it was just stand and deliver. Even though I was bone weary by the end, both my ability to keep my emotions in check and my ability to ad-lib proved valuable.

Television coverage of this national tragedy changed the country. It also changed the relationship people at home had with their television. Families sat riveted to their TVs for hours on end, almost as if sitting at a wake. Television became the medium that linked our people together in times of tragedy or disaster; it still fulfills that function today. TV coverage of the Kennedy assassination united the country in national mourning and set the stage for coverage of other catastrophes in the future, including the Robert Kennedy and Martin Luther King assassinations just five years later.

By now, the story of the assassination of John Kennedy has become an oft-told tale, and like most stories it has both gained and lost in the retelling. Sadly, two generations of younger Americans think they know a lot more about the death of President Kennedy than they do. Sadder still, much of what they know ain't so, having been gleaned from Oliver Stone's 1991 movie *JFK*. The film is not history. It is not a documentary. It is a Hollywood movie, a fictionalized story based—loosely—on historical events. The assassination still has many open questions, some of which may never be answered with certainty. Stone's disservice to history is that he sacrificed accuracy to entertainment. The script blends fact and speculation so seamlessly that it is very difficult to know where one leaves off and the other begins.

After the assassination, there was much condemnation of the Warren Commission. The country was reeling; speculation about a conspiracy was rampant. New rumors surfaced almost daily. Commission members were under tremendous pressure to get out a report as fast as possible so the country could begin to heal. Without question, some of the commission's work was not perfect, but that doesn't mean it came to the wrong conclusion. I may be one of the few people who actually read the entire commission report from cover to cover. My primary criticism is that they shut down too soon. After they issued their findings, it would have been far better to have left the door ajar, retaining a small Warren Commission office and a skeletal staff with the ability and the authority to investigate other leads that might surface in the future, or even to reinvestigate existing evidence based on new breakthroughs in forensic technology.

Was there a conspiracy? Keep in mind that for a reporter, there could not be any bigger story than to reveal that the assassination was not what it appeared to be. But the facts just do not go in that direction. I've now participated in four independent investigations, all of which attempted to prove that Oswald could not have been the assassin. Because there was a widely held belief that no one could get off that number of shots that accurately and that quickly at that distance, the most painstaking of these investigations involved an elaborate re-creation of the assassination. In the early 1970s, we spent more than half a million dollars of CBS's money on a re-enactment. We built a track for a Lincoln Continental and went through a precisely choreographed replay of the events of that dreadful day.

What we discovered was quite the opposite of what we set out to prove. We showed that the actual distance was not that formidable. We also demonstrated that it was possible for a shooter to squeeze off the required number of rounds in the allotted time frame. From the sixth-floor window of the Texas School Book Depository, what Oswald saw through the gunsight of his Mannlicher-Carcano rifle was his victim, first up close, then receding in a straight line, *not* crossing in front of him. In other words, even though the limousine was moving, President Kennedy remained in the crosshairs. At that range, it didn't take a super marksman.

Although there are many conspiracy theories about other sharp-shooters firing from different vantage points, there is no hard evidence to support that contention. If shots had been fired from the grassy knoll, as is commonly alleged, those bullets had to have gone somewhere. But where? No one has ever found any hard evidence documenting where those shots might have landed.

I don't want to leave any ambiguity about my belief that Lee Harvey Oswald was the shooter, the only shooter. For me, the primary issue revolves around the question of who, if anyone, assisted him. To date there is still little, if any, concrete evidence to support the conjecture that others were involved. I remain open-minded about the possibilities, but frankly, I do not believe that there was a conspiracy. That being said, I do think the time has finally come to put an end to all the theories and speculation. Along those lines, if the CIA has any further information, it should release it. Whatever the justification for secrecy might have been back in the day, surely it no longer exists. As a journalist, my position is that the American people have a right to know, and that the time for withholding information for the good of the country, emotionally or politically, has long passed.

One truism in investigations is that truth will come out. This applies especially to conspiracies, which by definition means more than one person is involved. People who have information eventually feel compelled to tell someone else. They whisper it to their priests, wives, children, girlfriends. Over five decades, this has not happened. There have been no deathbed confessions, no "now it can be told" first-person revelations.

Much of what we would have liked to know died with Lee Harvey Oswald. Now I fear the odds are getting smaller and smaller that we will ever know more than what we do now. For me as a journalist, it will continue to nag at me that I may never get to the truth. I have continued to follow leads and possibilities ever since that day in late November 1963, and I will continue to do so, but I don't have any expectation that these speculations about the murder of a president will be resolved in my lifetime, if ever.

I stayed in Dallas for about two weeks, covering the aftermath of the assassination. While there, my emotions about the murder of the president eventually did come to the surface. I did speak to Jean immediately and we shared the feelings that I imagine all Americans were feeling at that time. The children were of an age that they did not understand what was happening, but I asked them to sing some patriotic songs about America with their mother. By the time I left Dallas, I was no longer southern bureau chief, based in New Orleans. I was instead headed to Washington to cover our new president, Lyndon Baines Johnson, as chief White House correspondent.

Irvin "Rags" Rather, Dan's father, fishing

Dan's mother, Byrl Rather, holding Dan in front of the house in Wharton, 1931

Byrl Rather in front of a neighbor's car, 1931

Irvin Rather on his way to a job interview, 1946

As a member of the William G. Love Elementary School "rhythm band," Dan (last row, second from left) played triangle.

Dan, on the far left, in 3rd grade at Love Elementary School

Dan (far right, second row) at a Boy Scout gathering in Houston, 1945

Dan (center) spent his college days as the editor of *The Houstonian*, circa 1952

As a young Marine

Dan (who did play-by-play) with University of Houston football coach Harold Lahar, Rice coach Jess Neely, and color analyst Roy Hebert

At KTRH Radio,
circa 1959

Alone while covering Hurricane Carla in Galveston, Texas, 1961

Dan with his daughter, Robin, 1958

Dan with his son, Danjack, Christmas 1962

Dan with his wife, Jean, at the Beaverkill fishing lodge, just after it was built

Dan with Jean at a Christmas ball given by the Rathers for the CBS News staff, mid 1980s

With actor George Clooney (Michael Tran/ FilmMagic/Getty Images)

With Mark Cuban, founder of HDNet (Frederick M. Brown/Getty Images Entertainment/ Getty Images)

At the 1994 dedication of the Dan Rather Communications Building at Sam Houston State University, with Jean

With fellow anchors Brian Williams, Walter Cronkite, and Tom Brokaw (Evan Agostini/Getty Images Entertainment/Getty Images)

CHAPTER 5

Presidents I Have Known, Part I

In the modern era, the press and the presidency are joined at the hip, but this symbiotic relationship is imbued with an inescapable dynamic tension. The press and the public have an insatiable appetite for information. Divulging that information is not always in the best interest of any particular president. Let me explain.

In the White House, "free press" is a double entendre. The media represents the people's right to know, and the right to publish what they find out. This is what journalists mean by "free press." The White House uses the media to trumpet its successes and play down or explain away its failures. For them, press coverage is a simple extension of public relations or free advertising. For the White House, "making the news" offers an opportunity to place their own imprint or spin on events, gratis. This is an entirely different understanding of the term "free press."

In one capacity or another, I've been covering the presidency since the Eisenhower administration. Over that period, presidents have developed increasingly sophisticated strategies for dealing with journalists, and each president has carved out a different relationship with the press. Some have wholeheartedly embraced the media; others have been ambivalent or inconsistent; still others have sought to wall us out entirely. Almost all administrations, however, find reasons to try to manipulate the press for their own ends. For a journalist, therefore, to cover the presidency is to deal with politicization of the news.

White House efforts to control the flow of news, however, is a slippery slope. There are times when this involves legitimate issues of national security. It would not have been in the public interest for the president to have revealed details of the secret expedition to kill Osama bin Laden in advance. Other times, of course, national security is deployed as a smokescreen to shield events that are embarrassing or even felonious, such as Watergate, from public scrutiny.

Eisenhower

As supreme allied commander in Europe during World War II, Dwight David Eisenhower was responsible for the planning and execution of the D-Day invasion. After the war, he became everybody's first-choice nominee. Courted by Democrats and Republicans alike, he declined to run in 1948 but chose to run as a Republican in 1952. He was elected by a landslide with 442 electoral votes, compared to just 89 for Adlai Stevenson.

Eisenhower was our last president who was not press-centric. Perhaps it was his military background, or perhaps it was his enduring popularity, but Ike simply never felt the need to be concerned about the press all that much. Luckily, he had one of the best press secretaries in history. Jim Hagerty held that position longer than anyone else: eight years—throughout both of Ike's terms, start to finish. Nobody did it longer; nobody has done it better. Hagerty was surely one of the best informed and most influential press secretaries. He not only had Eisenhower's confidence; he had his ear.

My brief interaction with Eisenhower happened toward the end of his second term. Ike had scheduled a goodwill trip to Russia, Japan, Taiwan and the Philippines. At the time, I was news director at KHOU in Houston. Cal Jones, my boss, had the idea that I should go on the trip and do a one-hour special program on it when I returned. Unfortunately, the trip started falling apart before it began. Anti-American protesters in the streets of Tokyo made the Japan leg of the trip impossible. The Russian portion was scrapped in the aftermath of the U-2 spy plane incident and the subsequent exchange of pilot Francis Gary Powers for Soviet spy Rudolf Abel.

We flew with the president to Taiwan and visited Quemoy and Matsu, two Taiwanese island chains that had been claimed by Mainland China. Later that fall the islands became a topic in the debate between Kennedy and Nixon, but Eisenhower's visit was intended simply to demonstrate our support for Taiwan on the issue. Because so much of the trip had been scrubbed, to eat up time we then took a slow boat from Taiwan to the Philippines. Finally, the trip ended with a week-long vacation in Hawaii for Eisenhower, who played golf every morning.

It was a pretty big deal for me to be included at all. There were only two local station TV journalists on the trip, myself and Frank Reynolds, then with CBS affiliate WBBM in Chicago. None of us, including the dozen regular White House correspondents, had any real access to Eisenhower, but because I was a local reporter with no White House experience, I had no seniority, either. This was a real disadvantage, since everything was allocated according to your rank in the press corps pecking order, from seating in the bus (I was in the last row, over the engine) to who was selected to join the group watching Eisenhower tee off at the golf course.

I had a lucky break one morning in Hawaii, when one of the designated reporters dropped out and I was asked to go in his place. That particular morning, the president was late to the golf course. Ike could be snappy and downright standoffish, and at first observation he did not seem to be in a particularly good mood. But as soon as he flashed that disarming grandfatherly smile, the atmosphere immediately improved. Eisenhower had a command presence. As a five-star general, as president of Columbia University after the war, and as a two-time landslide president, he exuded a reassuring aura of confidence that left no doubt that he was the guy in charge.

These morning gatherings at the golf course were never supposed to be full-blown press conferences. Today we would call them simple photo ops. Eisenhower had had a heart attack in 1955, and this part of the trip was meant to reassure the press and the public alike that the president was healthy and vigorous. It was all strictly informal—reporters were allowed to ask a few softball questions and watch the president tee off. After that a White House staffer would say, "That's it, boys" (at the time, the presidential press corps was still all male), and we were ushered away.

On the plane coming home, I started to worry when I realized that I had nothing to show for having been on the trip. Having traveled with the president from Taiwan to the Philippines to Hawaii, I had virtually no newsworthy information about him whatsoever. I expressed my concern to one of the more experienced photographers, who offered to talk to Hagerty on my behalf. Hagerty was nice enough to give me an "exclusive" interview regarding the details of the president's assurances that we would protect Taiwan's sovereignty over Quemoy and Matsu. It was enough to save my bacon back in Houston, where Cal Jones understood that I had made the best of what were very slim pickings indeed.

The Eisenhower administration marks the beginning of a long run-up of corporate influence on the American political scene. Charles Erwin Wilson, aka "Engine Charlie," became president of General Motors in January 1941 and oversaw GM's transformation from a maker of family sedans into a manufacturer of tanks, aircraft and armaments—the linchpin of what FDR called "the arsenal of democracy." Wilson was still president of GM in January 1953 when Eisenhower tapped him to become his secretary of defense.

During his Senate confirmation hearings, Wilson was asked if he would be able to make a decision that was contrary to the interests of General Motors. He answered yes, but added that he could not imagine such a situation "because for years I thought what was good for the country was good for General Motors and vice versa." Wilson was not being facetious. At the time, the employee population of General Motors exceeded that of Nevada and Delaware combined. Ever since, Wilson has been famously misquoted as having said, "What's good for General Motors is good for the country."

Whichever way you put it, the concept developed a life of its own. The idea that the interests of big business and the interests of the United States are aligned has been with us ever since. The Eisenhower administration was unabashedly pro-business, and frankly most people didn't find this to be a problem. In Texas it was taken as gospel: When corporations do well, they do well for their workers. When workers do well, they buy products. It was an article of faith that we all believed in.

For several generations, we all reaped the benefits; now though, we're reaping the downside. Especially in the wake of the 2010 Citizens United ruling by the Supreme Court, it is an open subject whether today we still have a government of the people, by the people and for the people, or whether it has become a government of corporations, by corporations and for corporations.

Over the years, I have given the Eisenhower presidency much higher marks than was considered fashionable. Ike negotiated an end to the Korean War, broadened the reach of Social Security and built the Interstate Highway System. In 1957 he also federalized the Arkansas National Guard after Governor Orval Faubus called them out in an attempt to defy a Supreme Court ruling to integrate the state's public schools. Eisenhower was perhaps not so much pro-integration as he was anti-insubordination. As head of the federal government, no governor was going to be allowed to flout federal authority on his watch. In true commander-in-chief style, Eisenhower countered Faubus by deploying the 101st Airborne to escort black students into Little Rock's Central High.

To my mind, however, above and beyond these important accomplishments, Eisenhower deserves a special place in the history of American presidents because he gave what may be the second most important speech that any contemporary American president has delivered. (Given at the depths of the Depression, FDR's 1933 first inaugural address—"the only thing we have to fear is fear itself"—probably ranks first.) In his January 1961 farewell address, Eisenhower warned against the ascendancy of what he was the first to call the "military-industrial complex." "The potential for the disastrous rise of misplaced power exists and will persist," he said. "We must never let the weight of this combination endanger our liberties or democratic processes."

Eisenhower was the first president of the television era, but he did not use the medium well. Listening to that speech on radio, it is extremely powerful. Viewed on television, however, it loses its intensity; the screen is dominated by the top of Ike's bald head as he's reading. Eisenhower was not a gifted orator, and at the time he gave it, the speech did not resonate the way it should have. It is only with the benefit of hindsight that its importance has been realized. Would that we had paid more heed to his admonition.

Kennedy

My first contact with John F. Kennedy was when he became the Democratic presidential nominee at the 1960 convention in Los Angeles. I interviewed him at the time and came away impressed. It was evident even then that he was a forceful personality and a persuasive speaker. After that I covered some of his speeches; finally, of course, I was in Dallas for the campaign stop that ended his life.

JFK was the first president born in the 20th century. Young and handsome, he was very image conscious, even early in his career. It had little to do with vanity. As a politician with ambitions toward higher office, he knew his physical appearance was an attribute that could be exploited for political advantage. While still a senator, Kennedy retained the services of Howell Conant, Grace Kelly's favorite photographer. In all likelihood, Grace made the arrangements herself; the Kellys were to Philadelphia what the Kennedys were to Boston, and the two clans had first met sometime in the late 1940s.

Kennedy had no interest in sitting for an official portrait; instead, he gave Conant an unusual assignment. He asked to be photographed from every angle imaginable. The two then pored over the photos, studying them carefully. Kennedy wanted to learn which were his best camera angles and which were to be avoided. Conant gave him the same advice he gave to Grace Kelly. Both were counseled never to be photographed straight on—he because his eyes were set too close together, she because of her square jaw.

John F. Kennedy was truly our first TV president. Although television had come of age during the Eisenhower administration, Ike had dismissed it as an entertainment medium. Kennedy, on the other hand, was acutely aware of the power of television to sway public opinion. He seized the challenge and the opportunity of television and used the medium well. Not surprisingly, he was very involved with camera angles and lighting and makeup for his televised appearances, just as he had been with his still photography.

Televised news conferences had been initiated under Eisenhower's press secretary Jimmy Hagerty but were boosted into prominence by Kennedy and his press secretary, Pierre Salinger. These sessions showcased not only Kennedy's physical attractiveness, but also the fact that he was witty, articulate and quick on his feet. He came across as warm and genuine and comfortable in his own skin.

When it came to his relationship with the press, JFK was extremely accessible, as was Salinger. The two had a close personal relationship. Salinger was an adjunct member of Kennedy's "kitchen cabinet"; he had real access to the president, and Kennedy trusted him completely.

The White House used this easy access to generate positive coverage; it was a way to cultivate the image of the Kennedy administration as open and forthcoming. Salinger knew who President Kennedy liked in the press corps, and they unquestionably played favorites. They rewarded their friends, cold-shouldered their enemies and more or less gently herded those in between. They took this approach with both print and television media, but they went out of their way to cultivate TV journalists, often giving them preference over print reporters. On-air White House correspondents really became center stage for the first time during Kennedy's presidency.

Friends in the media were rewarded with greater access, not just in press conferences but for innovative special broadcasts as well. The Kennedys opened the White House to a televised tour, hosted by the first lady with my friend and mentor Charles Collingwood. It was an excellent use of television for an ostensibly nonpartisan activity, one of the earliest examples of what would become known as "campaigning from the Rose Garden."

Johnson

Things changed when Johnson became president, or as the wags soon put it, "Austin isn't Boston." Lyndon Johnson had learned a lot about television from Kennedy but couldn't match his image or his style.

It took him a while to find his own. LBJ ached to be a good TV president, but he went through some awkward phases in search of his on-air persona. First was the cowboy phase: hats, boots, everything but a bolo tie. He was comfortable—for him this was pretty much his native garb—but he was told that the image he projected was a bit too rodeo and not sufficiently presidential. Then he went into his teacher mode. Early on, he had been a teacher in the small town of Cotulla. Tweedy, however, did not suit him. After that he tried on the image of the businessman president, but even then he didn't get it quite right. He debuted the look wearing a dark suit with a piece of jewelry at the neck, where only the knot of the tie should have been.

Unfortunately, a lot of Johnson's image problem was physical, not sartorial. He was a large man with prominent ears and huge hands like a polar bear. He was hardscrabble. In sharp contrast with JFK, he was not born to privilege, and it showed in his craggy face. Soon after becoming president, he held a news conference in the East Room of the White House. The room was crowded with press; television cameras were set up everywhere. After it was over, LBJ viewed the videotape with Lady Bird, who was horrified. "Lyndon, your ears look enormous!" she is reported to have said. "You look like Dumbo." True enough. Johnson's big ears, viewed from the side, looked even bigger. Johnson's solution was a simple one: That was the last of the side camera shots.

Johnson always believed that he was his own best press secretary, and in many ways, he was. Pierre Salinger lasted less than a year with LBJ, having stayed on as part of the transition team after Kennedy's assassination. In August 1964, he was replaced by George Reedy. Even as Johnson was the antithesis of Kennedy, Reedy was the antithesis of Salinger. Salinger's MO was to pop a few back, smoke a cigar and admire the trailer on some woman walking by. Reedy was a pipe smoker, and I can remember going into his office and seeing him enveloped in curls of pipe smoke. He was a wonderful, gentle man, professorial, intellectual and academic. Johnson, as he could do with such people, beat him like a rented mule—psychologically, that is. Johnson was irascible. He went off on people, and frankly, Reedy was too decent a person to handle it. He didn't last long.

Bill Moyers took over for him in 1965 but was soon replaced by George Christian. Christian was a laid-back Texan, having been press secretary to Governor John Connally. He is not well known because he kept himself out of the limelight, but he was one of the best press secretaries in the history of the White House. It was George Christian who served as press secretary during the most tumultuous years of Johnson's presidency, from 1966 through 1969. By this time, the war in Vietnam was going badly, and LBJ was sinking in the polls. George worked hard at taking reporters aside, maybe in a small group, or more typically one on one. "Dan, can I see you a minute? I'm not bitching or moaning, and I want you to take this in the spirit in which I'm saying it, but you're off on this. Let me tell you why."

Christian was effective not just because of the way he handled the press, but because of the way he handled his boss. He was not fazed or intimidated by Johnson's choleric outbursts. Salinger, Reedy and Moyers had all tried and failed. A key part of Christian's strategy was to avoid direct confrontations with Johnson and come at hot-button issues obliquely.

One story George told me from early in his time as press secretary illustrates his approach. "Mr. President, I am pleased to be here and honored to be of service to you and to the country. But I am no miracle worker, and I want to disabuse you of that. I cannot turn things on a dime here. Let's take your problems one at a time. I am not going to try to solve everything. Give me the problem that worries you the most, and let me begin by taking on that one."

"George," LBJ responded, "everywhere I look those sum' bitches— the press—are quoting me as saying, 'I will not send American boys to do what Asian boys should be doing for themselves.' I am supposed to have said that early in our involvement in Vietnam, and George, I never said it. Still, it keeps coming back to haunt me. Now it's become some version of goddamn urban myth. I am tired of getting hit over the head with it. Fix it."

"Okay, Mr. President."

George returned after a few days to give Johnson a report on what he discovered. "Mr. President, I don't want you to get mad at me. I haven't solved this problem, but I want to show you the dimensions of it." At that, several interns entered the office carrying stacks and stacks of newspapers and magazines. "Mr. President, every one of these publications has you saying it—not just as an indirect quote, but in direct quotes."

"That's what I am telling you, George!" Johnson shouted. "They keep printing it, but it isn't true. I never said it."

A couple of days later, Christian returned to the Oval Office with a tape recorder. He placed it on the desk and said, "Mr. President, I don't want you to get mad at me, but the puzzle is deepening." With that, Christian pressed "Play" on the recorder, and there came the unmistakable voice of LBJ saying the quote.

Johnson's temper got the better of him once again, and he demolished the tape recorder with his polar bear paws. "Goddamn, George! I didn't realize what a complete idiot you really are. You know what these guys do: They piece these things together, they take a little razor blade, cut a piece here and add there."

"I believe you, Mr. President," Christian answered patiently, "but I wanted you to know that these recordings are everywhere."

About a week later, LBJ hosted a group of guests in the White House screening room for a showing of *The Alamo*, with John Wayne. George was in attendance. "Mr. President, I'd appreciate it if we could get together, just the two of us, after the movie. I have something I'd like you to see."

After the guests departed, Christian gave the signal to roll his footage. Up on the full screen came the unmistakable image of LBJ, standing on the bumper of a limo on a darkened street corner in Philadelphia. Johnson was speaking through a bullhorn, saying, "I will not send American boys to do what Asian boys should be doing for themselves!"

"Damn, George," Johnson said as the lights came back up. "You sure that's me?"

Despite his coarse demeanor, LBJ was actually quite intelligent. His great strength and expertise was that he knew where the levers of power were in Washington and knew when to pull them, or not. He was very aware that he had inherited an enormous amount of goodwill coming into the presidency on the heels of a tragedy. He also knew that goodwill would not last forever. He used his grace period to push through civil rights legislation and the rest of what he called the Great Society.

I covered him twice as White House correspondent, first in the immediate aftermath of the Kennedy assassination, and a second time after I returned from Vietnam. Johnson took JFK's cue about press access and ran with it, so much so that reporters actually got tired of seeing him. When I was on that beat, it was not unusual to be in the Oval Office five or six times a day, which was unheard of, before or since. Johnson would have frequent photo ops with visiting dignitaries, which afforded the chance to ask a question or two.

LBJ did have a great sense of humor, but most of his best lines were not suitable for television, or indeed for repetition in polite company. Profanity and salty innuendo were his stock-in-trade. One day he began talking about how public opinion was building up against him because of Vietnam. Another correspondent—not me, I'm happy to say—asked what effect that growing negative sentiment was having on him. "I'm like a bitch dog in heat," LBJ replied. "If I stand still, they stick it to me. If I run, they bite my ass."

Presidents don't talk like that anymore. God knows, Johnson could be crass. He'd have reporters up to the living quarters, and after 20 minutes or so he'd say, "Boys, let's break this off for a minute. I gotta go take a piss." And yes, he said it just that way. He'd go into the bathroom, leave the door halfway open, relieve himself, and then come back saying, "Now, where were we?" He did wash his hands, though.

LBJ and I had an awkward relationship. He was all Texas, and because I was a fellow Texan, Johnson always believed that entitled him to a free pass. It was a sore subject throughout his presidency. He seemed to expect some sort of Lone Star dispensation. That, of course, was something I just could not give.

Nixon

Oddly enough, I was immediately seared with the LBJ brand as soon as Nixon became president. I was sitting in a small café in Laguna Beach, California, when H. R. Haldeman, Nixon's chief of staff, slid into my booth. In 1969, he was perhaps the last civilian in America sporting a crew cut. I started to introduce myself, but he cut me short. "We know who you are," he said curtly. "You're an LBJ man."

I found this weird to say the least, especially since I had just been through all those years with Johnson and his people saying, "Rather, you're a Texan. What the hell is wrong with you? Why the hell don't you get on board and play on the team here, son?"

Once I recovered from my surprise I said, "I'm sorry you feel that way. I'm an independent reporter, and I work for a news organization that has a reputation for independent reporting. I hope to prove to you that I have no bias, but that doesn't mean you'll always like what I'm going to report."

Haldeman was having none of it. "We know who you are," he repeated. "You're a Texas liberal Democrat, and we'll be watching your ass." It wasn't quite menacing, but there was surely a cold look in his eye.

Nixon's press secretary was Ron Ziegler, a good-natured guy who was a member of what had been dubbed the "USC Mafia" on the White House staff. As a young man, his first job had been at Disneyland in Anaheim, where he started out as a jovial, wisecracking helmsman on the Jungle Cruise attraction. After working press for Nixon's failed run at the California governorship in 1962, he had signed on at the J. Walter Thompson ad agency, where he reported to Haldeman.

Why is Ziegler's gig at Disneyland relevant? Because those jungle riverboats run on a track. The job of helmsman involves no steering, and the witty commentary he delivered was completely scripted.

Being Richard Nixon's press secretary was pretty much the same thing.

The Nixon White House saw the press secretary as a minion. Ziegler's job was to go forth and speak from whatever libretto they handed him. He had virtually no access to Nixon himself, receiving all of his marching orders from his ventriloquist, Haldeman.

Dating from his 1960 loss to Kennedy, Nixon distrusted the press. Arguably, he distrusted our network in particular, since CBS had hosted the famous "makeup debate" that Nixon among others came to believe cost him the election. From that point forward, he sought to manipulate and control the media. Whenever possible, he did not enter any press landscape that he did not operate or command. Although he took questions from reporters while he was running for office, they were seldom spontaneous. Under Haldeman's direction, they'd stack the deck; questions were prearranged and topics were assigned to specific journalists.

During the campaign, virtually everything Nixon said was scripted and on message. That approach carried through into the White House. After the inauguration, the freewheeling days of easy press access to the Oval Office under LBJ instantly disappeared. The number of press conferences shrank drastically.

Every appearance by the president was carefully orchestrated. Haldeman micromanaged every detail. When I was granted a prime-time interview with Nixon in early 1972, I was told that Nixon preferred to be interviewed in front of a fireplace. Fireplace notwithstanding, when I arrived, it was like walking into a meat locker. The temperature was above freezing, but only just.

The thermostat was dialed way down because Nixon was extremely sensitive about his tendency to perspire heavily. He was what we in Texas used to call a sweater, but he did not want to be caught on camera dabbing at his upper lip. The fireplace, which was Haldeman's idea, was the ideal backdrop to project an image of warmth, warmth that Nixon was never able to conjure up personally.

I was very lucky to have Robert Pierpoint with me while I covered
the White House, and I valued him as a colleague. When LBJ was still
president, I'd been moved in over Bob as chief White House correspondent. Nevertheless, he had elected to stay on. He was a terrific reporter
and extremely savvy. As soon as the Nixon people came in, Bob made
what turned out to be a very prescient observation. "They'll try to
divide and conquer," he told me. "This is a very television-conscious
administration, and Haldeman thinks he knows everything about TV
because he's been in advertising. They're going to size up our situation,
see that they've got a somewhat older guy and a younger guy who has
been brought in over him, and they're going to try to drive a wedge
between us."

Bob was right on the money. To Pierpoint's everlasting credit, he
gave them nothing but cold steel every time they tried to wedge us,
which was often. Oddly enough, Nixon's people never seemed to get
it—the more they pushed, the less successful they became.

It's not that the Nixonites were uncomfortable with journalists; they
hated journalists. Nixon was driven by a toxic combination of cynicism
and personal insecurity, mixed with just enough hubris to make him
sure everyone else in politics was just like him. He was suspicious; his
mind leapt to thinking the worst of everyone. The presumption was
that you were an enemy until you proved otherwise. In short, Nixon
was a hater, and organizations take on the colors of their leaders.

How serious was this hatred? Deadly serious. In a recent book entitled *Poisoning the Press*, Mark Feldstein lays out the details of the plan
by Watergate conspirators E. Howard Hunt and G. Gordon Liddy to
murder syndicated columnist Jack Anderson.

Their plot was far more than mere conjecture. It was openly discussed on the secret White House tapes, and both Hunt and Liddy
admitted their participation under oath. In James Bond fashion, the
two consulted with a CIA toxicologist in search of a lethal pharmaceu-
tical that would leave no trace behind. One suggestion was to slather
a "massive dose" of LSD on the steering wheel of Anderson's sedan to
provoke a fatal hallucinogen-induced car crash. (The old-school idea of
simply rigging an accident was also considered.) Another possibility was

what they termed "aspirin roulette"—introducing one or two poison pills into the bottle of Anderson's headache remedy of choice.

Hunt testified that the directive had come from White House special counsel Chuck Colson, but Feldstein convincingly makes the case that Colson was not acting independently. Nixon never forgot a grudge, and the bad blood between him and Anderson went back a long way. Feldstein contends that during the 1960 campaign against Kennedy, Anderson had put out a story about a 1956 "loan" from Howard Hughes to Nixon's brother. Hughes had given Donald Nixon more than $200,000, ostensibly to shore up his financially troubled fast-food restaurant in Whittier. Anderson alleged that this had been a political payoff that had nothing to do with Donald and everything to do with his brother the vice president. He had a lot of compelling circumstantial evidence.

Just a few weeks later, the IRS granted tax-exempt status to the Howard Hughes Medical Institute, which it had previously denied. Twice. The loan was never repaid, and the burger stand went belly-up the next year, but the vice president and his wife, Pat, had purchased a brand-new home right after Donald got the money. Nixon blamed Anderson's column as a major factor in his loss to JFK, and the incident continued to rankle years later. Worse, Anderson never let up on Nixon; he kept publicizing embarrassing revelations in his "Washington Merry-Go-Round" column, including Nixon's effort to have John Lennon deported.

Homicide plots notwithstanding, the Nixonites' hatred of the press led them to do a lot of what they thought were smart things that turned out to be really dumb things. From my time covering LBJ, I prided myself on having sources inside the White House. So did every other White House correspondent worthy of the name. These sources were the assistants, aides, secretaries—folks you could reach by phone, take out for a drink, take out to lunch. In my case, there were also some guys I had known in Vietnam who were now in the Pentagon. I knew I could always give them a call, but under Johnson, we never had to go too far beyond the White House to work a story.

With the new administration, it was good-bye to all that. The Nixon people stonewalled everybody except known sycophants. With the change in administration, I had been looking forward to developing new sources, but it was made immediately clear that there would be no sources for me in the Nixon White House.

"Hi, I'm Dan Rather. I'd like to introduce myself, either in person or by phone."

"Do yourself a favor and don't ever call me again." Every overture ended the same way. All my sources in the White House dried up. Pierpoint's, too.

My job was to cover the White House, and the White House wasn't talking to me. But Washington, then and now, runs on talk. Even if Nixon's people weren't talking to me, they had to be talking to *somebody*.

The only thing to do was to branch out and cultivate outside sources—to get the story from whoever was on the other end of the line. A political reporter's contacts are everything; I began developing chiefs of staff of key congressmen and senators. Pierpoint had good sources on the Hill, as well as in the cabinet. I also made a conscious effort to expand my contacts at the Pentagon—to get passed along to other sources by people I'd known in Vietnam who could vouch for me.

The efforts began to pay off. I'd go with my notepad to a White House briefing, listen to Ziegler deliver the Jungle Cruise scripted message, then come back and work the phones to find out what was really going on. Sometimes my source would confirm what I'd heard from the White House. Other times I'd be told, "That's bullshit. Meet me tonight in Arlington for a drink, and I'll tell you what I know."

We broke story after story and monitored the rising consternation and anger within the White House. Nixon, Haldeman and White House adviser John Ehrlichman became obsessed with finding out who was leaking to the press. Their plumbers put a blowtorch to every source in the White House, but they never figured out that they were looking into the wrong end of the hose.

How bad did it get? Bad enough that in 1971, John Ehrlichman had breakfast with CBS News Div president Dick Salant to suggest sending me to Austin to open a new bureau, or on a year's vacation, Dick's choice. To his death, Ehrlichman swore that he was only kidding. And if you believe that, you believe that water runs uphill. In the Nixon White House, nothing was said in jest, especially not by John Ehrlichman or Bob Haldeman, the twin bulwarks of what was privately known as Nixon's "Berlin Wall."

In the aftermath of this very blatant effort to get rid of me, I demanded a face-to-face meeting with Ehrlichman. He was hostile from the outset. He accused me of going on air with stories that were deliberately wrong or misleading. I assured him that any correspondent with that kind of record for inaccuracy would be canned in short order. When I asked him for an example, he couldn't come up with one. Then he said something that has stuck in my mind ever since: "The problem with you, Rather, is that people believe you." That was my crime—not that I was wrong, but that people believed me.

When I first arrived at his office, Ehrlichman had been very specific about which chair I was to sit in. As I sat down, I noticed a briefcase nearby. I immediately wondered whether there was a recording device inside, but I dismissed the idea out of hand. "Too paranoid," I thought at the time.

This was before Watergate, but as the saying goes, "Just because you're paranoid doesn't mean they're not out to get you."

In April 1972, our daughter, Robin, by then a teenager, came into our bedroom at about midnight and woke us up. "I hear someone on the back stairs," she said. At that point I did what any Texan would do: I made sure the family was safe, then grabbed the shotgun.

Ours was a three-story house, and all of the bedrooms were upstairs. When I came out onto the top floor landing, I looked down the stairwell and saw someone coming out of the basement. "I don't know who the hell you are or what you're after," I shouted, "but you better get the hell out of here!" With that, I chambered a round in the shotgun.

Clack. Click. Clack. Click. This was a pump-action shotgun, and that sound is loud, unmistakable, and can be deadly in a hurry. Whoever was in the house got the message and fled. I found it odd that no valuables had been stolen. The intruder, however, had clearly rifled the files in my basement office.

We filed a police report and chalked it up as a garden-variety case of breaking and entering. At the time, the idea that it might have been more than that never occurred to either me or my wife. However, as Jean was describing the incident to a friend, the wife of a young Republican senator, she looked at Jean with alarm. "This is political," she said immediately.

On June 17, 1972, roughly two months later, five men were arrested as they broke into the headquarters of the Democratic National Committee in the Watergate Hotel. The group included James McCord, security director for the Committee for the Re-Election of the President (CREEP).

Coincidence, random events or part of a pattern of conspiratorial skullduggery? No one was ever caught in conjunction with the break-in at the Rathers' house. I doubt that we will ever have confirmation, but I know how I connect the dots. Our house in Washington was supposed to be empty that weekend. I was scheduled to go to Florida with the rest of the press corps to cover Nixon's trip to Key Biscayne. Jean, Robin and Danjack had planned to come along, but stayed home after Robin developed a fever...

...Their reservations on the press plane had been booked by the White House.

From the moment the Watergate story first broke in June 1972, Bob Woodward and Carl Bernstein of the *Washington Post* were way out in front with their coverage. They did a magnificent job. That said, all of us quickly realized that there could be more to the incident than first reported. CBS News Division made the decision to swarm the story, just as we had with civil rights and Vietnam. We very quickly formed a unit, which besides me also included Daniel Schorr, and of course Bob Pierpoint.

The Nixonites didn't like me, but they really despised Daniel Schorr. In 1971, the FBI had interrogated his friends, relatives and colleagues at the direction of the White House, ostensibly because he was under consideration for a post with the EPA. They also tapped Schorr's phones and went digging for dirt in his financial records. In reality, there was no such post; Haldeman eventually testified that he had authorized the investigation.

Especially in the initial stages, Pierpoint, Schorr and I could not match what Woodward and Bernstein were coming up with, but then again, no one could. We were running down every lead, but often enough what we had was just not as good as what they had. At that point there was a command decision, made by Bill Small, Washington bureau chief, and approved by News Div president Dick Salant, that we could report Woodward and Bernstein's breakthroughs on air, credit the *Washington Post,* and then supplement it with whatever else we had uncovered.

This made the White House apoplectic. Their prime damage-control strategy had been to keep it local. The Beltway was their Maginot Line; if they could hold the Watergate story within DC by chalking it up to the excesses of two junior reporters from the hometown paper, they had a chance of keeping a lid on it. The fact that CBS—*national* television—was picking up items from Woodward and Bernstein blew their containment strategy out of the water.

The White House fought back by playing hardball with Katharine Graham, publisher of the *Washington Post.* John Mitchell's famous threat that Mrs. Graham was going to "get her tit caught in a big fat wringer" if Woodward and Bernstein continued pursuing the story, became one of the pivotal moments in the film *All the President's Men.* In addition, Nixon himself privately threatened "damnable, damnable problems" with the FCC. The *Post* owned several very profitable television stations, which put them at the mercy of the FCC, just like CBS. If the White House thought Mrs. Graham would be cowed, they misjudged her. Katharine Graham deserves a lot of credit for standing up for her reporters.

The White House also tried to pressure Bill Small, pushing him hard to stop picking up stories from the *Post.* Small was repeatedly called in for what he called séances with various top Nixon staffers. The thing about Bill Small is that he is absolutely rock solid. He had confidence in my ability as a reporter, and in Schorr and Pierpoint as well. Beyond that, Bill was convinced that the story led up, way up.

Our ratings got better and better, in part because we finally got some traction and were reporting things other people weren't reporting. The pressure from the White House got more intense as we started finding things on our own. Pierpoint's sources started coming through for him. Often enough, if he dug up something he'd give it to me, because I could command airtime. We at CBS were running hard with the story from the first, even though ABC and NBC were not.

All of these factors swirled together as the story snowballed. And as it snowballed, it seemed to suck up everyone in its path—*All the President's Men* was well and truly named. From a break-in that supposedly had been perpetrated by a few rogue operators, it spread into CREEP, Nixon's reelection campaign committee, then into John Mitchell's Department of Justice, then into the lower echelons of the White House.

The story was moving in my direction, which meant that the pressure was coming my way as well. There was even pressure from within CBS News, in part because our Watergate coverage was so far out in front of the other two networks. Because ABC and NBC were much more wary of the story than we were for a long time, there were some within our own News Division who murmured that the Washington correspondents were being irresponsible. It was all sotto voce, but the finely tuned CBS bush telegraph picked it up nevertheless.

Some of the innuendo may have stemmed from a genuine belief that we were making too much out of nothing, or that we should have been giving more credence to the raft of denials issued by the White House. Sadly, more than a little of it was also the old ego monster. Within CBS, some of those keeping score thought I was getting far more than my fair share of airtime, which could only mean that they were getting far less. I never confronted those who said I was reckless in reporting Watergate, but Bob Pierpoint spoke up to defend all of us on numerous occasions.

Dick Salant, God rest his soul and now long since gone, was the epitome of journalistic integrity and the best News Division president in the history of the game. He backstopped Bill Small at every opportunity, and the rest of us as well. His attitude was, "We have good people in place—Rather, Schorr, Pierpoint. I have confidence in them." End of story.

Bill Paley always backed Salant, with only one exception that I know of. That occurred in late October 1972, in the immediate run-up to the November presidential election. Paley received what he much later described as a "vicious" phone call from Chuck Colson. Even then, Colson was known as Nixon's hatchet man; it was Colson who put together the Enemies List. After the call, Paley pushed Salant to cancel the second installment of a two-parter we had put together on Watergate. Salant was astonished; never before had Paley interfered at this level. Besides, the first segment had already been broadcast.

Salant refused to pull the second segment, choosing to truncate it instead. Paley hadn't told him about Colson's phone call; Salant learned of Colson's involvement only after the fact. Had Paley mentioned it, Salant later said, he never would have cut a syllable. The story stands as a vivid reminder of the enormous power that government officials, especially in Washington, possess and wield in an effort to manipulate the press. And as was the case here, most of the time those efforts occur in secret. I suspect that Colson implied FCC problems for CBS in the same way that Mrs. Graham had been threatened.

Paley was gingerly walking a tightrope. He still believed that the news was the news, but he was taking heat, not just from the Nixonites but from our affiliates as well. In an echo of what had happened during our coverage of the civil rights movement, there had been a lot of push-back from the local CBS stations, who complained that Watergate coverage was hurting them financially. In addition, many of those station owners were staunch Nixon supporters. Paley may have passed these complaints on to Salant; if he did, they stopped there. They never filtered down to us at all.

We reported the facts of the story as they emerged. We had the total and unwavering support of Bill Small and Dick Salant, and so far as we knew we also had the support of William Paley, which he gave at some personal cost. Paley had always dreamed of being appointed ambassador to the Court of St. James's. When Nixon first took office in 1969, Paley thought he was in line to get that job, but Nixon chose longtime pal (and far more generous contributor) Walter Annenberg, publisher of *TV Guide*. Although the White House still considered Paley to be friendly, Nixon and his staff harbored animosity toward CBS News, in particular toward Cronkite and me. As long as we were probing into Watergate, there would be no ambassadorship for Paley.

As Watergate continued to unfold, it affected me in a very personal way. I knew it was an important story, but I had an ambivalent reaction to it. On the one hand, following its twists and turns was investigative journalism at its best. On the other hand, against all evidence to the contrary, I kept hoping that it would not reach the Oval Office.

Going back to when I was first named White House correspondent, I always had a special reverence for the presidency—not for the man, but for the office, for the institution itself. I felt it particularly when I came back from Vietnam. By 1972, I had been walking through the White House security gate almost every day for six years, and I got to know the guys at the gate very well. "Hello, Mr. Rather. How are you doing?" Whenever I'd walk through the gate, I'd well up inside. I could control it to a degree, but what was welling up was patriotism—pride of country, pride in the office of the presidency and pride in the part it plays in our democracy. I know it sounds corny, and in some ways I'm sure it is, but many others in the White House press corps felt some version of the same.

Now, however, as developments in the story got darker and darker, there was a part of me that almost refused to believe what was happening. I'd go home at night and Jean would ask about my day. "Honey, you won't believe it," I'd say. "Every stone we turn up has another bunch of creepy-crawly characters underneath it." I knew what my reporter's instincts and a lifetime of covering politics were telling me, and I could clearly see that the trail of evidence was pointing where I did not want it to go. Still, I was reluctant to believe.

Did I feel stressed out? You bet. As the importance of the story burgeoned, Walter Cronkite got on the phone with me. "I know you're under a lot of pressure, Dan. We feel it here, too. Just know that I'm behind you."

I had been surprised and even a little shocked when Cronkite had replaced Douglas Edwards on the *Evening News* shortly after I joined CBS. My respect and admiration for him grew as he settled into the anchor chair. At first, I had little contact with him. It was not until the Kennedy assassination that we worked closely together. During that trying and testing time, my respect for him grew even greater, and I believe he gained a new respect for the way I worked.

In the years that followed, when I was at the White House and in Vietnam, and especially when covering Watergate, there was no tension, no problems between us. He became the country's premier television news anchor; I was one of his top field correspondents. He was helpful and supportive, and I reciprocated. We both thrived.

Cronkite's support mattered at a time when someone as powerful as John Ehrlichman was still trying to get me fired. The White House was maintaining that the Watergate affair was nothing more than an overblown media witch hunt in the wake of what Ziegler memorably termed "a third-rate burglary." I was still hearing whispers through the News Div grapevine that what I was doing was irresponsible. Those who did this will deny it to this day, but this is the truth as I experienced it. One very well known correspondent—a good man, and a good reporter—said, "Dan is moving too fast on this story, and he's out too far. He's going to wreck the network. It would be one thing if it just reflected on him, but he's going to bring the rest of us down with him."

The mess was spilling over into our family life. Robin had let me know that kids at school were asking her why her dad hated the president. A schoolmate of Danjack's had told him just the opposite—that he hoped I nailed the SOB.

Despite allegations to the contrary, I wasn't gunning for the president. I wasn't gunning for anybody. What I was gunning for was the truth. The problem was being ready to accept the personal consequences that might ensue when I found it. Gut check.

One night after supper, Jean and I were sitting at the kitchen table. We were having that kind of forthright conversation that husbands and wives have when there's a lot going on. Unquestionably, this was the best job I'd ever had. I loved what I was doing and thought I was doing good work, but times like these offer a cold, clear opportunity to second-guess yourself. Was it possible that the in-house whisperers were right, that I was out too far on the story? Or perhaps worse, did I have it right, but there would be hell to pay? What would happen if the White House came down full force on the network? Would I be the scapegoat somehow?

At some point, it wasn't just about me. Jean and I had slogged our way up from the bottom, but now there were car payments and a house note to meet, and kids' schooling to pay. Now it was all on the line. Unexpectedly, there was a silence, and we just looked at each other. "Are we going to make it?" Jean asked quietly.

I was taken aback by her question, but I surely understood where she was coming from. Jean, as always, is my best reality check. "Of course we're going to make it," I replied. "We always make it."

"We have a lot at stake here," she continued.

"It's true we have all our chips on the table," I said. "Everything is on the line. Either I'm right about what I'm doing on this story, or very soon I'm going to be doing something else for a living. I'll be selling insurance or real estate."

Jean being Jean, our conversation ended with her saying, "I'm not questioning what you're doing, but I worry. You know, as you've always known, that I trust your judgment. I trust you, and I'm behind you all the way."

That was all the reality I needed to hear.

Senate Watergate hearings commenced in May 1973, right after White House counsel John Dean was fired and Haldeman and Ehrlichman resigned. I went over to the hearing to get a sense of what was happening, but because my beat was the White House, I did not go very often. In July, the existence of the White House taping system was revealed. I immediately thought back to my session in Ehrlichman's office and my suspicion that I was being taped. In hindsight, of course I was being taped. Every other conversation in that office had been recorded, why not mine?

As soon as the tapes' existence became known, special prosecutor Archibald Cox asked that they be subpoenaed. Nixon fought their release on the basis of national security. Meanwhile, the hearings continued; most of Nixon's former staff was called before Sam Ervin's committee, including John Dean. The sessions were televised, and the nation was riveted by them. After Dean testified about Nixon's Enemies List, Dan Schorr was handed a copy. Schorr was live as he read the list on camera and was amazed to speak his own name aloud as No. 17: a "real media enemy." Thereafter he claimed that making the list was one of the greatest achievements of his career. (That particular list contained just 20 names. Eventually we learned that the White House had identified hundreds of enemies, including me.)

Nixon lost the battle to remain in office in stages. In April 1974, the White House tried to satisfy Judge John Sirica by releasing edited transcripts of some tapes and withholding others, but that tactic was rejected.

One of my most poignant memories of the last days of Watergate is Julie Nixon Eisenhower's impassioned 11th-hour defense of her father. On May 7, 1974, Julie and her husband, David Eisenhower, met with reporters in the East Garden of the White House. The bravery and loyalty of a daughter to confront the presidential press corps and tell us that her father intended to take this "constitutionally down to the wire" was entirely admirable.

To me, however, it was heartbreaking at the same time. By then, the facts had completely overwhelmed Richard Nixon. None of us in the White House press corps thought there was any way that he could weather this crisis. To a man—and woman—we all were certain that Richard Nixon would be driven from office or forced to resign. The only question remaining was when. We knew it was over. *He* knew it was over. Moreover, we knew that he was sitting in the Oval Office, only a few yards away, as his daughter spoke. He was allowing his child to defend the indefensible. I have a daughter, and I remember choking up and saying to myself, "Mr. President, for the love of God, find an aide, somebody, to call her back inside. Don't let her do this."

On May 9, 1974, formal impeachment proceedings began in the House of Representatives. In July, special prosecutor Leon Jaworski took the matter to the Supreme Court. (Jaworski had replaced Archibald Cox after Nixon ordered Cox's firing in October 1973.)

On July 24, 1974, the court voted 8–0 to order the release of all tapes. (On the tape of January 3, 1972, Nixon is heard telling his daughter Tricia, "Rather's a bastard.")

On August 5, the so-called "smoking gun" tape was made public. On the tape of June 23, 1972, less than a week after the Watergate break-in, Nixon's voice is clearly audible as he instructed staff to work through the FBI and CIA to kill the investigation. This meant that the president of the United States had ordered and actively participated in a conspiracy to obstruct justice, an impeachable offense.

Nixon announced his resignation on August 8, 1974, effective the next day, rather than face impeachment by the House and almost certain conviction in the Senate. In the end, Senate Republicans, among them Barry Goldwater, played a decisive role. After the release of the tapes, it was clear to them that Nixon was complicit. It was their duty to tell him that he would not be exonerated in the Senate.

What a long and bizarre downfall it had been. If you had tried to tell me that there would be more than 40 members of this administration convicted of felonies, that the president himself would be the ringleader of a widespread criminal conspiracy directed from the Oval Office, that there would be CIA operatives tapping phones and breaking into houses, that there would be hush money paid and a guy using his wife's dishwashing gloves so there wouldn't be any prints on the money, I'd have said that the odds were better of seeing Fidel Castro riding through the Capitol Rotunda on a giraffe.

The weird part is that it didn't have to be. Nixon was going to win the 1972 election, and he knew it. And he was going to win big. He didn't need to break into the Watergate complex and spy on Larry O'Brien and the Democratic National Committee. He didn't need Donald Segretti and his team of dirty tricksters (who, by the way, included a very young Karl Rove). This, however, is where Nixon's cynical and vindictive nature got the better of him. Winning, even winning big, wasn't good enough. Nixon's election to the presidency brought him redemption. To his everlasting shame, once in office, he turned to revenge.

Nixon came to believe that it was not sufficient to simply defeat your opponents; it was necessary to destroy them, both individually and collectively. He had to crush the Democrats, and to do so he resorted to extreme and illegal measures.

What happened after the break-in was so much more extreme than the worst I could possibly have imagined at the time the story first broke. This was not just the true believers in the White House going beyond their brief. Richard Nixon directed them—stopping only just shy of murder. In fact, it was only the arrests at Watergate that derailed the White House plumbers in their plot to assassinate Jack Anderson. To call them "plumbers" is to place a benign and somewhat humorous nickname on what was really an insidious, malicious gang of felons. The plumbers were a highly skilled group trained in the political black arts—wiretapping, home break-ins, use of federal agencies like the IRS and FBI against personal "enemies," and beyond—a paramilitary group recruited by the White House expressly for this purpose. This may sound like harsh judgment, but it is indeed supported by the facts.

Revisionist history has blurred the edges of the national memory of what happened. People not yet born, or not old enough to remember the early to mid 1970s, may be tempted to think that Watergate was just another political scandal. It was not. This was a constitutional crisis of the first order. The president was running what was, in effect, a crime syndicate from the Oval Office.

There have been many theories put forward about why Nixon did what he did. Many of them delve into armchair psychology, hypothesizing a sense of inferiority about his childhood, which begat his huge resentment of the Kennedys and all that they represented. (Following Neil Armstrong's "one small step" on the moon in July 1969, the watchword in NASA became "on to Mars." Instead, Nixon cut the space program off at the ankles. The reason? He saw it as a Kennedy program, not an American program. It took a great deal of convincing for him to go forward into space with even a minimal effort. The only project he kept was what was billed as a "space truck"—the space shuttle.)

The idea that Nixon was somehow less than responsible for what he did because he came up the poor way doesn't wash. There are millions of Americans who have risen above underprivileged childhoods who didn't end up running a crime syndicate, let alone one that operated out of the highest office in the land. Make no mistake: Nixon was not a victim. He was a perpetrator. The only reason he was an *unindicted* co-conspirator was because prosecutor Jaworski told the grand jury that on constitutional grounds, indicting a sitting president should be left to the Senate.

Watergate left the country reeling. Beyond its immediate damage, however, are its lingering toxic effects. Nixon injected the vindictive and malignant virus of "win and demolish" into the American body politic, where it has taken root and proliferated. It still flourishes today.

Four decades later, however, the memory of what happened has faded, and two generations of Americans have little or no inkling what Watergate was about. The public at large may have forgotten what happened during that time, but Nixon's people never did. In the aftermath, there was not a lot of contrition among the participants, not even among those who did time. Worse yet, they held CBS, and me, along with the *Washington Post*, responsible for what happened, and that animosity carried through into the Reagan and Bush presidencies.

Elephants, it seems, never forget.

CHAPTER 6

Presidents I Have Known, Part II

When Nixon won in 1968, I had wondered whether CBS would rotate me off covering the presidency, but the answer had come back no, they wanted me to remain. Now, barely a few weeks into Gerald Ford's administration, Dick Salant asked if I would leave my post as chief White House correspondent and take a new position as anchor-correspondent for *CBS Reports*. *CBS Reports*, however, originated from New York.

By that time, I had covered the White House for a decade, which was a considerably longer stint than usual. I myself had chosen to stay on after the transition from Johnson to Nixon. The idea of leaving in 1972, between Nixon's first and second terms, was rejected out of hand. "Whatever you may be thinking," Dick Salant had told me at the time, "you have to stay. We can't be in the position of appearing to yield to White House pressure." (For the record, I felt the same way.)

Now that Ford was president, Salant went to great lengths to convince not only the public but me as well that this reassignment was a promotion. I was not convinced. Ed Murrow had made landmark documentaries, first on *See It Now*, then later on *CBS Reports* before being pushed out. The show's title had since become an umbrella for network documentaries in general, but the format had languished. What message were they sending by making me the anchor of a show that had no regular spot on the schedule?

I suspected that the move might have been precipitated by an exchange I'd had six months earlier with Richard Nixon. In March 1974 at a presidential press conference before the National Association of Broadcasters, I'd stood up to ask Richard Nixon a question and was greeted with a mixed chorus of cheers and boos.

Although that spontaneous reaction pretty accurately reflected the diversity of public opinion over our reporting on Watergate, I suspected that a number of the boos might have come from our own CBS affiliates, especially those from the Deep South. Some local station owners were hostile because they were Nixon supporters; others objected because our coverage of the Watergate hearings was cutting into ad revenues from daytime programming, especially soap operas.

Before I could ask my question, Nixon, as surprised by the hubbub as I was, asked me one of his own: "Are you running for something, Mr. Rather?"

"No sir, Mr. President," I replied quickly. "Are you?" That instantaneous reflex response probably would not have kicked up any dust at all, except that I was the one who had made it, and Richard Nixon was already much besieged. In the wake of the exchange, Dick Salant received a barrage of letters criticizing me for being disrespectful to the president and demanding my reassignment.

Now it was late August 1974, and rumors were flying that I was being called back to New York because I had become the poster boy for animosity between the White House and the press. It was a very low period for me. Some southern station managers were actually taking credit for pulling strings to effect my relocation. The move was also difficult for me personally. Because our children were in their last years of high school, uprooting them would have been much too disruptive. I got a small apartment in New York and commuted to DC for family time on weekends.

Once I got to work, however, I wasn't in News Div headquarters in the old milk barn. The *CBS Reports* offices were blocks away in another building entirely. Although long-form journalism suited me, it still felt like I'd been shunted up and aside. Iced. About a year later, however, I was given yet another assignment. In December 1975, I made my first appearance as a correspondent on *60 Minutes*. The program had just been moved to its 7:00 p.m. time slot. The officially stated reason was so that it could better stay clear of professional football overtime, which had been newly instituted. Some on *60 Minutes* suspected that people in the Entertainment Division of CBS moved it there in hopes that it would die off in the more competitive prime time "fringe" of 7:00 p.m. (If so, little did the Entertainment guys know that this would be the making of *60 Minutes* as we know it.)

Ford

The 25th Amendment to the Constitution, which deals with presidential succession, was ratified in 1967. The first three times it was invoked all involved Gerald Ford. Ford was appointed vice president in October 1973 upon the resignation of Spiro Agnew after charges of bribery and tax evasion. He ascended to the presidency in August 1974 upon the resignation of Richard Nixon. In December 1974, Nelson Rockefeller was appointed as Ford's VP.

Gerald Ford was a genial fellow, easy to be around, and he got along extremely well with reporters. The press loved President Ford in no small measure because he wasn't Richard Nixon. Ford already had some media skills that he'd honed as House minority leader. He knew who was who in the press corps, who represented what, and who needed what. He also made himself accessible. Correspondents were a bit easier on him than they could have been, both because he took over the presidency when the country was aching for some stability and peace and quiet, and because it was acknowledged that he was a caretaker president.

Ford was truly humbled by the presidency—after all, the only constituents who had ever voted him into office were the folks in and around Grand Rapids, Michigan. In a way, he was a bit like a club-level prizefighter who suddenly found himself in a title match.

He was aware that the Watergate crisis had badly fragmented the country and that it needed to be pulled together, to heal. Toward that end, he used the media in his efforts to soften and elevate the public's negative view of the presidency and generally presented himself with great humility and self-effacing humor. To salve the wounds of Watergate, he deliberately showed us the human face of the man in the office. He allowed himself to be seen making toast and that sort of thing. Ford was Everyman as president.

That said, he will always be best remembered for his pardon of Richard Nixon. The grand jury had already named Nixon as an unindicted co-conspirator, but literally a month after taking over as president, Ford issued a blanket pardon, thus ensuring that Nixon would never have to answer under oath for what he had done, either before a jury or in the Senate of the United States. Because it was a presidential pardon, nobody could do anything about it. We say we're a people who want accountability for elected officials, but from that point forward, Nixon would never be held accountable.

Although he projected an image of being a regular guy, I don't think Ford acted out of bravery or any sense of nobility. I said as much the night he announced the pardon, and I have believed ever since that there was a deal in place when Ford became vice president after Agnew resigned in disgrace. I believe Nixon chose Ford in October 1973 because implicitly or explicitly he already understood how vulnerable he was. The noose was tightening. Nixon was still hoping against hope that he would slide through, but he was also a realist. At some point the question would have been asked, "If worse comes to worst, whom can I depend on?"

And I believe to this day that there was a deal, explicit or implicit, in place at the time Nixon resigned. If Nixon had gone to trial, he would have been convicted. If impeachment proceedings had been issued against him, he would have been impeached. Ford was a tough partisan fighter and a decent guy, but he understood that in politics, you can't always be decent, and you can't always play by the rules.

But it cost him. Jerald terHorst, who had covered Ford for the *Detroit News* for two decades, became press secretary when Ford became president in August 1974. In September, immediately after Ford issued the pardon, terHorst tendered his resignation because he could not in good conscience defend the pardon to the press and to the public.

Ford ran for election against Jimmy Carter in 1976. If Watergate had not happened, or even if Watergate had not been fully exposed, a case could be made that the Republicans might have won the 1976 election, but Carter came virtually out of nowhere and defeated Ford. The pardon certainly helped doom Ford's chances to be elected in his own right.

Carter

President Carter became a favorite of the press during the 1976 presidential campaign because he was something new. Johnson was pure Texas to the core, but that is different from being a Southerner. Carter sounded exactly like Georgia; more than that, he surrounded himself with people from Georgia.

In the beginning, he and the members of his new administration tried very hard to be different. Worse, Carter made a point of saying that different was better. He was certain that those fresh, beyond the Beltway Georgia voices were exactly what the country needed. The downside of that posture was that instead of embracing Republican and Democratic insiders, he stayed aloof.

Payback for Carter, as it is for so many in politics, was a bitch. After he walled off the DC establishment, they walled him off in retribution, which meant Carter couldn't get anything done. That became the central problem of his presidency. He was as tone deaf about the levers of power in Washington as Johnson was adept. Over and above bringing in his loyal but inexperienced campaign people to fill high positions in the administration, what he needed was a really good insider—a Beltway pit bull—to be his White House chief of staff.

That would have made him much more effective in getting his agenda through Congress, but Carter vowed never to be part of the Washington elite and tried to sell that to the press. The press knew better and was having none of it. "Excuse me, Mr. President, but by virtue of the office you hold, you are the ultimate Washington insider."

Those two elements pretty much decided how he was received. There was a testy side to Carter, and it would flash from time to time. By mid-presidency the press wasn't actively hostile to him, but the honeymoon was certainly over.

Carter was unquestionably a smart guy. Although he campaigned as the peanut farmer from Plains, he had graduated from Annapolis and trained as a nuclear engineer. That engineer mentality didn't necessarily serve him well. He loved being involved in the details, to the point of getting entangled by minutiae that should have been delegated to staff. That said, given any standard IQ test, he would probably score competitively with two of our brightest contemporary presidents, Bill Clinton and Barack Obama—perhaps higher, because Carter was so strong in math and physics.

One of the first interviews I did with President Carter made it clear that he was a very bright guy who wanted to appear as an honest, sincere person with the country's best interests at heart. He did, however, let himself go much too far in his "just folks" candor. At the suggestion of my producer, Steve Glauber, I asked him to grade himself as a president. A shrewder or more wily politician might have replied, "That's for other people to do." But Carter was into honesty, so he went down the line and actually answered the question.

"Let's see. On domestic policy, I'd give myself a C plus. I'm getting better on foreign policy, but I think I've only shown a C there. On economics, I'd give myself a B." He added a few more but stayed very modest.

I wanted to give him a way out, but by that time he had built his own trap. "Mr. President," I said, "by my calculations the average is a C plus." He was stunned. He certainly did not want to be a C-plus president, but he had graded himself. The interview went downhill from there.

One of the more endearing things about covering the White House is that each administration brings at least a tinge of the culture from which it comes. From Harry Truman forward, you did not smell whiskey anywhere in the White House at any time—not to say that people didn't drink in there, they surely did. Lyndon Johnson drank, not excessively by the way. Johnson always said to interviewers and others that he drank bourbon and branch water, which is a western expression. Fact is, however, he had a taste for Scotch, and most of the time that's what he drank.

I don't think Carter himself ever drank, but he had surrounded himself with some very talented good ole boys who had a penchant for elbow-bending. I remember walking into the Oval Office and getting just the faint, faint smell of bourbon wafting on the air, a smell I do know something about. I remember smiling and saying to myself, "That's kind of nice, actually." It made me feel a little better about these drawling southern guys.

During the 1980 campaign, it didn't take a political reporter to surmise that at the very least, Carter was going to have a tough time with Reagan. It wasn't in him to believe that, however. Perhaps more poignantly, it wasn't in Mrs. Carter to believe it, either. The two of them were sure, right up to the very end, that they were going to win. They convinced themselves; hope is father to belief.

As the elections approached, the Friday polls showed a dead heat. Having covered politics for a long time, I am aware that many folks don't make up their minds until the last minute, and there is often a shift over the last weekend before the voting begins on Tuesday. In a close race, that shift decides the election. I do think that if not for the hostage situation in Iran, Carter might have been able to pull out a victory over Reagan.

Reagan

When Ronald Reagan first vied for the Republican nomination in 1980, the Washington press corps was initially very skeptical about his chances. He had sought the nomination twice previously. The first time was in 1968, when he lost out to Richard Nixon. He put his hat in the ring again in 1976 and again lost out, that time to appointed president Gerald Ford. In 1980, however, he secured the nomination and went on to unseat incumbent president Jimmy Carter.

Reagan enjoyed a good relationship with the White House press corps and was at ease with them. As a TV and movie veteran, he knew how to use the media to great advantage. As we say in Texas, he had been to that rodeo many times. He was comfortable in his own skin, always ready with a quip or a joke, which was invaluable. Although not a scholar, he had outstanding people skills. Reagan had a wonderful sense of humor and never seemed to get mad at anyone. (Or if he did, he never let it show.)

He sometimes used the press as a foil. When he departed the White House for Marine One, he left enough distance so you would have to shout a question to him. ABC's Sam Donaldson made a whole career of shouting what became known as "the helicopter question" to the president.

The Reagan White House was skillful at managing photo ops for the president, and indeed at managing the press in general. Deputy Chief of Staff Michael Deaver often handled that responsibility, ensuring that whatever Reagan had to say had what they termed "good visuals" behind it. Their prevailing view was that the image Reagan projected on television was at least as important as what he had to say.

Reagan took office less than two months before I took over from Walter Cronkite at the *CBS Evening News*. In 1980, Walter had made the decision he wanted to leave the anchor chair and go out on top. He told me I was his choice to succeed him, for which I was deeply appreciative. When I came to the anchor chair in March 1981, he remained as supportive and encouraging as he had been earlier in my career. One of my first goals was to get an interview with Ronald Reagan. I talked with my longtime friend, White House correspondent Bill Plante, whose job it became to get the anchorman an interview with the new president. When the process of getting it set up seemed to be taking longer than it should have, I asked Bill what was going on. "Well, they're pretty choosy," he said, "and they're not too sure of you. Reagan's people are pretty hard-core conservative Republicans, and they're of the ilk that sees most people at CBS as left-wing liberals. You included."

Elephants never forget.

Several members of Reagan's press team had been in the Nixon White House. What they learned in the interim, however, was to be more clever at disguising their contempt for the press and far more subtle at managing coverage.

Finally an interview was set up, an hour-long session of the sort that isn't much done anymore. We had agreed at the start that somewhere about the halfway mark, we would pause for five or ten minutes to give both of us a break. Shortly before that, I had asked the president about race, and he had replied.

In general, I thought the session was going well, but Michael Deaver, the White House image-maker in chief, apparently was unhappy with the answer Reagan had given to the race question. During the break, Reagan himself took me aside. "Dan, on that last question I didn't respond as well as I wanted to," he said. "I'm not asking you not to use it, and I will understand if you say no, but when we resume, if we could revisit that subject, or if you could ask a follow-up question that would give me an opportunity to better express what I really feel, I would appreciate it."

There was nothing whatsoever threatening or unpleasant about his tone. Reagan could be tough, but one-on-one, there was a gentleness about him that was impressive. "I'll certainly consider that seriously, Mr. President," I replied. When we resumed, but not right away, I asked him another question on the subject, and he gave a gentler, more expansive answer. As I recall, when we edited the tape, we left both responses in the segment.

I thought the interview was very good and we played it in prime time, with the enthusiastic support of CBS executives. Shortly after the interview was broadcast, Bill Plante told several CBS executives that Reagan was not displeased with the interview, but that he didn't feel any particular chemistry with me. Reagan was a big believer in personal chemistry. I had felt very comfortable during the interview and I thought he did, too, so I thought that his comment seemed rather curious. The interview did not get rave reviews, but it didn't get blasted either. The later interviews with Reagan seemed equally comfortable for me and for him. Although I did not agree with all of his decisions, I liked him. I never believed President Reagan was personally racially prejudiced, but he wasn't as sensitive as he should have been about race relations. In particular, he did not seem to realize how some elements of the Republican Party tried to exploit racial conflict as a wedge issue for partisan advantage. There were many positives to the Reagan presidency, but his being a leader for improving race relations was not one of them.

Reagan really earned the plaudits that came with the handle "the Great Communicator." There was something very disarming about the way Reagan presented himself, both in his demeanor and especially in his tone of voice. It played, I believe, a significant role in his ability to avoid being implicated in Iran-Contra, which was potentially as impeachable an offense as Watergate, if not more so. He was indeed the Teflon president.

Reagan was a good combination of optimism and pragmatism. We talk a lot about the power of the American presidency. That power has many facets, but one of the most important, and in my opinion the most overlooked, is the power to persuade. This power is right at the core of the power of the presidency—the power to persuade Congress, and even more important the power to persuade the American people. And Reagan was masterful at it.

He was a superb speaker. Like a good actor, he knew how and when to pause in his delivery and when to emphasize a key word or phrase. Yes, they called him "the Great Communicator," but part of what made that possible was that he was a Great Deliverer.

Time and again he demonstrated that he had the right things to say and that he could say them in the right way. Yes, he had good speechwriters, among the best that any president has had, and yes, he worked off a script for his most important speeches. Peggy Noonan wrote extensively for him; Reagan did not write a lot of his own speeches. He wrote more than either Bush I or II, who wrote almost none of theirs.

What is overlooked, I believe, is that Reagan was very good at telling his speechwriters what concept he wanted to get across. Beyond that, he was emotionally engaged in taking responsibility for the content of the speech. After he'd been given the draft of the speech, he'd read through it aloud, write his own notes in the margins and edit it till he was comfortable with it. What he had to say and the way he said it resonated with the public, even with those who disagreed with him, and that's no small accomplishment.

Bush I

The term of George Herbert Walker Bush was in many ways the third term of Ronald Reagan. By the time he took office in 1989, he had one of the longest résumés in the Republican Party, having served eight years as Reagan's vice president, and before that as ambassador to the United Nations, Republican National Committee chair, and congressman from the Seventh District in Texas (Houston). He was also director of the CIA during the final year of Gerald Ford's presidency.

Bush is perhaps best remembered for facing down Saddam Hussein in the Gulf War, after Saddam had attempted to take control of the oilfields in neighboring Kuwait. In January 1991, Bush ordered the aerial assault on Iraqi troops, followed by the introduction of ground forces about a month later. After routing the Iraqis from Kuwait, Bush gave the order to stand down. His popularity soared because of the successful military operation, but many people remained puzzled by his decision not to push forward into Iraq and overthrow Saddam Hussein, especially since the Iraqi Army was in full retreat and the road to Baghdad was wide open. Bush explained by saying that overthrowing Saddam would have generated heavy casualties and expense and that "we would have been forced to occupy Baghdad and, in effect, rule Iraq." I think that it was a mistake, and when his son went into Baghdad, part of the reason was to repair his father's error.

I had always gotten along well with Bush Senior, and with Mrs. Bush as well. We had Houston in common. They were adoptive Texans out of Connecticut, having moved to Houston at the end of the Eisenhower years. I was a local boy made good, and we got along fine—at least until I interviewed him in January 1988. Bush was still vice president. He was gearing up to run for president, but his nomination was far from assured. Other contenders included Bob Dole of Kansas and Jack Kemp of New York.

The interview got off on the wrong foot immediately. As soon as I asked Bush a question about his role in Iran-Contra, he threw the issue of my six minutes of dead air back at me.

Dead air in Miami. This is one of those incidents that has stuck to me like a wad of old chewing gum on the bottom of my shoe. Less than four months earlier, I had left the set because we'd been put on notice that a semifinal tennis match at Forest Hills between Steffi Graf and Lori McNeil was going to run long. CBS Sports was carrying the broadcast, and they had let us know they would stay with the match to the end. We were set to go on the air at 6:30 with special coverage of the arrival of Pope John Paul II in Miami to begin his historic visit to the United States. We had a tightly scripted half hour, and the first we'd heard about the tennis problem was about 18 minutes before airtime. If we were going to have an abbreviated broadcast, we would need some time to determine how to cut it down. And of course, until the match ended, there was no way to know how much time we'd actually have. The only way to buy time to figure it out was to have CBS Sports stay on the air at the conclusion of the match.

Let me be clear: I did not walk off the set in a snit. Was I unhappy that tennis was being allowed to preempt the pope? Absolutely. I thought it set a very bad precedent, in effect telling viewers that sports was more important than news. But going to black is one of the great cardinal sins in broadcasting and not something I would have done just to make a statement. Not ever.

As we got closer to airtime, what I said—several times—was, "If tennis isn't off and you don't come to us at 6:30, don't come to us. I'll be in place, ready at 6:30, but not immediately after that if our newscast doesn't start. Give us a chance to regroup and get ourselves together. Have Sports hold it until we can know what we're doing."

I was in the chair at 6:30 but was told that the tennis match was still going on. Since I thought the plan was clear, I unhooked myself and went out of the studio. I understood that CBS Sports was still running the show. Sports understood no such thing. When the match ended at 6:33, Sports put us into black. There was no wrap-up, they just tossed the broadcast to News.

This was not anyone's finest hour. Within both the Sports Division and the News Division, there was surely enough blame to go around among executives, producers and directors. Some of it belonged to me, but I was urged to hold my peace and let our corporate spinmeisters deal with damage control. Their way of doing that was to lay the incident squarely at my feet.

Which is exactly where George H. W. Bush picked it up, like a brickbat, during our interview.

Bush's use of the dead-air incident was a red herring meant to derail any further questioning from me about his role in Iran-Contra, but there was nothing accidental about his doing so. His media campaign consultant, Roger Ailes, was in the studio with him, holding up cue cards out of camera range, telling him what to say. (Ailes today is president of Fox News.)

The vice president and I had a contentious and confrontational nine minutes. I asked what I thought were the right questions but got very little of substance in response. As soon as I got off the air, I realized that he had never answered the Iran-Contra questions. Bush's spokesman later termed my questions about Iran-Contra an "ambush," saying that the campaign had no expectation that the subject would be raised during the interview. This is about as plausible as Captain Renault being shocked, *shocked* that there is gambling going on in Rick's Café during the movie *Casablanca*. The network had promo-ed the Bush interview for several days, making the particular point that Iran-Contra would be on the docket. If the Bush campaign was unaware of our intentions, they had spent a great deal of time down the rabbit hole.

At the end of the interview, the CBS phone lines lit up with calls from irate individuals complaining that I had rudely hectored and browbeaten the vice president and that I deserved to be strung up for it, or words to that effect. I asked Jean whether I should apologize. "Don't you dare!" she replied. Eventually we learned that many of the calls came from Republican phone banks that had been set up across the country—set up in advance, for exactly that purpose. Ambush indeed.

My interview with George Bush made the news, but the reporting that night and the following morning focused on the kerfuffle, not on whether Bush really had been "out of the loop" on Iran-Contra. The sound bite that was broadcast over and over featured Bush asking, "How would you like it if I judged your career by those seven minutes when you walked off the set in New York?"

It was six minutes, not seven, and Miami, not New York, but I was in the eye of one of those media maelstroms that had quickly taken on a life of its own. For the moment, the truth scarcely mattered. I had asked a serious question about a scandal that involved backdoor funding of a clandestine effort to overthrow a foreign government, the deliberate breach of a law passed by Congress expressly to prohibit this activity, the sale of arms to an enemy nation in exchange for the release of hostages and a pattern of lying about it afterward. Much like an aircraft carrier under attack in the open ocean, Bush had responded by laying down a smokescreen. His retort about the dead-air incident was an effort to equate Iran-Contra, which involved significant impeachable offenses, with something far more petty.

Bush was obviously very proud of his macho performance. "It was like combat. Bastard didn't lay a glove on me," he crowed the next day, thinking his microphone had been turned off. "He makes Lesley Stahl look like a pussy."

Elephants never forget.

The incident certainly provided more fodder for those who were convinced that Dan Rather really had it in for the Republicans, but journalists of integrity ask questions. Especially when an interview subject is involved with allegations of serious wrongdoing in public office, and especially when that individual is a candidate for the presidency, journalists have a responsibility to ask the hard questions and to keep on asking them until the subject answers, or until it is clear he refuses to answer.

It took a while for the dust to settle and for it to become apparent to more people than just me that the vice president had never answered my question. As was later made clear, however, Bush definitely was vulnerable on the issue. Although he repeated his contention that he was "out of the loop," at the very end of his term Bush pardoned six officials prominently implicated in Iran-Contra, including former secretary of defense Caspar Weinberger and former assistant secretary of state Elliott Abrams. Several were pardoned before they came to trial, hence before they were convicted of any wrongdoing. After those pardons and after the inauguration of Bill Clinton, Bush turned over his 1986 diary to independent prosecutor Lawrence Walsh, a diary whose existence he had denied for many years.

And in a way, Ailes's tactic worked. This incident remains a classic example of the trivialization of the news.

A year before the dead air episode, something else happened to me that also got far more attention than was warranted. In the fall of 1986, I was mugged by a stranger on New York's Park Avenue. The assailant escaped after sucker punching me from behind. Who he was and why he had attacked me remained a mystery for almost 10 years. His identity was not discovered until 1994, when he fatally shot an NBC technician outside the *Today* show studios. William Tager confessed to that murder, and in the process confessed that he had also assaulted me. The NYPD and the district attorney's office confirmed that he unquestionably was my attacker; when questioned, he related details that only he and I could know.

Apparently Tager had also planned additional armed assaults on other media personalities, but had failed to carry them out. The reason he gave for the assaults was puzzling, if not downright bizarre. Tager was convinced that the media had him under surveillance and was relentlessly beaming hostile messages to him. As he attacked me, he demanded that I tell him the frequency being used to transmit these messages. The statute of limitations prohibited his being prosecuted for assaulting me, but William Tager was convicted of murdering the NBC technician and is serving a long prison sentence. My biggest regret is that he wasn't caught before he killed someone.

Clinton

Bill Clinton first came on my radar screen when he was a very young man, having become the governor of Arkansas at the age of 32. When I had breezed through Arkansas prior to the election, he was the talk of the state. It was clear even then that he had presidential aspirations, and I knew not to bet against him. His time as governor was initially rocky; he was defeated in his first bid for reelection but came back and was reelected four times thereafter.

Sometime in the 1980s, a friend of ours told me offhandedly that her friend, Arkansas governor Bill Clinton, would be visiting New York, and that she'd like for Jean and me to meet him. She didn't say so, but implicit in her invitation was the idea that Clinton was a political comer, which I already knew.

We met up on a hot New York Saturday afternoon at the corner of Madison and 82nd Street, then strolled for a little bit to a local place that specialized in different beers. We had a lively conversation, and I came away impressed with Clinton. Hillary was with him, but very quiet and very much in the background. Surely no one thinks of her that way anymore.

When Clinton won the Democratic nomination in 1992, George H. W. Bush was favored; the incumbent president generally has the advantage. Bush, however, ran a terrible campaign. Among his other gaffes, he got caught flatfooted in a supermarket, marveling at this new-fangled device called a scanner, something that homemakers had known about for years. It surely pegged him as out of touch with regular folks.

It was the entry of upstart populist billionaire Ross Perot, however, that helped create the conditions for Clinton's election. Perot's platform was a mixed bag of liberal, moderate and conservative positions and included a balanced budget, gun control, an end to job outsourcing and a pro-choice stance on abortion. In the end, Perot siphoned off more votes from Bush than he did from Clinton. If Perot had not been in the race, it is likely that Bush would have been reelected.

As president, Bill Clinton had a terrific relationship with the press, despite the fact that he got off to a very difficult start. He was perhaps the first president to have literally no honeymoon period. As soon as he took office, he proposed health-care reforms—sound familiar?—but ran into a tsunami of lobbying and opposition from the other side. His first term never really recovered from that. When the Republicans took the House in 1994 with Newt Gingrich and his "Contract with America," Clinton regrouped. There was a persistence married to resiliency in Clinton throughout his political career. He took stock, made changes and was reelected in 1996, defeating Bob Dole. Much of his second term, of course, was bogged down in the Monica Lewinsky scandal. Despite the fact that under Clinton the country was both prosperous and peaceful, the scandal and the ensuing investigation and impeachment stopped his presidency in its tracks. His second term in office could have carried with it a dazzling array of new directions and possibilities. Instead, it was one long replay of the Lewinsky affair. Arguably, however, he has been one of the best and most influential retired presidents in history.

I got along well with him; we only had one uncomfortable time, and that was the exit interview as he was leaving the presidency. There had been a lot of competition as to who was going to ask the questions, and finally I was selected. I conducted the interview and allowed him to talk about his successes as president, but then I had one question and one follow-up about the Monica Lewinsky affair and Mrs. Clinton's reaction. I basically said, "You've gone through all of that and it's behind you. You've had time to reflect on it. Any thoughts?"

It was really a softball question, at least I thought it was, but he didn't hear it that way. He let me know after the interview that he did not appreciate it, but I think he was naïve to expect that we were going to cover his entire presidency and not deal with the affair and the impeachment threat. His reaction showed me that the wounds were still raw, both his own and Hillary's as well.

Bush II

The most important aspects of my relationship with George W. Bush have become public knowledge and have already been covered at length here. The last time I was in his presence was shortly after we'd gone through what we can call "the Bush case." Every year before the State of the Union address, Bush would host a lunch for a small group of reporters from the major networks and wire services. This was a tradition many presidents observed. The lunch included a preview of the State of the Union and offered us a chance to ask a few questions.

In 2005, I was invited. I was not sure I wanted to go, but I was curious about what he would say in this State of the Union address. I asked two lightweight questions, and he gave easy answers. As we were all leaving, Bush came up and wished me well and expressed the hope that I would have a good retirement in Texas.

Perhaps a good way to look at Bush II is to compare his approach to problems with that of his father. Although only 12 years separate the beginnings of their presidencies, they are light years apart in how they handled the office. Bush I, for example, would no sooner allow his vice president to equal him—or even near equal him—in behind-the-scenes power than he would do a half-gainer off the Empire State Building. His vice president was Dan Quayle. Even though I never thought Quayle was as dumb as he was presented in the press, he knew his role and played it quietly.

Contrast that with Vice President Cheney. Dick Cheney was no "spare tire," which is how Quayle was often described. On the contrary, he was at least the assistant president, and there was nothing quiet about the role he played. In fact, Cheney was the driving power of the Bush II administration.

Bush I had quite a bit of legislative experience—he had been in Congress for some time and had been vice president under Ronald Reagan for eight years. His son had zero experience in legislative processes. Equally clearly, he had zero interest in legislation.

Bush I was curious about everything (which is one sign of a good mind, I think). Bush II seemed to have little curiosity about anything other than baseball. Bush I held his own views, but he was always searching for common ground with his opponents for the good of the country. There was very little of that in his son. Bush I inherited a shaky economy and worked with Republicans and Democrats alike to bring it back under control.

Bush II inherited a surplus and a balanced budget. Under the guise of being a fiscal and social conservative, Bush II very nearly spent the country into oblivion, in particular on the wars in Iraq and Afghanistan.

George H. W. Bush had been forged in the fires of war. He enlisted in the Navy on his 18th birthday and got his wings as World War II's youngest naval aviator just days before he turned 19. While serving in the Pacific, he was at the stick of his torpedo plane on a bombing run against a radio station when he was hit by antiaircraft fire. Despite severe damage to the plane, he "continued his plunge toward the target" before bailing out. For his bravery, he was awarded the Distinguished Flying Cross. He has said that his experiences in wartime gave him what he called a "sobering understanding" of the human cost of war. In contrast, Bush II has often been accused of leading the country rashly into war without a good understanding of cost, either in blood or in treasure. The fact that neither he nor his very powerful vice president ever saw combat is, I think, a contributing factor.

Bush I had some semblance of respect for the role of the press in a democratic society. I don't want to say that Bush II had no respect for the press's role, but more often his administration used it as a means to advance their own political and ideological agenda.

Obama

Shepard Fairey's iconic campaign poster from 2008 showed the image of Barack Obama with the word "HOPE" underneath. In the run-up to the election, Obama built a glowing bonfire of hope and tied it to the message "Change You Can Believe In." Much of the electorate believed that his would be a transformative presidency, one that would indeed effect the changes our society so badly needed.

The expectation turned out to be way too high. At a time when most expected the economy to take center stage, Obama turned to healthcare reform instead. I believe that it was a mistake. I think it was also a mistake to remain convinced that he could do business with the other side, despite all evidence to the contrary.

You have to give the Republicans credit for being well organized and well disciplined. They made it clear from day one that their top priority was to make Obama a one-term president, and they said as much, out loud and often. Nevertheless, Obama continued trying to make Washington work in a conciliatory, bipartisan way. One can certainly argue that that is the way Washington *ought* to work, but in the attempt, Obama negotiated away meaningful portions of his agenda, perhaps unnecessarily, and in the process alienated many of those who had elected him.

The message he put forward was, "I really am a nice guy. I really do care about the country, and I really do want to do business." No one should have been surprised by this approach. This is how he got to be editor of the *Harvard Law Review*. This is how he has made it in life and politics this far. He really is a nice guy who is open to compromise. He is a smart guy with good character, intellectually and emotionally ready to be president. On paper, as a package, he looks like presidential material.

His mistake was in underestimating the adversarial determination and solidarity of the Republicans. Most of them think he is too far left. Some even think he is a socialist, a Communist, a Muslim. This name-calling is untrue, but when has truth ever been a useful tool in politics?

On foreign policy, Obama gets pretty high marks in my book. His selection of Hillary Clinton as his secretary of state was bold and controversial, but she has been good. Staying with the decision to aggressively pursue Osama bin Laden was another important decision, and he deserves credit for that, too.

I think that he has put some good people around him, but not in the area he needed the most help—the economy. He has depended upon the same old clique of economists—the Wall Street big corporation guys—who have not had the answers to help our sluggish economy and unemployment disasters. Obama ran a strong, successful presidential campaign in 2008. If his reelection drive succeeds, I hope that he will open the windows in the White House and let the fresh, new talents of the 21st century come into his administration.

CHAPTER 7

Washington, London, Vietnam

But we just got here!"

Jean was understandably exasperated at the prospect of relocating again so soon. Late in 1964 I came home with the news that we were moving to London; I was to become London bureau chief. Less than 12 months earlier, we had pulled up stakes to move from Houston to Washington when I had been named chief White House correspondent. This next assignment meant that our daughter, Robin, would be enrolling in yet another first-grade class in a single school year—her third—and this time overseas, no less.

Frankly, I was more than a little surprised when I got the word, but the London posting was not negotiable. Fred Friendly had just become president of CBS News, and Fred had very firm ideas about what he wanted. I did not know him when he worked with Ed Murrow, but long before becoming head of the News Division, he had been Murrow's producer for many years. Fred had produced both the hard-hitting 1954 *See It Now* segments that helped precipitate Joseph McCarthy's downfall and the landmark 1960 *CBS Reports* documentary "Harvest of Shame," exposing the plight of migrant farmworkers.

Murrow aside, by now Fred was pretty much a legend in his own right. He was a big bear of a man, both in physical appearance and in demeanor, which meant he tended to dominate any landscape that he occupied. He was passionate about his work and demanded excellence from everyone, including himself. He wouldn't take anything less than his best work, or yours.

CBS was still chasing NBC in news ratings, and Friendly had the idea that someone better known than I was should be covering the White House. And by someone better known, he meant Harry Reasoner. At the time, Harry was seen as a possible successor to Walter Cronkite in the anchor chair. Harry was a writer by nature, and had a writerly heart and writerly ways, which meant he took a lot of time off. Fred thought that Harry was an underutilized asset, and the way he chose to get more work out of Harry was to make him chief White House correspondent.

As for me, getting assigned to London felt a bit like exile. It was a letdown, especially since I thought I'd done a pretty good job covering the 1964 elections, in which Lyndon Johnson trounced Barry Goldwater. Was I being punished somehow? Fred, however, called me himself to cushion the blow. He told me straight out about the need to give Harry a higher profile. He also reaffirmed that sending me overseas was part of a larger network plan for me. I was still on the grow, and Fred wanted to develop me as what he called a "complete correspondent." To complete that transformation, he insisted that I be based in London for at least two years.

"If you're going to send me someplace overseas, send me to Vietnam," I told him. "It's going to be the great story of this time."

"If it were only up to me, I'd let you go," he told me, "but my hands are tied. The feeling among most senior people here is that we shouldn't be sending fathers and husbands to Vietnam." Friendly then laid it on pretty thick about the significance of my becoming London bureau chief. Not only was London our No. 1 overseas bureau, it was venerable, almost sanctified—the place where Ed Murrow had founded broadcast journalism as we know it.

The transfer meant giving up the house in Georgetown where we'd been living. For those covering official Washington, there were two places to live: a suburb like Chevy Chase or McLean, or the city itself. Our small-bordering-on-tiny house just off Wisconsin Avenue on the edge of Georgetown had been a deliberate choice; we'd picked convenience over square footage. "You're working all the time, Dan," Jean had reasoned. "If we get a house in the suburbs, you're never going to be home. We need to be near the White House, so you might be able to get home for dinner, or to put the kids to bed."

It was in its way a wonderful jewel box of a house: narrow, as most Georgetown row houses are, full of architectural detail and historic, built around 1835. None of that mattered to Jean's father, however. Jean is from Winchester, Texas, population 35—20 of whom are her family. Her father, Martin, was the quintessential Texan, country born and bred, rangy, well over six feet tall, big boots, ten-gallon hat, the works. He came to see us shortly after we moved in, because he'd volunteered to drive our family car up from Houston. Although not especially accident prone, as soon as he entered the house, Martin began turning black and blue. Within hours he began banging into every architectural detail in the house, hitting his head on the door frames, barking his shins and tripping on the stairs with their worn, nonstandard tread. For him, everything was out of scale. It was Gulliver in Lilliput, a graphic and painful demonstration that folks were a lot smaller in 1835 than they are today.

When I got up the next morning, Martin's bags were already packed. He was headed back to Texas, and nothing we could say would change his mind. We were puzzled, but he eventually confessed to Jean that he had fled because he was sure there was something deeply wrong with our marriage—because there was something deeply wrong with me. "Dan better straighten his ass out pretty quick," he warned her. "He's got to be into drugs or gambling or something. You're living in a goddamn chicken coop!"

The Rathers arrived at Heathrow in the dead of London winter, January 1965, just before the death of Sir Winston Churchill. His passing marked the end of an era in more ways than one. Previously, bureau chiefs were expected to sink themselves deep into the culture and politics of the country where they were stationed. Paris bureau chief David

Schoenbrun had been at least as French as Charles de Gaulle, but my job in London was no longer just to become immersed in the complexities of Parliament, Buckingham Palace and 10 Downing Street. The first game changer was jet travel. The second was broadcast technology: Satellites and videotape were coming into wider use. Taken together, these factors meant that our foreign bureaus—not just London, but all of them—were becoming springboards for covering a much bigger beat.

As a result, I spent a lot of that summer away from home. In quick succession I covered the Apostasia in July, a political crisis in Greece precipitated by the resignation of Prime Minister Georgios Papandreou (Greece's "Old Man of Democracy" and the father and grandfather of two future prime ministers), and the Indo-Pakistani War in August and September. This was an old-fashioned shooting war (the second) between the two countries over the disputed province of Kashmir and my first time witnessing full-scale combat. I spent some time with Gurkhas; I watched Indian and Pakistani forces clash in a pitched battle on the ground and in the air. I witnessed tank and artillery exchanges. (Somehow, the network prohibition on sending family men into war zones did not seem to apply to the Indian subcontinent.) What I saw looked like something out of a World War II newsreel, and it made a deep impression on me, to say the least. It also made me even more eager to go to Vietnam.

A few months earlier, Bill Leonard, a fine correspondent who had just segued into management as vice president of CBS News, had passed through London. During his visit, I'd reminded him of my willingness—my desire, actually—to go to Vietnam. I made what I would describe as an impassioned plea—arguably, some might call it begging—and I could tell that it made an impression. U.S. involvement was starting to escalate, and both of us knew that Vietnam was on the verge of becoming a much bigger story. At the time, he made no promises, except to say that he would carry the fervor of my request back to New York.

Bill was as good as his word. When I came off of covering the Indo-Pakistani War in the early fall, he called me. "I have good news for you," he said. "If you still want to go to Vietnam, you're going to get your chance—provided you talk it over with your wife and kids and get their okay." CBS was sending correspondents to Vietnam on three months' rotation. Morley Safer, young and single, was being rotated out. Leonard successfully argued for me to replace him.

As soon as I hung up, we held a family council to discuss it, but the outcome was never in doubt. "Go," Jean told me simply. "Go because you've got to go." For better or worse, she understands me. In a craft that is littered with the carcasses of marriages, she has been my rock. I called Bill back within hours and said, "I'm ready to go, and I can leave this afternoon."

With a three-month stint, I'd miss the holidays, but I'd be back in England before winter's end. After that, the original plan called for me to stay on in London for another year at least, and as far as I knew, that hadn't changed. With those expectations, Jean, Robin and Danjack remained there after I left for Saigon.

I arrived in Vietnam in time for my birthday in late October. It didn't take much to understand that the American top brass, both in Saigon and in Washington, were ecstatic to see him depart. That August, while I was in India, Morley had gone out with some Marines on a search-and-destroy mission. The Marines had orders to take out the village of Cam Ne, which they did.

On camera.

They calmly torched every thatched roof in the village, some with flamethrowers, others with Zippo lighters, about 150 houses in all. The huts were empty, but still the scene was startling and disturbing.

The segment was a demonstration of the power of television. Safer's cameraman, a Vietnamese, captured the tears and terror of elderly men and women and the wailing of mothers with their children as they were driven from their homes. People who already had so little now had nothing. It was alarming and heartbreaking to see; it is still so today. In any conflict, Americans see ourselves as the heroes, the good guys, but Cam Ne was not good guy behavior.

In the aftermath, CBS was swamped with angry phone calls criticizing the network for showing American troops in such a negative light.

None was quite so vitriolic as the call CBS network president Frank Stanton received at his home the next morning.

Stanton was awakened at dawn's early light by the insistent ringing. "Frank, are you trying to screw me over?" the caller bellowed when he finally answered.

"Who is this?" Stanton asked sleepily.

"Frank, this is your president, and yesterday your boys shat on the American flag." Or words to that effect.

LBJ and Stanton were friends, but Johnson always did have a hair-trigger temper, not to mention a flair for colorful profanity. That particular morning he was apoplectic, certain that Safer's Cam Ne segment was proof positive that Morley was anti-American. It didn't help matters when he was informed that Safer was a Canadian. Johnson was happy, however, that Morley would soon be leaving. This led to the unfortunate speculation that I was going to Vietnam to replace Safer because of Cam Ne. It had nothing to do with Cam Ne. The truth was that Bill Leonard, Frank Stanton and all of CBS News had a lot of faith in both Safer and me. LBJ was about to find out how much faith.

My first impression of Vietnam from the air was that it was an emerald green, beautiful place, but as was always the case in Vietnam, nothing was as it appeared. Almost immediately I learned firsthand that it was in fact a jungle hell for our servicemen and women. The brass in Da Nang arranged for me to board a chopper that was headed out, and I found myself in the middle of a firefight. A Marine had been caught in the crossfire and was very badly wounded. They asked my help getting him out, and of course I agreed. Here was this young man, much younger than I, cut down. I said to myself, "My God, this is somebody's son, this is somebody's brother, somebody's husband."

As soon as I settled in, I realized that there was a decision to make. What did I want to cover? There was surely the "big picture" story—the kind you read in the history books—of sweeping troop offensives, counteroffensives, internecine rivalry within the government and diplomatic maneuvering. But there was also the "little picture"—what it was like, day in and day out, for American troops. I thought this was much more compelling, both in narrative and in image.

This was what I had seen that first day, and this was what I wanted to show to the American people. Real mud. Real blood. The screams of the wounded and the moans of the dying. Or as Ernie Pyle had put it, "Here is your war." During the Second World War, Ernie Pyle was a newspaperman who wrote about the infantrymen he called "dog-faces"—in today's slang the grunts—the guys in the foxholes on the front line. My priority as I saw it was to communicate to the nation the reality of what the war was like from their perspective. (I brushed aside the unfortunate fact that Pyle had been killed on Ie Shima, an island off Okinawa, while doing exactly that.) I wanted to walk the ground, to see, feel and smell what combat was all about and to be an honest broker of that information. What I wanted to do in Vietnam was what Ernie Pyle had done in World War II.

By the time I arrived, there were many more grunts in Vietnam than there had been even a few short months earlier. In March 1965, a contingent of 3,500 Marines had been ordered to Vietnam to defend the perimeter of U.S. air bases. At Lyndon Johnson's directive, they were followed by wave after wave of rapid and massive new deployments—a "surge," if you will—as we transitioned out of our fig-leaf role as "advisers" to the Army of the Republic of Vietnam (South Vietnam) and into direct military engagement with the North Vietnamese and Vietcong. By the end of 1965, the conflict had escalated dramatically, and we had committed almost 200,000 American troops to the war. (At the time of the Tet Offensive—January 1968—there would be upward of half a million U.S. soldiers in Vietnam.)

Morley Safer stayed in Saigon long enough to pass me the baton—to run down his sources with me and give me their vital contact information. High on his list was a fellow named Pham Xuan An. An was actually every correspondent's go-to guy. Some of the biggest names covering Vietnam, including David Halberstam, Peter Arnett, Stanley Karnow and Neil Sheehan, depended on him and used him extensively. Vietnamese by birth and educated in the United States, An was a fully bilingual journalist. He had attended Orange Coast College in California and then interned at the *Sacramento Bee*.

From 1965 on, An was a staff correspondent for *TIME* magazine.

Beyond that, he was witty and extremely personable. He had a reputation as Saigon's best dog trainer, specializing in German shepherds.
He collected rare birds and bought and sold them at the Bird Market.
He was nicknamed "General Givral" after the Saigon café where he
could often be found, chain-smoking and shooting the breeze. (Givral
itself, recently demolished, was during the war something of a center of
intrigue, not unlike Rick's in the movie *Casablanca*.)

By reputation, An was the best-connected source in Saigon. He
could explain the Vietnamese to the Americans, and the Americans
to the Vietnamese. As the new kid in town, I got a briefing from him
when I arrived. To double-check, I vetted him with the wire services.
They confirmed An's trustworthiness and recommended strongly that
I rely on him, just as my predecessor had. Pham Xuan An had great
information—by God, he had great information. He had sterling contacts at the highest levels within both the South Vietnamese government and the South Vietnamese military. He regularly attended highly
sensitive off-the-record briefings with U.S. military leaders. I knew that
I could bust my ass for days and not get as much as I could from one
conversation with General Givral.

In the end, however, I never really used him. Part of my reluctance
was orneriness, but part of it was seat-of-the-pants instinct. I just didn't
take to this guy. To me, there was always a niggling, intangible something about him that didn't sit quite right. Mostly, however, it was my
Ernie Pyle vision of how I wanted to cover the war that led me to avoid
him. The bottom line was that I just wanted to get out into the field and
experience things for myself. An's high-level connections weren't much
use to me if my first priority was to head for the front lines to talk with
our own GIs about what it was like on patrol.

Again, nothing in Vietnam was as it first appeared. Turned out that
Pham Xuan An was a spy for North Vietnam. He had been a part of the
movement since he was 16 years old—even before he went to college
in California. While flawlessly maintaining his cover as a *TIME* magazine journalist, An was gathering valuable intel and passing it on to the
Communists. In January 1976, less than a year after the last helicopter
left Saigon, Pham Xuan An was made a Hero of the People's Army. The

citation is the equivalent of our Medal of Honor and one of the highest accolades Hanoi could bestow. Every American correspondent who had befriended him was astonished.

An's activities both during and after the war were chronicled by Larry Berman in a book entitled *Perfect Spy: The Incredible Double Life of Pham Xuan An*. His exploits make any character in a John le Carré novel look like Ned in knee pants. Walking his German shepherd through Saigon neighborhoods, his obedient dog lifted his leg to pee on specific trees, marking them as dead letter drops. Late at night, An photographed documents at home, while his wife stood guard. With the help of his longtime courier, an illiterate betel-nut-chewing woman named Nguyen Thi Ba, An's film was smuggled out of Saigon in meat rolls wrapped in banana leaves, or in bars of soap. He wrote messages about what he'd learned in U.S. briefings using rice water "ink" on ordinary wrapping paper—ink that disappeared as soon as it dried. An then used the wrapping paper to cover spring rolls—spring rolls that he gave to Ba at their rendezvous in the Bird Market.

Pham Xuan An died in 2006, disillusioned with what his country had become. He was saddened that Vietnam apparently had simply replaced an American presence with an even harsher Russian presence. At his burial, his final request was not to be buried too close to Communists.

CBS headquarters in Saigon was located in the Caravelle Hotel. My quarters were in the hotel as well. ABC also had its bureau there, as did the *New York Times*. In addition, it was home to the embassies of Australia and New Zealand. Built in 1959, by Vietnam standards it was state of the art. It was one of the few really well air-conditioned places in Saigon; it also had its own generator. Still, the faint smell of *nuoc mam*—fish sauce—wafted through the corridors.

The Caravelle's rooftop bar was the de facto press club; I spent less time up there than some correspondents did. I had no interest in hanging around Saigon, attending daily military briefings (a banquet of misinformation that came to be known as the Five O'Clock Follies), and going to tea and dinner with the wives of diplomats. I got out into the field as much as I could, and like every other correspondent who left town, I became a hitchhiker. The only way to get anywhere was to beg rides with combat troops and medevac pilots. We learned pretty quickly that the medevac helos were a great way to get to where the action was. The very fact that they'd been called in told us that there was fighting. Sadly but conveniently, we also knew for certain that not only were they going in, they were coming back out.

I traveled with my cameraman, Jerry Adams; I'd known him since my days in Houston at KHOU. Jerry had seen action in World War II, and I was grateful to be working with someone who had combat experience. As we had in Dallas, we stuck story materials—film, audio, script—into one of those bright yellow grapefruit bags. The next challenge was to get the bag back to Saigon, even if we were staying on in the field. The footage didn't always make it. Some of our best work might still be in the remnants of grapefruit bags in the underbrush somewhere, tossed out with the ammo and spare parts to a unit that was under fire.

One of the first things I did when I got to Saigon was to get outfitted with fatigues. When covering the civil rights movement, I had dressed in a suit, because it was important to look like a reporter, a professional. In Vietnam, being professional meant dressing in field gear and being able to fend for yourself.

Getting off the helicopter, you often didn't have a lot of time to make a good impression. It was important to be able to immediately reassure the commanding officer that you weren't going to need coddling or impede the mission. Over the months in Vietnam, three simple but essential rules of the "Rather Guide to Covering Combat" evolved. With revisions and amendments for changing local conditions, they still apply today.

• **RULE 1:** *Dress the part.*

Wear a dark safari jacket or fatigues and proper footwear for the terrain. When I first got to Vietnam, I was kidded and called "Mr. GI," but from the beginning my attitude was to get into the field, stay in the field as long as I could and get as close as possible to combat. That's the way I operated. There were some correspondents who looked like backpackers out of college. I didn't have a problem with people who dressed down or took fewer things; I had a problem with people who were not prepared.

When a platoon leader is looking you over, his eyes always go straight to your feet. On one occasion, Jerry and I met up with a Special Forces unit that was to attack a communications target and create a diversion in advance of a larger action. Another highly respected correspondent was going along as well, and he had already arrived. I could see the commander looking at this guy's shoes with absolute disdain. He was wearing Gucci-style loafers—the ones with the little metal horse bit across the top. Any credibility he might have had was draining right out of him, but he was clueless. There is no faster way to lose credibility with a combat unit than to appear in loafers.

- **RULE 2:** *Make sure you are self-sufficient.*

Don't be a burden.

- **RULE 2A:** *Make sure that you are **obviously** self-sufficient.*

Officers and noncoms sizing you up for the first time need to know right away that you won't be needing anything from them except access and information. Two canteens tells them that you won't be asking for water. Maybe you open your pack so they can see that you have your own food. Usually I bring peanut butter and protein bars. In Vietnam I also took what I needed to take care of myself for the night, including a poncho, a hammock, medical supplies and personal items. I carried these in a butt pack attached to a web belt around my waist. The butt pack attached to the web belt at the rear, nestled in the lumbar region between waist and rump. Canteens hung from the web belt as well, one on either side. The web belt and attachments were supported by web suspenders over the shoulders. Sometimes I carried a full backpack instead of or in addition to the butt pack. In a backpack I could carry extra clothing, a tent and a lot more, but with just the butt pack, I was far more mobile and able to run farther, faster. All too often, that was important.

Be ready to carry your own medical supplies, including hemostatic bandages. Especially hemostatic bandages. These are also called "blood stop" bandages—if you get a bullet hole and you slap it on, it forms a seal and stops the hemorrhaging. It's not that the grunts wouldn't share with you—they would—it's just that they're thinking, "If this guy gets hit, then I have to give up my bandage." When you carry your own, it also marks you as someone who knows what war is.

I did not carry a weapon in Vietnam, although there were some correspondents who did. I'm not a combatant; if captured, I didn't want anybody to think I was a soldier. On the other hand, I didn't want to give the impression that I was completely useless, either. When I was trying to hitchhike with a unit, the CO would almost always ask if I was armed. "No sir," I'd say, "but I know how to use one. I can disassemble and reassemble both an M16 and a Kalashnikov." If he needed convincing, I'd ask to have a look at an infantryman's rifle, break it down, and put it back together.

- **RULE 3:** *Find the captains and sergeants.*

They are the keys to any effective fighting force. It's fine to talk to corporals and generals, but when you want to know what is really going on, straight/no chaser, your best bet is to talk to the captain of the forwardmost combat unit and his most experienced sergeant. The captains tend to be young, but not too young, and the sergeants tend to be old, but not too old. I was 33, old enough and young enough to talk with all of them.

In all my time in Vietnam, I never had a captain or a sergeant lie to me, or dress it up, or give me the official line, or tell me what he thought I wanted to hear. I'd crawl into a hole, mortar rounds going over, to talk with them. "Dan Rather, CBS News. Can you bring me up to date on the situation?"

These men were honest and straightforward, sometimes brutally honest and straightforward. "We're getting our asses kicked. We're taking very heavy casualties, and if the weather doesn't clear up soon so we can get the helicopters in so we can get the hell out of here, we're all going to be dead." Then he'd look me in the eyes to add, "And that includes you, too, Mr. Rather."

We were overrun a couple of times. One night it was raining like hell. I had taken my hammock and tied it between two trees, then strung another piece of rope above it and slung my poncho over that to create a makeshift tent. (See Rule 2.) And by the way, you knot two used socks—the more used, the better—on the hammock, one at either end, because if there's a snake, he's not going to crawl past those socks. There was a Japanese fellow, another journalist, sleeping on the ground below me. He didn't have a poncho, so I had offered him a chance to sleep beneath me to have at least some protection from the rain. He was wet, but not nearly as wet as he would have been otherwise.

Meanwhile, the rotten weather had enabled the Moving Hats, as the VC were called, to infiltrate our position. Suddenly, there was a lot of confusion, and a lot of shooting in the dark. The Japanese correspondent froze like a rabbit. He was scared shitless, which was an entirely reasonable reaction—I was more than a tad concerned myself. I didn't know whether to pick up a weapon or not. This was one of those occasions when I instantly had that ever-so-basic debate with myself: If it really gets down to it, life or death, shoot/don't shoot, would I grab a rifle and pull the trigger? The truth is that I went back and forth about this crucial decision. I didn't know then and, thank heavens, I doubt that I will ever know.

Fortunately it was all over pretty quickly, but incidents like this were to be expected if you were going where the story was—where our troops were. The footage we took when we went out on patrol, the footage that people eventually saw on TV, was genuine. We tried our best to tell it as it was. We went out where the war was being fought and captured what was happening, first on film, much later on videotape. At first, we were sending our film footage out to be processed in New York. Between the difficulty of getting materials to Saigon, finding a commercial airline that was flying on a regular basis and working on a script with no telephone service, that could take as long as a week. The big difference came when television began to use videotape, commercial airlines were faster and flights more frequent and satellites became more reliable and less expensive. All satellite feeds in those days were sent out from Tokyo or Bangkok. Such feeds were not possible from Vietnam. Live coverage of the war was thus impossible. With luck, sometimes we could bring our story delay time down to two or two and a half days—but this happened only rarely. Luck, like everything else in Vietnam, was in short supply.

I realized that portions of my children's childhood were flying by in my absence, but keeping in touch was a challenge. You couldn't just pick up a phone in Vietnam and place an international call. There was, however, a telephone call center in Saigon. When I called Jean and the children, I minimized any discussion of the danger. I suspected, however, that I wasn't fooling Jean in the slightest—she was perfectly capable of figuring this out on her own. One aspect that did help was that Jean and the kids were still in London. The BBC ran pieces from CBS only rarely, so in general they were spared seeing me reporting from the field with rounds coming in overhead.

In my time there, I saw a good deal of Vietnamese countryside, from deep down in the Mekong Delta up to the DMZ on the border with North Vietnam, from the coastline at places like Da Nang and westward over the Ho Chi Minh Trail into Laos. I saw a lot of the war, and the more of the war I saw, the more I realized that what was being said in Washington about the situation did not match what I could clearly see was the reality on the ground. And for our troops, that reality was a minute-by-minute, hour-by-hour, day-by-day death struggle.

You couldn't be with our soldiers in that incredibly lethal environment, thousands of miles from home, see and share the reality of what they were going through, and then hear people in Washington describe a war that did not exist. The Johnson administration deliberately exercised what was called "minimum candor" in providing facts to the press. This clumsy attempt at managed news was a failure. Worse yet, it severely damaged public trust in any information coming from the government about the war, creating what came to be called the "credibility gap."

In any war, particularly a protracted war, there has to be a strong degree of communicable trust between the leader and the led. In the beginning, Americans had that trust in Johnson and in his conduct of the war, but as it dragged on, that public trust was eroded. President Johnson and the rest of the leadership in Washington, both civilians and the Pentagon, wanted to paint a picture of the war as told by Hans Christian Andersen. Everything was always going well, and those aspects that weren't going well were always improving.

Bullfeathers.

I knew better, because the captains and the sergeants knew better. And it was their truth that we put on the air. That's why I and most other reputable journalists boycotted the military's Five O'Clock Follies. Every night on the *CBS Evening News*, our footage of GIs on the front lines trumped the Pentagon's whole-cloth statistics.

The war changed the way Americans thought about television, and television was a major factor in changing the way America thought about the war. CBS led the coverage of Vietnam. In the same way that Ernie Leiser and others realized that civil rights was a big, important story and wanted to swarm it and franchise it, we did the same with Vietnam.

We brought the war into the living rooms of America. In and of itself, however, that was not sufficient to change American opinion about the war. What happened, I believe, is that increased television coverage paralleled the surge in troop deployment, and rapid escalation of the war produced a marked and sudden increase in casualties. Soon enough, most folks around the country had heard about someone from their hometown who'd been killed or wounded, even if they didn't know him personally—the boy down the street who had been the star quarterback for the football team, or the lad who had delivered the morning paper. When these local young men started coming back without their limbs, without their eyes, without their sanity or in flag-draped coffins, that's when most people began to seriously question the war.

And this is where our Ernie Pyle "little picture" coverage of the soldiers in Vietnam and the "big picture" coverage of the geopolitical issues about the war converged. As had been the case with civil rights, and would later be the case with Iraq and Afghanistan, what folks saw on television was increasingly at variance with what they were being told. That dichotomy would eventually call the whole U.S. commitment into question.

LBJ understood this all too well. His anger at our coverage of Cam Ne was just the beginning. Throughout the war, Johnson tried to compel the kind of positive, upbeat war coverage he believed patriotic Americans were duty-bound to provide. In short, he tried to deal with the media the way he had always dealt with his colleagues in the Senate, by cajoling, and if necessary bullying, to get his way. It didn't work.

I don't think I ever heard President Johnson personally blame the media for making the war unpopular, but many in the upper echelons of government and the military surely felt and stated that television incited antiwar demonstrations. To them, the press was the real enemy, at least as much as Ho Chi Minh or the Vietcong. At the time, Republicans generally supported the war. But so did many Democrats and supporters of LBJ. Many from both parties began to say, "The war is really going well. It's just those press people (like Dan Rather, like CBS, and many others) who are accentuating the negative and turning the country against the war."

This made things increasingly uncomfortable at Black Rock, CBS's brand-new corporate headquarters. Lyndon Johnson and CBS president Frank Stanton had been friends for about 30 years, but Vietnam seriously tested their relationship. Stanton had long been at ease in Washington, working (with Johnson's clout firmly behind him) to benefit broadcasting in general and CBS in particular. Johnson railed that what CBS was doing was a disservice to the country. Stanton pushed back, arguing that the role of the press in wartime cannot be reduced to that of a cheerleader. As the war escalated, it became harder for Stanton to reconcile his personal relationship with LBJ with his responsibility to protect the integrity of CBS News. Eventually, it would become all but impossible.

The heightened tension and distrust between the press and the government is still with us today, but it can be traced back to our coverage in Vietnam. As a journalist, I didn't go to Vietnam with any antiwar sentiment. When I arrived, I had no opinions about the war, other than that it was a big, important, developing story. I didn't go in with any agenda. I had no agenda while I was there. I had no agenda when I came out, except to put on the American television screen the war as it was, as opposed to how some were trying to convince people it was.

Was this aiding and abetting the enemy? Did that make us journalists unpatriotic? Hardly. The members of the press I have known have been every bit as patriotic as any American, especially in time of war. And if my country is at war, I want my country to win, whatever the definition of win is. That, however, was one of the enduring problems of Vietnam. There never was a satisfactory definition of winning.

It is not my purpose to paint the press in some kind of heroic light, but instead to point out that the press is an essential part of how government of, by, and for the people is supposed to work. The people have a right to know what is being done in their name, and when the press finds out that something's not right, we have an obligation to call attention to it.

If this was something Lyndon Johnson tried to forget, it was a principle about which the Supreme Court saw fit to remind his successor, Richard Nixon. "The press was protected so that it could bare the secrets of government and inform the people," wrote Justice Hugo Black at the time of the Pentagon Papers. "Only a free and unrestrained press can effectively expose deception in government. And paramount among the responsibilities of a free press is the duty to prevent any part of the government from deceiving the people and sending them off to distant lands to die of foreign fevers and foreign shot and shell."

I left Vietnam in 1966. I was not back in London by Valentine's Day, or even by the Fourth of July. My three-month stint stretched into the better part of a year, but Vietnam stayed with me for much longer than that. For about three or four years after I left, I had nightmares. I had seen a lot of terrible things, and it was as if they wouldn't let go of me. A jukebox came on in my head and replayed the horror over and over, and there was nothing I could do about it. I can only imagine what it was like for those who fought there, what it may still be like for some who fought there.

Not long ago, there was a reunion of reporters in Saigon—now Ho Chi Minh City—who had covered Vietnam. I was invited, but I couldn't bring myself to go. I had an opportunity to visit several parts of Asia on a cruise ship in March 2011. And, honestly, I would not have gone if Jean had not wanted to go. Jean made it a better trip for me, and I narrated some of my experiences during the war for her. I was nevertheless uncomfortable; it was anything but a sentimental journey. One of the strong feelings that I had was that the country of Vietnam has made a lot of economic progress. But then again, I think of how much economic progress they might have made if they had real political freedom.

I am still conflicted in my own mind about Vietnam, about what happened there and how it happened. I am *not* conflicted about the men and women who served there. I have the utmost respect and admiration for them. I've always felt very strongly about the people who fought the war. The entire country is soaked with American blood. It may have been the wrong war, for the wrong reasons, in the wrong place, but those who fought that war did so because we asked them to go and because they love their country. I used to have a habit of visiting the Vietnam Memorial on each trip to DC; I still do from time to time. I know a lot of people whose names are etched on those black tablets; their faces are etched in my memory. I stop to remember and communicate.

The quagmire of Vietnam and the inability of the national leadership and the military to define success gave rise to the Powell Doctrine, first enunciated by Colin Powell shortly before the Gulf War (1990–1991). At the time, Powell was chairman of the Joint Chiefs of Staff. For the United States to put troops in harm's way, he said, we should have a clear mission, a clear exit strategy, popular support, and a clear definition of what constitutes victory. Powell had served in Vietnam as a junior officer, and he had a clear grasp of the problems the military had faced there.

How quickly we forgot.

By the time Powell became secretary of state, we were watching a Vietnam-style dynamic play out in Iraq. In 2003, after the theatrics of "shock and awe," we stormed into the country knowing virtually nothing about it, its history or traditions. We "took" Baghdad expecting to be greeted as liberators—Paris, 1944. After Baghdad fell, however, things quickly bogged down, not that Washington would admit it.

And as was the case in Vietnam, nothing was quite as it first appeared. I made many trips to Iraq, and whenever I got out beyond the Green Zone and spoke with the captains and the sergeants, often off the record, a very different and far more pessimistic picture emerged— a picture that was completely at odds with "Mission Accomplished" and the rest of the message that was coming from the Pentagon and the White House.

I wish I could say that Afghanistan is better. Perhaps we might have learned in Vietnam how difficult if not impossible it is to remake a society. Now that we are in our second decade in Afghanistan, however, the familiar echoes of Vietnam are sounding louder and more haunting. We are fighting massive government corruption, trying to revamp the Afghan legal system, trying to teach literacy, trying to improve the status of women, trying to oversee free elections. We are once again hearing about the need to win the hearts and minds of the people. Afghanistan and Vietnam are different. The only thing that is the same is the mistakes we made in both situations.

How quickly we forget.

CHAPTER 8

Afghanistan

I must have been quite a sight that March afternoon in 1980 in the open-air bazaar in Peshawar, Pakistan. Under the supervision of Mirwais, our 20-year-old guide, I was decked out in native garb—secondhand, of course. Everything was earth tones—grey and brown and olive drab. It was impossible to tell whether this had been the color when the clothes were new, or whether it was an acquired veneer of dust and dirt. Furthermore, it was a question I preferred not to ask. I also did not want to know what had happened to the previous owner. But there I was, clad in baggy drawstring pants made of rough cotton and a loose-fitting long tunic. My pajama-like outfit was topped off by a combination shawl and blanket—the local equivalent of a serape—and an instant reminder of why those little coverlets crocheted by your maiden aunt were called "afghans." If only the impeccably tailored Charles Collingwood could have seen me then.

This was the birth of "Gunga Dan," and I've endured a fair share of ribbing about it ever since. The clothes were, however, absolutely necessary for the journey. With Mirwais and four others, I was getting ready to leave our hotel in the dead of night to sneak into Afghanistan—on foot.

I'd already more or less snuck out of New York. After persuading Don Hewitt, producer of *60 Minutes*, to let me make the trip—no small accomplishment—Don and I had sort of forgotten to ask permission from the higher-ups in News Div, because we didn't want to risk getting no for an answer. Only my family and a few staffers within 60 *Minutes* were told the itinerary. I knew it would be dangerous; Jean, who by now was all too accustomed to sending me off on these kinds of journeys, was very aware that this was more hazardous than most. She wept as I left. So did my daughter, Robin.

I had some of the best veteran CBS staff with me: producer Andy Lack (now CEO of Bloomberg Media Group), cameraman Mike Edwards and soundman Peter O'Connor, as well as the excellent cultural historian/translator Eden Naby. Mirwais Yasini, our guide, had been "volunteered" to lead us into the country by his tribal leader. In terms of trusting him or not, Andy and I had nothing but the seat of our drawstring pants to go on.

Peshawar is located near the eastern end of the Khyber Pass. Leaving the ancient city, we hiked northwest through the pass like salmon headed upstream, walking against an oncoming tide of refugees headed out of Afghanistan, fleeing the war. Some carried meager belongings; many had nothing at all. In late December 1979, the Soviets had sent 100,000 troops into Afghanistan. In blitzkrieg fashion they had quickly occupied the major cities and installed a new head of government, after having the sitting president executed. Two months later, the Russians were in control of much of the country.

By then, there was almost no official U.S. presence in Afghanistan. Our last ambassador, Adolph Dubs, had been kidnapped in February 1979 and subsequently was killed during a botched rescue raid on the hotel in Kabul where he was being held. After his death, and particularly in the wake of the Soviet invasion, the U.S. embassy was operating with a skeleton staff. Make no mistake: We weren't supposed to be there at all. We were a CBS News crew walking into Afghanistan with no official authorization to enter the country. We carried no passports or diplomatic papers that would help us. If any of our group were to be apprehended, it would not go well.

We wanted to show Americans the face of the war in Afghanistan, a war that most people had little or no knowledge about. There had not been much initial opposition to the Russians during the dead of winter, but as the weather warmed, local fighters, called mujahideen, had increased their activity, striking back against the Soviet invaders in classic guerrilla fashion. Not far from the Afghan-Pakistan border, we hooked up with an Afghan resistance leader also named Yasini (I believe he was an uncle of Mirwais). We traveled with him and his squad of fighters all around the Kunar Valley. He eventually took us to within a couple of football fields of the end of the runway at Jalalabad Airport, where Soviet helicopters, fighters and other aircraft were clearly visible. Cameraman Mike Edwards and I accompanied Yasini's fighters high into the mountains. Once there, what began as a recon mission turned into a firefight, followed by a breathless escape from Russian troops across rice paddies and poppy fields.

At a primitive makeshift field hospital, we filmed casualties and recorded conversations with doctors and patients. Both victims and medical personnel confirmed that the Soviets were using napalm and some sort of toxic gas on the noncombatant civilian population, forcing people out of their homes in order to starve out the mujahideen. They also used bombing and infantry attacks to level villages and destroy crops and livestock. The secondary goal was to generate as many refugees as possible. Judging by the flood of people we'd seen streaming into Pakistan, this brutal strategy was having the desired effect.

To keep from being discovered, we often moved by night. We took refuge in farmhouses and lean-tos, and in one case in a scorpion-infested stable behind a mosque. To keep our health, we adhered as closely as possible to Rather's Rules for Survival:

- Don't drink the water (without boiling or purifying).
- Don't eat the meat.
- Don't even think about looking at the women. Don't even look in their general direction.

Our diet was unusual, to say the least. We subsisted on naan, the local bread (insides only—there's no telling what might have made contact with the crust), tinned Vienna sausages, peanut butter, and nips from a flask of Wild Turkey. We were inside Afghanistan for almost two weeks. By that time, despite the water purification tablets, two in the group had come down with dysentery, but Mirwais got us out and safely back to Peshawar. He proved to be a reliable and brave young man. He now, these long years later, continues to play an important role in the revitalization of Afghanistan as a member of the Afghan parliament.

Andy and I didn't have time to shower or change before racing for the airport for the first leg of our journey home. We barely made it onto the plane, lugging our precious yellow grapefruit bags of film. And, despite airborne efforts at hygiene in the aircraft lavatory, we were still a sight—and stench—to behold on the Concorde that took us on the last leg back to New York. After our reports aired, the Russians were mightily displeased by our revelation that they were gassing civilians, so much so that their radio broadcasts into Afghanistan offered a bounty for my death or capture.

Made my day.

Our reports caught the attention of Texas congressman Charlie Wilson. Like me, Charlie was a graduate of Sam Houston Teachers College, but we were not there at the same time. I knew him, but not well. He was Texan to the core. While in Las Vegas he saw the piece about Afghanistan and called me. I told him about the refugee camps, which were probably the worst human conditions I had ever seen. I had no idea that he was going to throw himself into this subject as completely as he did.

I have been back to Afghanistan about a dozen times since, never in quite such dramatic fashion, but each time I have been awed by the size and scope of the country, and by the seeming intractability of its problems. Most of all, I am humbled by how much I do not know. How much we *all* do not know.

Larger than France, Afghanistan is a landlocked country that shares long borders with the Asiatic republics of the former Soviet Union on the north (Turkmenistan, Uzbekistan and Tajikistan), Pakistan on the east and south and Iran on its western flank. It even abuts China for roughly 50 miles high in the Pamir Mountains, along the ancient trade route known as the Silk Road.

We think of it as a nation, but it is not, at least not by our western understanding of the term. In truth, Afghanistan is a collection of provinces inhabited by tribes. Although no ethnic group has a majority, Pashtuns and Tajiks make up roughly 40 and 30 percent of the population respectively. Hazaras and Uzbeks constitute another 10 percent each. That said, many of the tribes have subsets, and even some of the tribal subsets have subsets.

Although civilization here is very old, civility is not. Fiercely held tribal and ethnic loyalties have given rise to grudges, hostilities and hatreds held for centuries, if not for millennia. These are coupled with a split-second readiness to settle quarrels through violent and often lethal confrontations. Afghanistan is an entire country of Montagues and Capulets, Hatfields and McCoys, Corleones and Barzinis.

These warring tribal factions, together with its daunting geography, have kept Afghanistan divided into quasi-independent districts and territories, and thus kept it from being the aggressor against its neighbors. This has also, in turn, kept Afghanistan from being conquered.

Many, from Alexander the Great in 330 BC, to Genghis Khan, to the 19th-century British, to the Soviets, have tried. All have controlled some of the country for a period of time, but never all of it, and never for long. And in every case, the effort has been costly in terms of blood and treasure. Afghanistan's nickname—"Graveyard of Empires"—is richly deserved.

In October 2001, President George Bush ordered U.S. forces into Afghanistan in hot pursuit of Osama bin Laden. Their objectives were:

1) To catch the mastermind of 9/11
2) To dismantle his organization, al-Qaeda
3) To overthrow the repressive Taliban regime that harbored him

Because of their many human rights abuses, the Taliban were widely despised among the Afghan populace, and the third objective was easily accomplished within weeks. Bringing bin Laden to justice, however, would take another president, almost another decade, and the extraordinary combined efforts of the National Security Agency, the CIA, and Seal Team 6. In December 2001, our Special Forces did have bin Laden trapped in a cave in the mountains of Tora Bora, but word came from Army CENTCOM in Florida to hold off. The thinking at the time was that it would look better if Muslim forces captured him. The top brass ordered our Special Forces to stand down and wait for the tribal leaders to come get him. In the interim, of course, bin Laden slipped away.

The logical next step for our forces should have been to continue pursuing bin Laden and to finish eliminating the power and influence of the Taliban. One of the teachings of the U.S. military, all through its ranks, is "Exploit success." Whether at the squad or theater command level, leaders are taught that when you are succeeding, that's the time to follow up and pour it on.

Inexplicably, instead of pressing our advantage after toppling the Taliban, President Bush did a version of moonwalking in the end zone and turned his attention to Saddam Hussein and Iraq. Using the pretext that Saddam had weapons of mass destruction, the Bush administration launched Operation Iraqi Freedom on March 20, 2003. To support that mission, they starved the Afghan war for resources, men and materials.

It was a strategic blunder of historic proportions.

Looking back today on our original objectives in Afghanistan, taking out bin Laden satisfied objective No. 1. With his death, al-Qaeda's influence in the Middle East is clearly waning, putting us well on the way to meeting objective No. 2.

But that may be as far as we will ever get. When the Bush administration refocused on Iraq, it allowed the Taliban to regroup, which now makes accomplishing objective No. 3 on a sustained basis more difficult than we ever could have imagined. After losing control in Kabul and the other major cities, the Taliban, which we had all but vanquished in 2001, established a new and more deeply entrenched foothold in the rural provinces.

The question for the Obama administration became what to do

about it. In quest of objective No. 3, what started out as a concise, clearly defined mission has morphed into something far more nebulous. In Vietnam we made the mistake of not understanding the people and the culture. We did the same thing in Iraq. In Afghanistan, we compounded that error many times over. We have now taken it upon ourselves to remake Afghan society in the face of staggering odds. In a fragmented country with no history of democratic institutions, we are trying to establish a legitimately elected central government, create a national army and police force, bring equal (or at least better) status to women and teach children and adults of both sexes to read. We are also trying to wean farmers off Afghanistan's leading cash crop, opium. This is what the Pentagon terms "mission creep," but in this case it's on a grand scale.

Today, our continued presence in the country flies in the face of the lessons we thought we learned in Vietnam, as summarized by the Powell Doctrine. More than a decade after we first went into Afghanistan, it is now far more difficult to understand why we are still spending billions of dollars and thousands of lives in this war. It was easier to justify when Americans were asking why a $25 million price on bin Laden's head didn't bring more leads, and why thousands of U.S. troops combing the mountains of Afghanistan couldn't find him. The answer to the first question is that it would have been a death sentence for anyone to have given up Osama bin Laden. And you only need to see the rugged mountains and the honeycomb of caves and tunnels to understand why bin Laden could easily escape, no matter how many American troops were searching for him.

The fact that Osama bin Laden was able to live comfortably for years in Abbottabad, Pakistan, in the shadow of the Pakistani equivalent of West Point, is another matter entirely. In Afghanistan, as in Vietnam, nothing is as it first appears, and the fate of Afghanistan is inextricably linked with that of Pakistan.

The Pakistanis are masters of double and triple and quadruple games. What the so-called official Pakistani position is depends on whom you ask, and when. There also exist serious rifts and rivalries among various civil and military factions in the government. These factions frequently work at cross-purposes and easily change their allegiances if they think it is to their advantage.

Before 9/11, head of the Pakistani army Pervez Musharraf had sent Pakistani soldiers into Afghanistan to fight side by side with the Taliban. Musharraf became president of Pakistan just months before the attack on the World Trade Center, after which he allied himself with the United States against the Taliban.

At least, so it appeared. At the same time, he tacitly gave permission for Taliban forces to freely cross the border and use Pakistan as a sanctuary, so long as they did not attack Pakistani troops. Papers released by WikiLeaks confirmed these and many other suspicions about the Pakistanis, beginning with their sharing of intelligence information with the Taliban and their protection of Osama bin Laden for years after 9/11. We were only able to find and kill bin Laden by taking Pakistani intelligence out of the loop. Given the immensity of what we are trying to accomplish, it should not surprise anyone that we are not "winning" in Afghanistan. It should also not surprise anyone that popular support is eroding at home. The echoes of Vietnam are growing louder and louder as the military and the administration keep trying to give us the good news—and only the good news—about a situation that common sense suggests is either stagnating, or deteriorating, or impossible to sustain in the long run.

The Pentagon's core technique in this regard is what they call "strategic communications," which is less a tool designed to convey information than one intended to bend public opinion. The linchpin of this strategy is stringent control of the conditions for media access. The Pentagon considers this a lesson learned from Vietnam, but it strikes me that they took away the wrong conclusion from that war.

Important high-ranking officers remain convinced that military victory in Vietnam had been within their grasp but that the press turned against them, and then turned the country against them. In short, they believe that the press is to blame for the U.S. defeat. This is revisionist history at its most absurd. As I heard repeatedly from captains and sergeants from the Mekong Delta to the DMZ, victory in Vietnam was nowhere in sight.

Nevertheless, "strategic communications" means that control of the flow of information is now considered an integral part of any war effort. In order to "dominate the information environment," the Pentagon has clamped down on press coverage. In Vietnam, accredited reporters were allowed to go everywhere we wanted to go. We could ask any helicopter pilot for a lift; many correspondents, including me, hitchhiked all over the country. That is no longer permitted. Beginning with the Gulf War, the military started to control not just who could go, but when and where and how long. In Afghanistan, unless you have your own independent transportation, all press trips must be carefully planned out and vetted by the military. Generally speaking, you just make a request to the Pentagon. If, however, you have a relationship with someone in Afghanistan, you might be moved along more quickly by the Pentagon, and even be granted more access.

The Gulf War was also the beginning of the embed strategy, which permitted journalists to attach to certain units. On the face of it, embedding perhaps does not sound so bad. Reporters go where they might not otherwise have access, and they get a chance to talk to real troops, one-on-one. And as in Vietnam, soldiers patrolling the wire will always answer a straight question with a straight answer. Reporters also get to see the war "up close and personal," as the saying goes, perhaps more up close and more personal than they would like. Indeed, at first glance it does not sound that much different from my first visit to Afghanistan, when I was "embedded" with Yasini's mujahideen.

The negatives of the officially sanctioned embed program, however, are significant and violate many of the core principles of independent journalism. Embeds come and go with their units; they generally are not allowed to stay behind or move to another location on their own. This means that once they are embedded, they lose control over their own itinerary. The military is also free to determine which units take on embedded journalists and which do not. There have been suggestions that those trying to "dominate the information environment" might be inclined to permit more embeds in parts of Afghanistan where things are going well and fewer in provinces where they are going poorly.

The Pentagon anticipated that the embeds would bond with the soldiers they traveled with, in effect becoming adjunct members of the military's propaganda team. That is often what happened, and some members of the press became advocates for the orthodox military point of view. Sy Hersh has called it "the worst single thing that has happened to journalism in the last decade and a half."

Hersh and a few others have protested, but on the whole there has not been nearly enough vehement objection from journalists about any of this. One of the aspects of our involvement in Afghanistan that is not talked about is the failure of the American press—or *any* press—to really cover the war. Sadly, Afghanistan no longer gets much play on the front page or on the evening news. Part of the problem, of course, is the new budget-conscious attitude toward covering the news. Wars are expensive, not just for our armed forces, but for the media as well. There is no well-staffed Kabul bureau for any of the major networks; some have no bureau at all. Most news sources now rely on stringers and occasional visits by correspondents, if that. Even those, however, are less frequent than they were in prior conflicts. This dearth of coverage is unconscionable, given that we have young Americans in peril fighting wars we signed off on.

It often strikes me in a war zone how much a small percentage of our population (probably 1 percent or less) sacrifices for the sake of the other 99 percent, most of whom have little idea of what the military does. It is especially humbling to see the sacrifices these soldiers make when you have just flown from New York or some other place where Americans have very little understanding of the situation in Afghanistan. I am always deeply troubled by coming upon bodies—either Afghan or American—who have given their lives, their futures.

We at *Dan Rather Reports* have probably put in at least as much time in Afghanistan as other electronic and broadcast media. I am often asked where I sleep in Afghanistan. It depends upon where I am. In Kabul, I try to avoid major hotels. I have a few downscale, out-of-the-way hotels that are comfortable by Afghan standards. The big hotels, where the beds are better and the phones work better, are targets. I practice what the security people call "passive security." You do the best you can. Do not come and go at particular times, and change rooms frequently, if possible.

There is no such thing as complete security. The point is to break your routine. You have to avoid being predictable—or complacent. When traveling in Afghanistan, I find that little personal security procedures learned long ago in Vietnam are still valuable. In 1965 I was staying at the Caravelle Hotel in Saigon. CBS had an office there, together with a couple of rooms on the same floor. Because I had seen what I considered to be unsavory characters hanging around the hotel, I was more than a little concerned when it seemed to me that someone had tried to get into my room. After that I began sleeping on the floor, facing the little balcony. On the second night, someone—maybe more than one someone—came over the balcony and into the room, checked the bed (where I had stuffed some pillows to look like a body) and left immediately. Were the intruders just robbers and thugs, or were they somehow connected with the war? I do not know. But I did not stick around to find out. I went immediately to another floor and did not have another incident.

Ever since that experience, I have tried never to be a sleeping target. In Afghanistan, I don't necessarily stay in the room where I'm registered. Often enough, I don't stay in a hotel at all. Afghans will sometimes invite me to stay in their homes.

I believe we have to confront the nonsense of "strategic communications," of American journalists being embedded with U.S. troops and the need to beg permission from the military to cover the war in a certain way. If this sounds like yet another echo of Vietnam, it should. During the Vietnam War, those in power felt that they couldn't tell the American people the truth, that we at home couldn't take it. They deliberately created a fairy tale about the situation that prevailed in Vietnam, presuming that if the American people had an accurate picture of what was happening, they would not support what we were doing. Of course, when the American public finally *did* learn the truth of what was going on in Vietnam, what was being done in our name, our worst fears and suspicions were confirmed.

As Bill Moyers, a key insider in the Lyndon Johnson White House, recently put it, "We circled the wagons and grew intolerant of news that didn't conform to our hopes, expectations and strategies for Vietnam, with terrible, tragic results for Americans and Vietnamese, north and south. I say, 'Never again!'"

Except that this is *exactly* what is going on—again. In Afghanistan, first the Bush administration and now the Obama administration are managing the news, and for exactly the same reasons. It is at the core of the Pentagon's attempt to control the flow of reportage from Afghanistan.

There are many formidable problems to deal with in Afghanistan. Of those, three stand out as our biggest obstacles to achieving anything permanent there:

• *A government that is not only corrupt, but inefficient.* Hamid Karzai was first elected president in 2004; he was elected to a second term in 2009, accompanied by widespread and vociferous allegations of fraud at the ballot box. Karzai acceded to U.S. pressure for a runoff election but canceled it on short notice and had himself declared the winner. I have spoken with President Karzai four times, and it is difficult not to like him on a personal level. He is very smart and well educated. He can talk, in English, about a broad range of subjects—literature, art, music or politics. All I have ever seen from him is a gentle demeanor. On the other hand, there is no doubt that his government is corrupt and inefficient. Although he is on record as being solidly behind efforts to eliminate opium cultivation, Ahmed Wali Karzai, his late brother (assassinated in 2011), was the man behind the curtain in Kandahar, the epicenter of the Afghan drug trade. As a journalist, I am not blind to Karzai's flaws, and I think it was a mistake for the United States to back him for the presidency in 2009.

• *Huge dependence upon opium.* Afghanistan is arguably a narco-state, producing 75 to 90 percent of the world's opium, and Ahmed Wali

Karzai's assassination did nothing to slow opium exports. Although the United States is striving mightily to promote and even subsidize the planting of profitable legitimate crops such as grapes and pomegranates, it is tough to compete with poppies for income generation. Moreover, poppy cultivation and the opium trade run long and deep in Afghan tradition. Virtually no one in Washington talks about it, but it is a livelihood for more than 3 million farmers. For the farmers it is basic agriculture, but for many members of the government, both local and national, the opium trade is the express lane to wealth and privilege. It is also one of the major financial underpinnings for the Taliban.

For *Dan Rather Reports*, I went to Afghanistan to investigate the poppy problem with Thomas A. Schweich, the man who was the deputy assistant secretary of state for law and drug enforcement in the Bush administration. He went to the major poppy growers and told them that if they were not willing to shift 60 percent of their land to crops other than poppies, the American military would burn all of their poppy fields and make them unusable in the future. He convinced a few growers in Jalalabad to do so, but President Karzai opposed the idea and it didn't succeed.

• *The Islamic mullahs.* Not all, but many of them preach in their Friday-night sermons that Americans are simply another brand of infidel. I am definitely not anti-Islamic, but these clerics are a hard-line group of older men who advocate the killing of Americans. And I do not think that is right. When we first went into Afghanistan, there were a few mullahs who understood that we were not there to conquer. We were there to stop the flow of terrorists. Some of them began to work with the elders of each tribe, and it is a good situation, because the Americans are doing exactly what they want—winning hearts and minds of average Afghan citizens. And both the elders and the cooperative mullahs are getting what they want—money and American expertise.

It's not that we aren't having some successes in Afghanistan; we are. For the past two years or so, the battlefield situation has reflected many positives. U.S. and NATO forces have had many wins; the momentum of large-scale combat clearly has swung against the Taliban—not without exceptions, but overall. On the other hand, ambushes and small-scale actions are on the rise. It would appear that the Taliban is following the time-honored battle plan of the guerrilla playbook. From Mao to Ho Chi Minh to the mujahideen, the guerrilla blueprint is clear:

- When the enemy is strong, retreat.
- When the enemy becomes strung out, harass.
- And when the enemy is weak or off guard, attack.

Distressingly, casualties from improvised explosive devices, or IEDs, are also increasing. In the last couple of years, IEDs have become the biggest cause of death and injury for our troops. Hidden in roadside debris, or even in animal carcasses, they are hard to detect because they generally lack metal or electronic parts. It is perhaps worth noting that four out of five IEDs in Afghanistan contain components and chemicals manufactured in Pakistan.

We are now trying to train the Afghans to be better able to deal with the Taliban on their own after we leave. Progress clearly has been made in efforts to build a reliable Afghan army and a national police force. This has been led by Lieutenant General William Caldwell, who has turned a not-very-good effort around and now has it pointed in the right direction.

Whether General Caldwell and those working with and under him are accomplishing this fast enough and with any real hope of sustainability is an open question. He believes that they are. He told me that he is convinced that by the current deadline, set by President Obama as December 2014, Afghanistan will have a viable military and police force that can sustain itself. There are many experienced observers who fear otherwise. They applaud Caldwell's efforts and what he has accomplished so far, even as they doubt his predictions.

A huge obstacle is illiteracy. Statistics vary, but overall literacy in Afghanistan is no greater than 28 percent. For women, it is much worse: Less than 13 percent of women over the age of 15 can read and write. These already dismal figures mask a wide disparity between major population centers, where literacy is somewhat higher, and rural areas, where literacy rates are much lower.

Another obstacle is infiltration: Taliban operatives and sympathizers have infiltrated training units and active duty posts, both in the military and police. Extensive vetting reforms have been instituted. How effective they are is an open question. (Afghan intelligence services are likewise permeated with supporters of the Taliban, and in some cases with supporters of al-Qaeda.)

Nevertheless, there is still reason for optimism in Afghanistan. Over the years, I have known a number of Afghans. They offer two major reasons for hope.

• *The women.* Afghan women do not wish the Taliban to return to power. They have no desire to be forced back into total subjugation. Under the Taliban, girls stopped going to school at the age of eight. Beatings and other forms of violence were commonplace, and condoned. Women were prohibited from holding a job. Today the United States is seeking to support and empower Afghan women by promoting literacy and by recruiting them into paying jobs, including the police force.

• *The hearts and minds.* Most Afghans do understand that Americans are not like Alexander the Great, the Mongols, the 19th-century British or the Soviets. They are aware that we do not seek to keep Afghanistan as some sort of colony. Winning hearts and minds is our main objective, and that's the biggest thing we have going for us.

The current official timetable announced by President Obama calls for the withdrawal of American combat forces to be completed by December 2014. (The prior deadline had been July 2011.) President Karzai has declared that by that time, his country will be able to shoulder the entire responsibility for both the army and the police force.

In theory, at that point we should be able to declare victory in Afghanistan, but as was the case in Vietnam, Washington has not done a particularly good job of defining what victory might look like. It is highly improbable that we will be able to eliminate all vestiges of the Taliban by then, if ever. With the death of bin Laden, however, that is the only one of our original objectives still remaining. Because it is far more likely that objective No. 3 will long remain beyond our grasp, we are desperately seeking a way to leave Afghanistan without leaving the Taliban in power.

About the best we can expect is a negotiated settlement, but it is not at all clear that is possible. Both sides hold numerous mutually inconsistent deal breakers. The United States is likely to hold fast on these issues:

• The Taliban would not be allowed to tolerate or harbor any Afghan or foreign individuals or groups that conspire to carry out acts of violence on other states.

• The Taliban would have to accept the current constitution of Afghanistan as the governing document for all people.

• The Taliban would not be allowed to oppose women's education, choice of work and freedom of dress.

• The country would have to halt all opium production.

For the Taliban, it is difficult to see how they would agree to anything that did not include the following three agreements:

• A strict and prompt withdrawal of all NATO and U.S. troops from Afghan soil.

• Strict Islamic law—including the subjugation of women—would be the legal system of the land.

• Release of all Afghan prisoners from Afghan and American prisons.

As is apparent, there is not a lot of middle ground on any of these issues. Despite the deadline, even withdrawal of U.S. troops is likely to be an issue, since the Pentagon is on record as saying that our troop levels will be "conditions-based." Intimations persist that some sort of American presence will remain far longer than the end of 2014, especially if General Caldwell and his successors are unable to stand up an effective, independent Afghan army and police force by that time.

Winning wars is about firepower, willpower and staying power. There is no question that the United States can mount formidable amounts of firepower, both strategic and tactical. For a long time, I was convinced that if we could marshal the staying power to remain in Afghanistan for 35 to 50 years, as we did in South Korea, it might eventually be worth it. Since the early 1950s, South Korea has become a functioning democracy and has a relatively thriving economy.

It is clear, however, that the American public no longer has the willpower, and certainly does not have the money, to persist in Afghanistan. Moreover, our citizens are tired of the waste and corruption, both in Afghanistan and at home. In its final report to Congress, the Commission on Wartime Contracting found that upward of $60 billion had been lost during the wars in Iraq and Afghanistan through various forms of corruption, including graft, mismanagement, payoffs to warlords and tribal leaders and to the Taliban itself, and to good old garden-variety stupidity.

On balance, where do we come out? To date, the war in Afghanistan has cost the United States roughly $450 billion, or $15,000 for every Afghan man, woman and child. Perhaps it might have been simpler to have handed each of them a check.

CHAPTER 9

9/11

In my head, there is a huge rack of videotapes tucked away in my mental museum. They are lined up like records in an old-fashioned jukebox. Sometimes I'll deliberately select one out and have it play for a while—a fond memory of catching the winning touchdown pass in a high school football game, of the little church ceremony in which Jean and I were married, or of my first sight of our children when they were born.

At other times—often at odd, unpredictable times—one will slide into place unbidden and begin playing. Frequently these are of the not-so-fond variety, unpleasant things I witnessed in unpleasant places: a racial beating in a small southern town, a mortar attack in Vietnam, starving children in Africa. One of the mental videotapes that plays most often is the events from September 11, 2001. The shock and disbelief, the despair, the sorrow and grief, the anger, and then—not always, but often—the memories of the bravery, resilience and determination of my fellow Americans.

The most unforgettable events of my lifetime are Pearl Harbor, V-J Day (the day World War II ended), the assassination of President Kennedy, the resignation of President Nixon (as leader of a widespread criminal conspiracy) and 9/11. Of those, September 11 stands out in my mind as the most compelling story I have covered as a journalist.

That day is embedded in my heart and in the museum of my mind forever. What I was thinking, feeling, experiencing—and most of all what I saw—I will truly never forget.

That fateful Tuesday morning at about 8:50, I had finished shaving and just stepped out of the shower when the bathroom radio mentioned that a plane might have hit the World Trade Center. It was unclear whether this was a confirmed fact, and the early speculation was that it was a small plane. Two things clicked in my mind: First, initial reports are frequently wrong, and second, if an aircraft did hit the World Trade Center, it was potentially a big story, no matter what size the plane was. I was a kid of 13 when a B-25 inbound to LaGuardia crashed into the Empire State Building. The pilot had become disoriented in the fog. That was July 1945, and it was big news; we talked about it for weeks, even in Texas.

I called out to Jean to turn up the kitchen radio and turn on the television. She was already on it; by now she knew the drill. She's had a lifetime of this: Anytime there's even the hint of possible breaking news, we go heavy into media mode at home. I was hastily putting on my shorts and trousers as I raced to the small balcony outside our apartment. We live on the East Side, not too far from Central Park and the Metropolitan Museum of Art. Our home is on an upper floor; the balcony faces south and west. Standing there on that crystal clear blue morning, I could see billowing smoke coming out of the World Trade Center, a few miles to the south. Meanwhile, the radio was blaring bits of extremely sketchy and very cautiously worded details. They knew almost nothing, and there seemed to be confusion about what little they did think they might know.

Been there, done that. I've been in front of a live microphone many times when a possible big breaking story hits, and there is always confusion when the first reports come in. Always. The radio people were doing the right thing. They were handling what little they were hearing carefully, very carefully. I don't recall much of what, if anything, television news was doing. At this very early stage, just before 9:00 a.m. and when half-hour program slots were ending (usually with a slew of commercials), Bryant Gumbel on CBS's morning show was doing the best he could with what scant information he had.

But the huge plume of smoke was all I needed to see. It was not clear at this point whether this was an accident or a terrorist attack. From my window, however, I could see the increasing amount of smoke. With that much smoke, there had to be a lot of fire, and with it a lot of chaos as well. With Jean's help, I grabbed a shirt, socks, shoes and a tie and sprinted for the elevator outside our door. "Got your hearing aids?" and "Remember to stay steady," were Jeannie's last words as I disappeared into the elevator.

I was far from camera ready, but at least I had all my moving parts covered, more or less, by the time the doors opened on the ground floor. I bolted out of the elevator like a man shot from a cannon; I'd have time to put on the rest of my clothes in the taxi. On the nearest corner, I hailed a cab. The driver happened to be a turbaned Sikh, one of many who drive New York cabs. I like Sikhs; I have ever since I covered the India-Pakistan war in 1965. At the time, I had roomed with a Sikh family for a few days in Amritsar, India, and visited for the first time their holiest site, the Golden Temple.

I often chat with Sikh cabbies about the temple, their history and the Indian subcontinent. Not this time. I tumbled into the cab and asked the driver to turn on the radio, tune it to the CBS all-news station, and make it loud. He never turned around to look. "Sure, Mr. Rather," he said.

His eyes now shifted slightly from straight ahead to his rearview mirror, and he smiled. "Recognized you from your voice," he said.

Voice recognition happens more often than I ever would have imagined when I first became a full-time daily anchor. When one is on television each day, and on for extended hours in the case of big breaking news or for long events like election night, one eventually comes to realize that voice as well as picture recognition becomes common. There is, after all, a speaker built into every television set. Not only what's on the screen, but also the sound coming out of the speaker becomes embedded in viewers' memories. Perhaps this became especially true in my own case, because besides doing the *Evening News* and other television work, I was on radio every day. This included a daily afternoon drive-time radio report of "news, commentary and analysis." And

I had been doing it for a long time: week-in, week-out, month after month, for many years.

Nevertheless, no matter how many times it happened, and it happened quite often—standing behind someone in a line or in a taxi—I was always a bit taken aback, pleased and, yes, humbled and honored by it. That said, it also made me a bit uneasy. To have strangers recognize your face in various parts of the country is one thing. To have them recognize your voice, especially after only a few words, is another.

I settled myself in the cab and began to finish getting dressed. I thanked the driver for recognizing my voice, then added, "I'll hit you with a Jackson if you make it to the CBS Broadcast Center in record time." The prospect of a $20 tip had the desired result, and the Sikh instantly became Dale Earnhardt.

We reached the corner of West 57th Street and 10th Avenue, just a few steps from the entrance to the CBS Broadcast Center, faster than I would have thought possible. I hurriedly gave the driver his fare plus his Jackson and jumped out before he had come to a full stop.

I quickly glanced down 10th Avenue. In the far distance, I could see large groups of people flooding up from Lower Manhattan. A second plane had struck the other tower. At that point I felt certain that America was under attack, from whom, for what purpose unknown.

I rushed up the steps to the entrance. If I had flung the doors open any harder, I would have bent the hinges.

I quickly dashed past the building security desk and down the long hall leading into the deep interior of our cavernous broadcast center. I got to the newsroom, which was already an anthill of journalists—my CBS News colleagues, many of whom I'd worked with for years. There was no chaos; far from it. There was lots of activity, but professionalism reigned. Everybody was worried, but we were all trying not to show it. By this time, we had confirmed that the first plane had hit the North Tower at 8:46 a.m.; the second had struck the South Tower at 9:03. What had started as a trickle of information was fast becoming a flood.

The anchor desk is perched on a raised platform inside the newsroom. Beside it is a small pit that holds a mini–control station, where anchor assistants sit while we are on the air. They are electronically connected to the big main control room in another section of the building. They're also equipped to be in contact with the nerve center a short distance away within the newsroom itself.

In the pit, waiting for me as he had done so often over the years, was my friend Wayne Nelson. Wayne supervised technicians for my "suiting up," a phrase TV news borrowed from the space program, because the process is akin to a scaled-down version of what an astronaut does before being launched into space. John Reade usually served as my anchor desk "pitman" and all-around assistant for live, special event broadcasts. John, however, was in Italy and would be stranded there for several days. Wayne Nelson stood in for him, as he often had before.

Every anchor has his or her own version of the suiting-up ritual. It may have been a little more complicated at CBS, because on big, breaking news live events, I preferred to have two earpieces, one in each ear. This enabled me to be in contact from the anchor chair with both the control room and the editorial desk, or in this case, desks.

I had worked this way for years. I got instructions from the control room in one ear and information from an editorial desk in the other, often while I was on air saying something completely different to the camera and the audience beyond. I know it sounds impossible, or at least crazy, but it's neither. It certainly is not a high skill, but it does require talent and practice, as anyone short of one or both will tell you. Actually, it's as easy as simultaneously rubbing your stomach and patting the top of your head—while also singing the second verse of "The Star Spangled Banner," hopping on one foot and juggling two raw eggs and a cantaloupe.

Piece of cake.

For me this was a skill acquired and then honed over years of doing live, unscripted, extended broadcasts. I started in college, with all of those nights and days doing play-by-play sports at KSAM in little Huntsville. I got better at it at KTRH radio and KHOU-TV in Houston, doing more play-by-play, plus covering breaking news, like hurricanes. Once I got to CBS, I spent many years ad-libbing all kinds of live events—election nights, political conventions and inaugurations, as well as disasters and tragedies.

Experience breeds confidence. And as you gain confidence, you broaden and polish your skill set. You also develop a real knowledge of what you can handle and what you can't; in short, you develop a comfort zone. It had taken me a while, but by this stage of my career, getting information from two earpieces while talking to the camera—generally without teleprompter or notes—fell squarely within my comfort zone. By that fatal morning, I'd been doing it for decades. Some might say I've never been really good at anything, but flying without a net on a breaking news live broadcast is something I knew I could do, and do well.

Wayne watched carefully as listening devices were placed in each ear, then strung down the inside back of my jacket. Jacket off, then back on. Now a small microphone was clipped to my tie; the attached wires were hidden down my shirt. He checked to make sure everything was working. I was good to go. Now I was in harness, about to ascend the raised anchor desk platform, get in the chair and go on the air.

I made a quick telephone call to Jean at home. Very much on my mind was that she was home alone and that our son, Danjack, and his family lived not far from the World Trade Center. We were unable to reach him, which was disturbing because about the time the planes hit, he would have been taking our grandson to his Greenwich Village preschool.

Jean's voice was full and firm. "I've got everything on this end covered, and what I don't know enough about yet, I'll get covered. Go. Do what you have to do. Do your duty. And do it great. We all need you— your country needs you—to do that now." Pause. "I love you."

I did indeed want to "do it great," but it had nothing whatsoever to do with ego. I knew that compared to the responsibility shouldered by first responders, police officers and firefighters, I had but a small role to perform. For whatever it was worth, however, I wanted to do it excellently. All of us in the newsroom wanted to be at our absolute best, and indeed, every journalist with whom I came in contact felt the same way. We were humbled, usually not a word associated with most journalists, especially those on television. But we were humbled during these times—humbled, but dedicated and determined to be on this story as good as we could possibly be.

That was it. I said a short, silent prayer and climbed into the anchor chair. I knew I'd not be leaving anytime soon.

The CBS *Early Show*, at that time with Bryant Gumbel anchoring, is broadcast from a separate, stand-alone goldfish bowl studio on the ground floor of the General Motors Building, across from the Plaza Hotel in Midtown. That's about eight blocks from the CBS News world headquarters where I was sitting, and where all other news programs originate. A handoff needed to be made, with Gumbel and *The Early Show* throwing control of airtime back to me in our news center on the West Side in Hell's Kitchen. The irony and tragedy of Lower Manhattan and much of the city now being a literal Hell's Kitchen did not occur to me at the time. Too much on my mind. The enormity of what was happening was consuming me.

I took the air at about 9:35. This was to be a time, and I knew it from the outset, when I would have to fight my emotions. As was the case with the Kennedy assassination, I was hit by wave after wave of personal emotional grief, anger and confusion. This was happening to New Yorkers all over the city, and to Americans everywhere. It is an absolutely natural human reaction, but I knew that I could not, absolutely must not, give in to it. I had to tamp it down, down strong, and down deep. Focus on the job at hand; focus hard. Get "zoned," which is to say focus completely on the one most important thing you have to do. Suppress or seal out everything else. Bury it deep inside. Be a pro.

For the next couple of hours, it took everything I had to be able to do that.

Soon after I went on the air, we were hit by a numbing and brutal lightning sequence of events, nothing less than a seismic jolt to the soul. With both towers aflame and spewing debris, people facing incineration on the upper floors started jumping to their deaths on the pavement below. Confirmation came that American Airlines Flight 77 had crashed into the Pentagon. We then received preliminary reports that United Flight 93 was believed to have been hijacked. There were suspicions that it was headed for the Capitol.

A minute before 10:00 a.m., the South Tower of the World Trade Center collapsed. There was no warning. It took all of ten seconds—there it was, right before our eyes, collapsing in a fiery, smoke- and debris-filled heap, taking countless lives with it. Surreal. I literally gasped.

Four minutes later, Flight 93 crashed into a field outside Shanksville, Pennsylvania. We would eventually learn that passengers had rushed the cockpit to battle the hijackers and divert the aircraft from the Capitol. Not quite 15 minutes later, the damaged portion of the Pentagon's E Ring fell in. And less than 15 minutes after that, the North Tower of the World Trade Center collapsed. All of this happened in the breathless span of 48 minutes: 9:41–10:29 a.m. From the time the first plane hit the North Tower (8:46 a.m.), less than one hour and 45 minutes had elapsed.

It seemed a lifetime. From the pictures we were seeing, and from the deluge of reports we were receiving of death, injury, destruction and continuing potential danger, it felt as if we had been plunged headlong into the ninth circle of Dante's inferno.

I could feel the anger rising within me. It quickly threatened to envelop me. I'm a Texan, and not just by birth—it's who I am. But New York had been my home for many years. By that September morning, both Jean and I had come to know and love the city. That made the attacks personal. And for me on the air, it created another layer of powerful emotions.

I got mad. "Whoever did this must pay!" I thought. My knees began to shake; I was grateful that they were hidden by the anchor desk. I knew I was having a visceral reaction to the scene unfolding before me; I also knew I had to put a stop to it before my whole body began to quiver.

"Get a grip. Can't let the audience see you quaking. Steady."

"Steady." It had been one of Ed Murrow's favorite words, and I remember him saying it often during his broadcasts from London during the Blitz. Now, 60 years later, it seemed all too appropriate in New York.

"Steady," I kept repeating under my breath, as rage and reason duked it out in my gut. "Steady." In addition to listening to the feeds in both ears and talking out loud to the camera, I was now talking to myself as well.

I managed to get it under control, at least on the surface. All day long I was the pivot man, conveying the news of the staggering events of the day, absorbing instructions coming in through my earpieces, doing on-air interviews and debriefings of witnesses and throwing to correspondents, experts and officials at remote locations. My mission was to be an honest broker of information and to present a calm, reliable and resolute face and voice to the audience.

Behind that on-air façade, however, my anger continued to smolder amidst the constant grief and worry. In addition to my concerns about Danjack, his wife, and my grandson, I knew that many others in the newsroom also had loved ones who were unaccounted for. There were maybe a hundred colleagues who were doing their duty while trying to find out what happened to people they cared about. Our director didn't know where one of his children was; he thought it was more than possible that the child had been at Ground Zero. We assigned someone to track down his family and prayed. Meanwhile, the professionalism he and everyone else in the newsroom displayed was unbelievable.

Steady. At times such as these, network news coverage becomes the national hearth. People gather around television sets to absorb what has happened (and what is happening), just as our forebears did around fireplaces, as Comanches did around their campfires. It had happened with the Kennedy assassination in Dallas, with the midair explosion of the space shuttle, with the assassinations of Martin Luther King and Bobby Kennedy and during various natural disasters, such as big earthquakes and hurricanes, as well as when presidents declared or ended wars. As people gather around the hearth, the Speaker—in the television era, the Anchorman (or woman)—carries the narrative. He or she calls on others and uses pictures and graphics to help but is responsible for driving the narrative of the story.

I was on the air, in the anchor chair, driving the narrative, for almost 14 hours of that first day and into the wee hours of the next. For food, I mostly lived on energy drinks; I long ago had developed my own recipe for a blended concoction. Bathroom breaks were few. Too few. When necessary I relieved myself in a version of the old "motorman's friend," proving once again that there is no dignity in television.

I telephoned home several times during the short intervals when I had tossed to Washington or some other remote. It was a huge relief when Jean confirmed that our son, his wife and our grandson were safe. Danjack had been able to pull his son out of preschool moments after dropping him off. Together they saw the second plane hit the towers. Each time we talked, and the times were few, Jean was reassuring and strengthening. Our family's Great Encourager was at her best. Many hours later, we found out that our director's child was also safe.

Pretty much from the first moment, our police, firefighters and first responders were constantly in my thoughts. As a much younger man trying to make myself into a reporter, I had spent a long apprenticeship covering the fire and police beats. From my experiences in Huntsville and Houston, I knew firsthand what police, fire and emergency crews did, how they did it and how very dangerous it could be. Now, a psychologically and emotionally toxic mix of concerns about those public servants working in the dark heart of the disaster areas, all of the dead and wounded and their families—so many of them, so very many—was ever present within me on the air. I had to fight myself to prevent those thoughts from taking over.

Steady. From somewhere deep in my memory, one of my late workingman father's favorite sayings about tough, challenging tasks floated up to the surface. "Just keep putting one foot in front of the other. Just keep on keeping on." It helped.

Shortly after 2:00 a.m. on the 12th, it was suggested that I get some rest. There had always been a cot in my office at the Broadcast Center. I'd often used it to sleep over during one crisis or another. Initially I said I'd go to it, but then I thought of Jean and how she and I—symbolically, if nothing else—needed me to be home, for however long it could be. She needed it, and frankly, so did I.

I went home and slept for about two and a half hours, then got ready to go back to the Broadcast Center. "Honey, don't forget this is a marathon," Jean said as I was leaving. "You're going to be broadcasting day and night for quite a while. None of us has ever been through anything like this. Pace yourself." A pause. Then a smile and, "Be great."

As the days wore on, it got a little easier for me to maintain my game face and stay in the zone. We were on the air day and night; I didn't really leave the Broadcast Center except to go home and sleep. And even that wasn't much. There probably had not been a night when I'd slept more than four hours.

When I finally did lose it, it was almost a week later, on the Letterman show. It was David's first show back on the air after the disaster. Even then, I stayed in the Broadcast Center till the last possible moment, arriving in Letterman's studio just in time to slip into the chair beside him. When he is serious, David is an excellent interviewer. We started talking about 9/11. I was fine, at first—until I tried to quote one of the later stanzas of "America the Beautiful":

> *O beautiful for patriot dream*
> *That sees beyond the years*
> *Thine alabaster cities gleam*
> *Undimmed by human tears.*

By the time I got to the gleaming alabaster cities and the human tears, I was overcome. Everything I'd successfully held inside for the past week welled up in a rush. It was grief—pure and simple. One doesn't apologize for grief, and I don't apologize for showing my feelings on the air, but when it washed over me, I was astonished. It came as a complete surprise. It had not entered my mind until that very moment that all those emotions that I had pile-driven deep down within me would eventually come back out. I certainly did not expect them to burst forth so powerfully at that particular time.

As we started to get some perspective on the events of that day, I came to realize that for me—and I think probably for others—the full impact of September 11 was revealed not in any single moment but in a series of snapshots. Beyond the enormity of the towers falling, there are small scenes I carry with me still:

• The images of doctors and nurses gathered outside St. Vincent's Hospital, waiting to perform triage on thousands of wounded. We went back to that on the air a couple of times before I realized that they were waiting in vain. There would be no wounded, or at least very few; those who had not escaped before the towers fell had died when the buildings collapsed.

• After the first tower's collapse, the dedicated CBS News employees—there were several of them—calling in while still trying to recover from being nearly overcome by the choking cloud of dust and smoke.

• After the second tower's collapse, a woman new to the city told of having her life saved by a New York City fireman. With fire and debris raining down and roiling all about, this firefighter pressed her against a wall. She could feel his heart beating against her back. She had been certain, she said, that this was how she would die.

• The heart-wrenching pictures from all over the city of one broken family after another, many of them young women with children, holding photos of the missing and coming to realize that their husband and father could not possibly have survived. In some cases, of course, it was a young man with children, realizing that the wife and mother was gone. And for me, multiplying the painful impact of these images was the fact that these families were a true cross-section of New York—so many different races, ethnicities and religions, including Muslims. The killers had been indiscriminate. They didn't give a damn.

These moments march side by side with the big-picture indelible images of the first day that are seared into my memory. They and others that followed in succeeding days deepened our understanding of the attack's toll. All together they confirmed how great was our loss, and how great the challenge we now faced.

Years before, I had told an interviewer, "Part of growing up is realizing that not everybody is going to love you." I had said it in the context of becoming a mature and seasoned journalist. Now I was thinking of a companion statement: "Part of growing up as an American is realizing that some people are going to hate you." There are people—truly evil people, capable of extreme cruelty—out there. They want to kill us, our children and our grandchildren, and they want to destroy our country and our way of life. They hate all for which we stand. That's a fact. A brutal, hard but true fact. We forget it at our peril. I told myself that first day, and have tried to repeat it to myself every day since, "I will never, never, ever forget." For a long time after 9/11, when I was still doing the *Evening News*, I often closed the broadcast—especially after some ending report having to do with September 11—by saying, "Lest we forget."

And we had better not. Osama bin Laden himself has been brought to justice, but others responsible for those attacks are still on the prowl. They ache to come back for an encore. I, for one, will be surprised if we are not similarly attacked sometime in the future. I hope I'm wrong. But that's not the way to bet it, no matter how much we wish it were otherwise.

In the seventh grade, back at Alexander Hamilton Junior High School in Houston, a teacher quoted Abraham Lincoln from a speech he made as a young man, while still a member of the Illinois House of Representatives. On January 27, 1838, he told the Young Men's Lyceum of Springfield, Illinois, "All the armies of Europe, Asia and Africa combined, with all the treasure of the earth (our own excepted) in their military chest; with a Bonaparte for a commander, could not by force, take a drink from the Ohio, or make a track on the Blue Ridge, in a trial of a thousand years."

Why that stuck in my memory I don't know, but it did. And now it came back to mind in the context of 9/11. Those who struck us had done what no attackers had done since 1781, when Cornwallis surrendered at Yorktown. They didn't drink from one of our rivers or leave footprints, but they surely did leave a shadow.

As I wrote in a preface for the book *What We Saw*:

Long ago, when America was still young, Nathaniel Hawthorne wrote, "Time flies over us, but leaves its shadows behind." For now and for the foreseeable future, we all stand in the shadow of that terrible, clear morning. We live in a world remade by the attacks of September 11. Years will pass, and the photos and videos will age and fade. Our memories of the feelings attached to them in real time will also dim, as they already have. But echoes continue to reverberate from that date.

For more than 44 years, reporting for CBS News gave me a front-row seat on history. When big events occur, they always loom large in the present, but there are times when the television screen enlarges what the perspective of years will show to be stories of only passing importance. (The O. J. Simpson trial comes to mind as just one example. Hurricanes, unless they are exceptionally large, strong and produce historic levels of death, injury and destruction, are another.)

Television is a great leveler. The inherent drama of the special report, the importance implied by the interruption of regular programming and the modern electronic phenomenon of "blanket coverage" have a way of giving equal gravitas to the various calamities that set them in motion. If one were to judge importance solely by the total number of television news hours devoted to covering an event, one might come away with the impression that the plane crash that killed John F. Kennedy Jr.—John-John—was as important a news story as the assassination of his father, John F. Kennedy Sr.

This isn't a question of ranking tragedies but of gauging historical impact—the far-ranging repercussions—of an event. And it is rare, in the fury and haste of the moment, that these historical implications are reckoned with accuracy.

September 11, however, was surely one of those times. We knew from the outset that we were watching history unfold. In real time we witnessed a line—a shadow—fall over the newsreel of our lives, one that would forever mark the days to come as separate from all the days that had gone before. We immediately understood that we would remember, and that we would someday be telling our grandchildren where we had been and what we had been doing when we heard the news.

The TV screen did not overinflate the importance of that day, not when New Yorkers could see the Twin Towers burning with their own eyes, not when people in our nation's capital could see a cloud of smoke billowing from the Pentagon and not when people in rural Pennsylvania could see aircraft wreckage and a hole in the ground that, but for the actions of a brave few, might have been a hole in the Capitol dome. If anything, television reduced those horrific images to a scale that could be comprehended.

Of course, the historical impact of any event depends on the reactions that follow in its wake. The attacks of September 11 provoked not only a direct response—or series of responses—but also a larger and more profound change in how our nation interacts with the rest of the world. From the Middle East to South America, from the Persian Gulf to Central Asia and the Pacific Rim, the war on terrorism now provides the impetus and the context for American foreign policy. Indeed, an atmosphere of change prevails all around the world, in ways we could not have imagined at the time of 9/11. Alliances have shifted and continue to do so. In danger zones around the globe, there is a sense that once fairly static situations are again in play. Some historians have compared the state of affairs that began with 9/11 to that just before the outbreak of World War I, when the great powers sought political advantage in Europe. Others have invoked the years that immediately followed World War II, the period of rising tensions that gave birth to the cold war. Whatever the point of comparison, the message was and remains clear: Our time is witness to a tectonic shift in international relations.

Today, the United States is more engaged in more ways with the rest of the world than ever before, with the possible exception of World War II. We have never been this engaged with the global Muslim community. And our economy has never before been so intertwined, so interdependent, on a worldwide basis. Not all of this can be directly attributed to September 11, but much of it can. The same can be said about the weaknesses and volatility of our economy, which began to be exposed in the latter part of the 21st century's first decade. It isn't all because of the 9/11 attacks, but a lot of it is.

Such are the aftershocks that have continued and will continue to follow the earthquake that was September 11. We Rathers, as one little family, and we as a nation were united in anger, fear, grief and determination. Resilience, compassion and courage quickly became our watchwords, our creed—as a nation, as one small family and as individuals.

The attacks of 9/11 changed us as a country, as a people. Much has been written and said about the effect of September 11 on America: that it awakened us from our illusions of invulnerability, that it shattered the sense of insularity that complacency, materialism and prosperity had let creep into our national discourse. These observations sting, but there is truth in them. And like so many Americans of all professions, those of us who report the news were forced by September 11 to reevaluate what we do and how we do it. For me, for my colleagues at CBS News and for others in the craft whom I know well, the scale of the story—and the many stories that have flowed from it—gave us an opportunity to do the kind of journalism to which we aspire. An opportunity and a challenge. It is a chance to perform a public service, to report news that is not only gripping but that also matters.

From what I've seen in the years between then and now, it is a chance that has been seized upon by much if not most of America's press. Yes, it was stronger and more evident in the first days, months and first few years after the event. Journalists increased their focus on what was important. International coverage went up, way up. News coverage reflected and informed America's renewed outward gaze. And, yes, all of that unfortunately has waned and dissipated some as we enter the second decade after the attacks. But for many journalists it is still there—the intention, the spirit, the determination—and within some of their places of employment as well. We are not able to do it as much as we once did in the immediate wake of 9/11. But speaking for myself—and I know many other journalists who feel the same—I have not forgotten, nor shall I ever forget. It is in my marrow, part of my DNA, and shall remain so.

Not a day passes that I don't still think about September 11; not a day goes by that I'm not inspired by it. So many gave so much during that time and in the wars that followed—including those who gave the ultimate sacrifice—that I find myself constantly rededicating myself to be the best that I can be, for my country, for my family and for my fellow humans. If that sounds over the top or overstated, so be it. It's how I feel and what I try to do.

However painfully, we Americans have received an education. But it has not been an education of the mind alone. Our hearts have learned much, too. We have been confronted by the courage of the firefighters, police and other first responders who answered the call at the World Trade Center and at the Pentagon; by the ordinary citizens who gave their lives to divert United Airlines Flight 93 from its murderous path; by family members who have to cope every day with the loss of loved ones killed in the attacks; and by the fighting men and women who travel far and give so much to defend our country.

The exhaustive labors of emergency workers and volunteers at Ground Zero have taught us new lessons in loyalty and love. Each flag-draped stretcher and coffin, every moment of silence, has given us a new appreciation of the word "respect." The dry rattle of a funeral drum, the plaintive wail of bagpipes keening "Amazing Grace"—these sounds summon our deepest feelings with a new sincerity and to a degree that might have made us blush in the past.

But the past, as it has been said, is a foreign land. It is in the spirit of understanding the distance we have come over the years that we remember—remember the day, and the days that followed, when we were first pulled, blinking and confused and very much against our wills, across the border into the lives we now know.

CHAPTER 10

Rather v. CBS

The tragic events of 9/11 took place just nine months after George Bush was first inaugurated. The controversy over the Bush/Guard broadcast came in the fall of 2004, as Bush was seeking a second term. Within hours after the outcome was clear, I was asked to leave the anchor chair. The 15-month period that followed ranks as one of the low points of my life, right up there with having rheumatic fever as a boy. In the immediate aftermath of Bush's win in November, the negotiations to get me off the *Evening News* had involved a delicate back and forth about what would happen to me after I stepped down. The plan was for me to stay on at *60 Minutes Wednesday* for as long as it lasted, and since everyone knew it was doomed, then segue to the regular Sunday *60 Minutes* broadcast. My agent, Richard Leibner, secured a letter of intent, a commitment signed by Leslie Moonves, which said CBS would finalize a new long-term financial arrangement with me within the year.

Richard thought a lot of Les. Despite everything, in many ways so did I. Richard kept assuring me that Moonves was trying to do right by me and that he would take care of me. When Les and I spoke, he looked me in the eye and convinced me that he was sincere in what he was saying about wanting me to stay with CBS for many years on *60 Minutes*. I trusted him as a man of his word.

I just wish I'd remembered that he'd started his career as an actor.

In May 2005, CBS axed *60 Minutes Wednesday*, which was supposed to mean that I would be regularly on the air on *60 Minutes* Sundays beginning immediately. Jeff Fager said that it would be impossible to get me on the air during the remainder of spring because their lineup of segments was already full. I didn't like that, didn't agree and was worried about it. But Jeff said, "Use the time to come on with a big start in the fall." That meant I had the end of spring and all of summer to get a jump on possible segments. I had been part of the *60 Minutes* team before, but not since 1981. I expected it might take a while to work back up to full speed, but that was never CBS's plan. My contract stipulated that I was to be a "regular correspondent," but once I got there, there was nothing regular about it. It was made clear to me on a daily basis that I did not have the same standing as the other regular correspondents on the roster.

I had trouble getting pieces approved, and those that were approved seemed to fall under heavy criticism during the review process. Whatever we did, there was something wrong with it.

In June 2005, I proposed doing a piece on Lebanon. When I submitted the proposal, I spelled out exactly what I had in mind. Lebanon was supposedly emerging from the ravages of a decades-long civil war. That past Valentine's Day, however, Rafik Hariri, Lebanon's former prime minister and still a major political figure, had been assassinated in Beirut. The massive car bomb that killed him was detonated in front of a luxury tourist hotel on the Mediterranean. Twenty-two others also died.

Rumors had been flying about who was responsible. Some blamed Israel's Mossad. Others accused Hezbollah in collusion with Syria, which at the time of the assassination had about 15,000 of its own regular army troops occupying Lebanon. Hariri's murder set off a chain reaction of other political assassinations. The situation was serious enough that the UN sent in its own commission to investigate. The piece I proposed was going to be about whither Lebanon, and why Americans should care. It was finally approved.

In July 2005, Mike Rosenbaum, a former CBS Middle East region chief based in Tel Aviv, and I set out for Beirut. Mike is terrific, everything you want an international reporter to be, and he had great sources in Lebanon. We were there for 10 days. We reported and shot our hearts out, really dug into the story. We crisscrossed the country interviewing leaders of all the major factions—Sunnis, Shiites and Druze. We even talked to Hezbollah. We also made contact with Detlev Mehlis, the German who headed up the UN team investigating the murder. Mehlis was no lightweight. A career prosecutor, he specialized in cases of terrorism, and in 1986 had led the investigation into the La Belle discotheque bombing in Berlin, which ultimately was traced back to Libya. Mehlis told us that he expected to hand in his special report to the UN in September or October. That was great news, since it would correspond with when we thought our piece would air.

Mike and I put together what we both thought was a dramatic, content-rich segment on Lebanon, its turmoil and its political future, a piece that closely fit the description of the original proposal. At the screening, Jeff Fager, who was now running 60 Minutes, hated every second of it. He wanted more of a travelogue. He wanted to see young people enjoying open-air cafés and discos.

Travelogue? What I had seen in Lebanon was fresh in my mind. This did not strike me as a good time to encourage vacationing Americans to hop a flight to Beirut and hang out in cafés.

After Jeff demolished the piece, we left the screening pretty much deflated. Mike Rosenbaum was mystified. "I don't know what's going on here," he said.

Mike was a friend of Fager's. I thought of myself as Jeff's friend as well—I had done a lot for him along the way, as he had for me. Mike and I both knew that Jeff had always prided himself on his dedication to hard news. In that way, he's a lot like me. Travelogue?

I was baffled enough that I grabbed one of my reporter's notebooks and wrote down what I believed about journalism. Looking back, it pretty much shows why I was in hot water with CBS corporate.

RATHER'S CREED

I believe in hard news.
I do not believe in news lite.
I believe in CBS News.
I do not believe in Viacom News.
I believe in independent—
fiercely independent when necessary—reporting.
I do not believe in Viacom's version
of go-along-to-get-along reporting,
Nor do I believe in reporting to serve the corporate interest
at the expense of the public's interest.
I believe in news of value to the country,
not in news simply for stockholder value.
I believe that a news network should not be operated
just as an owner's asset.
I believe that a news network is a public trust.
This I believe.

I submitted a lot of proposals to *60 Minutes*; most were rejected. Those pieces that did get approved were poorly treated. Once they were in the can, they were aired at odd hours, what you might call waste-pit country. A piece on Clinton ran the night after New Year's. A segment on North Korea played on Oscar night. The Lebanon piece, recut as a travelogue, as ordered, aired the night after Christmas.

For most of those 15 months, I walked around pretty much shell-shocked. I couldn't figure out what the hell was going on. I became all but invisible. It was as if I'd gone through the looking glass. On the one hand, I was angry and probably more than a little depressed about how I was being treated. On the other hand, I had my agent soothing my ruffled feathers, assuring me that "Les is going to take care of you."

On April 5, 2006, Katie Couric was announced as the new anchor of the CBS *Evening News*, taking over in September. I had nothing against Katie personally, but I had hoped they would promote someone from within, someone who had CBS News in their DNA. But that, apparently, was exactly what they didn't want. Publicist Gil Schwartz told me that Moonves wanted a break with the past; Moonves himself had said the same thing both publicly and privately. But why? He should have been proud of our history, our tradition, our accomplishments. Instead, he wanted to wipe the slate clean and forget what Ed Murrow had started.

This is where I fault myself. By this time it was clear to everyone but me that I was being erased. Nevertheless, I refused to believe what my eyes were seeing and my ears were hearing. I was in denial. Les Moonves and Jeff Fager were no longer behaving like the people I thought I knew. I was dismayed; when Les Moonves had said he'd take care of me, I never imagined that he meant it in the Paulie Walnuts/ Bugsy Siegel sense of the term.

In May, I went to the funeral of George Crile, an excellent longtime CBS journalist and author of the book *Charlie Wilson's War*, on which the film was based. The service was a reminder to me that nothing is promised. It was a wake-up call to be more aware of my time remaining and to use it to the fullest. That realization put me at ease about forgoing the golden handcuffs I'd been offered—a stipend, a desk, a secretary and an airtight confidentiality agreement; in other words, a vow of silence forever after.

I still felt that I had journalistic work to do, but it was clear that I wasn't going to get to do it at CBS. "I can see the end," I wrote in my notebook, "and the beginning."

By this time there was a new president of CBS News, Sean McManus, who had added that title to the one he already had as head of CBS Sports. McManus had been chosen by Moonves, and there is no doubt in my mind that he had been assigned to get rid of me. Moonves, however, made the decision. McManus simply carried it out. He and Moonves got confused in their statements about who had been responsible, issuing statements that were directly contradictory. My departure was announced on June 20, 2006, but looking back, the handwriting had been on the wall for 15 months. It just took me that long to decipher it.

It was time to get that tattoo off my backside. Shortly thereafter, I reached an agreement with Mark Cuban to produce an hour-long news show each week, beginning that fall. That story is told in the next chapter. Even before I started, however, I knew that the schedule was tight, damned near impossible. I became newly energized and more determined than ever with all the work to be done. This was my chance to do the kind of reporting I always wanted to do, on my own terms.

On the other hand, I had to come to grips with what had happened to me at the end. While I was still at CBS, my hands had been tied. After I was gone I had more options, but as soon as I signed on with Mark Cuban and HDNet, there was little time to pursue any of them. That first season I was fully occupied getting *Dan Rather Reports* up and rolling. By the summer of 2007, more than a year after I left CBS, we had carved out a little breathing room, enough for me to stand back and take stock.

The intervening months had given me a better perspective. I knew that there was still a great story in the Bush case, especially since the Thornburghers had taken such pains to avoid finding it. Out of my own pocket, I hired an investigator in Texas to look further into Bush's lengthy unexcused absence from the Air National Guard and the curious disappearance of even the most perfunctory paper trail of his military record during that missing year. The investigator turned up several extremely promising leads, but George W. Bush was still the sitting president, and after all, this *was* Texas. People continued to duck and dodge, and the investigator had neither carrot nor stick to make anyone talk with him.

Meanwhile, I was hearing troubling stories from former CBS colleagues about bizarre and chaotic goings-on, both in News Div and at Black Rock. Some had to do with the immediate aftermath of the September 8 Bush/Guard broadcast, but more were about what had taken place in connection with the Thornburgh investigation. I realized that beyond Bush and his vanishing act at the Texas Air National Guard, what had happened to me at CBS was itself a good story. The problem was confirming what I'd been told. Moonves was still there;

Redstone was still in his aerie. I was stonewalled at every turn. As my investigator found in Texas, there was no way to make people divulge what they knew without the muscle of the judiciary system to compel them.

For the first time, I began to consider pursuing the truth through the courts. I started having conversations with my friend Martin Gold, a good and decent man and an excellent attorney, to see what my options might be. "More than anything," I told him, "I want to find out what happened. Tell me how this would work."

"Expensively," he said simply.

Martin braced me for the idea that taking on CBS/Viacom would cost me several million dollars, not to mention a whole lot of my time. "Do I have a case?" I asked.

"Yes, but they will have good lawyers who will mount a vigorous defense. Once you file, they will be relentless. And it won't just be in the courtroom—it's possible that they will delve into your personal life, and that of your family. And whatever they find, be prepared for them to use it against you somehow, perhaps even *National Enquirer* style. They will harness every ounce of media power they have to make you look bad. Beyond that, they will do everything they can to spend you into oblivion. It's not that CBS has deep pockets," he said. "It's that they have *bottomless* pockets. The money they're spending isn't their own. It's the shareholders'."

"If you were in my shoes, would you do it?"

"No," Martin replied, "but I'm not you. You're a public person, and they damaged your reputation."

He surely had that right.

It was time to consult the others who would be directly affected—my family. My wife Jean was thumbs-down on it. She has always handled the family finances, and the idea of spending millions in pursuit of something that was stuck in my craw didn't strike her as a wise use of our money. "If you decide to do it, I'll be right behind you till hell freezes over," she said. "And after that, I'll even cut through the ice, but I don't think it's a prudent thing to do. Know, however, that if you choose to go forward, I will be your rock, and we won't have any more of these conversations. Once you've made your decision, I will be completely supportive, whatever happens. No laments, no regrets."

I made a point to talk to each of our children, separately. My daughter, Robin, the lionhearted Rather, did not hesitate. "Dad, this is not a choice," she said. "You have to do it."

"You need to know," I told her, "that I'm going to have to spend some of the money you would otherwise one day inherit."

"Spend every penny," she replied.

I thought my son, Danjack, who is an attorney, might be more cautious. Not this time. Courageous and steadfast as always, he immediately sided squarely with his sister. "Dad, you're never going to be at peace if you don't do this," he declared. "Ever since we were little, you always said, 'Don't back up. Don't back down.' You're the one who taught us never to quit."

"You know, of course, that there are no guarantees I'm going to win this," I told him.

"Some things are worth fighting for, win or lose," he replied. "This is your moment to stand up for all those things you believe in, for what you think is important. Go for it."

My family had weighed in; now it was up to me. Part of the problem was that I had to decide fairly quickly whether or not to proceed—I was running up against the statute of limitations to file a lawsuit. It was either do it right away or don't do it. Ever. It was now late summer of 2007, and I'd have to file by the fall.

I jumped in the Jeep and drove out of the city to go think it over. There was only one place to go. I headed for the Catskills, where we have a fishing cabin on the Beaverkill River, one of the great trout streams in the country. It's a revered place in the family and a really important refuge for me. I go there when I need to be alone and blow away all the clutter in my head.

It's isolated, but people can reach me if there is some sort of emergency. That said, it's not easy. I know everybody up there; the guy who patrols knows where I am on the river and how to come find me. Mostly, though, they just let me be, which is exactly what I want, and in this case, what I needed.

I spent the whole day fly-fishing on the river. I went out just before dawn, taking a sandwich. Sometimes I take a skillet with me and grill a trout streamside instead. I fished for three or four hours, then stretched myself out on the riverbank and watched the clouds go by. After that, I fished for another three or four hours—twilight is great fishing time.

I got back to the cabin at 9:30 or so and opened up a can of pork and beans. At that time, in that place, it tasted as good as the best meal any three-star Michelin chef could prepare. Better, maybe.

The last thing Jean had said to me before I left for the cabin was, "You're the only one who can say whether or not you'll be eaten up by this."

As is nearly always the case, she was right. And what I figured out there, up to my knees in the cold rushing water, was ultimately pretty basic. All my life, all I've ever wanted to do was to find and report important true stories. Not being able to do so gnaws on me. My entire career has been about getting as close as I can to the truth at the core of any story. And now, what was really eating on me was the prospect of closing the door on a piece of my life, walking away from my own story, without ever knowing the truth of what really happened.

It's amazing how clearly you think when life gets down to simple choices. After a couple of days on the Beaverkill, I drove back into Manhattan and went to see Martin Gold. "I'm all in," I told him.

Despite his strong admonitions to me beforehand, I think that as my friend, he was happy that I decided to go ahead. "I'll do my best for you, Dan," he said. "I think it's outrageous what they've done to you. This won't be just another case for me."

We filed suit against CBS and Viacom on September 19, 2007. The suit alleged, among other issues, breach of contract, interference with prospective economic advantage, and fraud, based on CBS's "intentional mishandling" of the aftermath of the Bush/Guard story.

We asked for compensatory damages of $20 million and punitive damages in the amount of $50 million. It was not a number plucked from thin air. We could document what my market value was, both as a journalist and as a public speaker, before the fall of 2004. We could prove how CBS set out to damage my marketability in the aftermath of the Bush/Guard piece. The $70 million was big enough to get their attention, but it was also intended to be an object lesson, a cautionary sum meaningful enough to prevent other companies from doing this to someone else.

For me, however, the suit was never about the money, and it was never about vengeance. Part of my soul-searching on the Beaverkill was to look deep inside and satisfy myself that a thirst for retribution wasn't the driving force. I knew that I would be accused of seeking payback no matter what, but I was clear in my own heart and mind about my motives. I filed suit on principle—to find out the truth and to stand up for the importance of a truly independent free press in a democracy. I genuinely believe that as a journalist, I have an obligation to uphold freedom of the press—especially the broadcast press—against big government and big corporations. I think all journalists shoulder this responsibility, but at that moment, I could see that I was in a better position than most to do something about it.

The two inescapable questions rose up before me. If not me, who? If not now, when?

With this court action, I was seeking to confront the grave issues raised by bald-faced corporate and governmental intimidation of journalists and by the chilling intrusion of these special interests into newsrooms across the country. If you believe as I do that a free press is a constitutional bulwark—in effect the red, beating heart of democracy—then you understand that the corporatization and politicization of the press is an issue that endangers the health and well-being of our country. From the outset, my plan was to donate whatever was left from my award after expenses to organizations that support and defend journalists.

In addition to CBS and Viacom, we also named Leslie Moonves, Sumner Redstone and Andrew Heyward as defendants. Andrew Heyward, ousted as president of the News Division (with a very large, very golden parachute) and now an unemployed private citizen, was included as a defendant because we were alleging fraud.

In the law, fraud is a false statement made to induce somebody to rely on that false statement to his or her detriment. My complaint alleged that in the immediate aftermath of the Bush/Guard broadcast, Heyward was double-dealing with me a lot, which led me to do things I would not otherwise have done, including apologizing on the air and nailing Bill Burkett to the wall in that grueling three-hour interview. I alleged that there were misrepresentations that convinced me not to go forward with actions that I would otherwise have undertaken, above all the assurance by CBS that it would launch a thorough and impartial investigation to prevent me from commissioning one myself. Heyward obviously didn't have the horsepower or the initiative to do this all on his own, but if at your employer's behest you hit someone over the head with a two-by-four, you can't just tell your victim to sue the corporation. You bear some personal responsibility for your actions.

Our suit was filed with the Supreme Court of the State of New York. We drew Judge Ira Gammerman to hear our case. Judge Gammerman, since retired, had a reputation for being tough but fair. We knew we wouldn't get any breaks from him, but we also knew we wouldn't get any prejudice from him, either—which is as it should be. Martin was pleased. Of the judges we could have drawn, he said, Judge Gammerman was about as good as we could have hoped for.

The sessions were held in the classic New York State Supreme Courthouse, one of the great architectural treasures of New York City. Our forebears clearly understood the importance of symbolism: If you close your eyes and conjure up a stately urban courthouse, it probably looks a lot like this. Indeed, if you have watched any episodes of the TV series *Law & Order*, you know this building well. It's practically a mainstay character in the show and is instantly recognizable by its graceful Corinthian columns and the long, dramatic flight of steps leading up to it.

Inside there is a rotunda, with a huge WPA mural entitled *Law through the Ages* that covers the ceiling. The magisterial atmosphere of the courthouse extends into the courtroom itself. It looks exactly like you'd want a courtroom to look. It was a little tatty around the edges, showing the earmarks of the fiscal austerity of the times, but nonetheless still dignified. It was clearly a place for serious business, spare, almost spartan, but not quite. Judge Gammerman had made an effort to soften the severity of his courtroom by adding a few plants, an effort that unfortunately was not successful. The plants were droopy and anemic, perhaps because the chosen vegetation was never intended to spend its life indoors.

It didn't matter. Inscribed in the courthouse is "Equal justice under the law." The entire building, from the exterior to the rotunda to the courtroom, reeked of justice, which I found to be immensely reassuring. Walking in there made me feel humbled, yet proud to be an American citizen, proud that this is the people's house.

CBS/Viacom was represented by a phalanx of lawyers from Weil, Gotshal & Manges, LLP. James Quinn was their lead attorney. Quinn had been doing this long enough that he appeared every inch like what he was. He fit the stereotype perfectly: distinguished looking, early 60s, razor-cut grey hair, expensive, well-tailored suit. Hollywood would cast him instantly as the hired-gun big-time corporate lawyer.

From the outset, he and Mindy Spector, his No. 1 assistant, had this peculiar good cop/bad cop thing going. He was poker-faced, curt but polite—good cop. She was the bad cop—always borderline insulting, sometimes over the border. She also had a decibel modulation problem. On several occasions, her vitriol was so loud and so toxic that Judge Gammerman barked at her, sternly ordering her to pipe down and to behave in his courtroom. Even when silent, however, she seemed to make a point of looking at me with disdain, if not outright disgust—as if I had not bathed since the Nixon administration. If she'd stuck her tongue out at me, I wouldn't have been the slightest bit surprised.

Actually, she got to make faces at me a lot, since I was there for every court date. Most people involved in a lawsuit leave it to their attorneys. Not me. I'm a reporter, and one who started his career covering the courts at that. I asked Martin if there was any potential downside to showing up. There wasn't. There was even a potential benefit, he said, so I attended each session in Judge Gammerman's court. When I told Martin I wanted to see this through, I meant it literally.

The bulk of Judge Gammerman's day was taken up with cases that were further along than ours, cases that were approaching trial. We were still in pretrial motions—and there were a boatload of them—which the judge heard at the close of business, generally from 3:30 or 4:00 on. A courtroom like this is a veritable cross section of legal life in the United States. Martin and I would arrive and wait for our case to be called. Because we never knew whether we would be first, middle or last, we sat through other cases on the docket in Judge Gammerman's courtroom on that particular afternoon. I listened as the estranged partners in a Chinese restaurant argued back and forth over a business dispute, followed by a vicious, high-stakes clash between two international business conglomerates, followed by two blue-collar folks wrangling over the ownership of an Archie Bunker house in Queens.

Not surprisingly, the first motion filed by Quinn et al. asked that the entire suit be dismissed out of hand. He made the argument that we were suing for damage to reputation, which the courts generally interpret as libel. Libel has a statute of limitations of one year; if their argument prevailed, the statute of limitations was already up, and I was beyond my "sue by" date. Judge Gammerman took the motion under advisement but soon turned them down. That happened regularly thereafter, and always with the same result.

I soon began to see, however, what Martin meant when he had warned me about CBS's strategy of spending me into oblivion. We demanded documents from them; they demanded documents from me. Documents by the tons, including all of my handwritten reporter's notebooks from the period. And of course, it wasn't like I could just hand over the originals; each page had to be photocopied and labeled. Some portions had to be redacted, which meant they had to be covered up, page by page, before they were photocopied, page by page. Each page in the burgeoning pile had to be assigned a unique five-digit number and stamped "Produced Solely for Litigation." It cost a fortune, but what we were getting back in return made it all worth it.

CBS fought us tooth and nail every step of the way—just like Martin said they would. Martin brought in trusted SNR Denton partners to develop the case against CBS. Gary Meyerhoff led the charge on issues related to the Bush/Guard broadcast, its aftermath and the Thornburgh commission's report. Eddie Reich and associate Rebecca Hughes Parker focused on CBS's retention of investigators to look into the Killian documents and on CBS's actions after removing me as anchor of the *CBS Evening News*. With this team in place, we started to make some real progress.

One important revelation was the discovery of an unreported e-mail exchange in December 2004 between Thornburgh and White House communications director Dan Bartlett, about a month before CBS had released Thornburgh's report. George W. Bush had already been reelected, and Thornburgh's law firm had spent several months conducting interviews and reinterviews of the CBS News team and other witnesses. In the e-mail to Bartlett, Thornburgh was asking President Bush to answer directly, once and for all, the questions that had surfaced about his National Guard service.

His e-mail to Dan Bartlett, subject "CBS Investigation," reads:

Many thanks for your cooperation in the above matter. As I mentioned by phone, we are in the homestretch of our assignment and would find it very helpful if we could secure written responses from the President to the following questions so that we can tie up a couple of loose ends. These questions all derive, as you will recognize, from material contained in the September 8, 2004 "Sixty Minutes Wednesday" segment on the President's Texas Air National Guard Service.

> (1) *Was there a waiting list to become a pilot of the Texas Air National Guard at the time you entered?*
>
> (2) *Do you recall Colonel Killian being dissatisfied in any way about your National Guard service in 1972 and 1973?*
>
> (3) *Were you ever ordered to take a physical in May 1972 or at any other time?*
>
> (4) *Did Colonel Killian say in May 1972 that you could do Equivalent Training for three months or transfer?*
>
> (5) *Do you recall being suspended from flight status on or about August 1, 1972? If so, how was that suspension communicated to you?*
>
> (6) *Why were you suspended from flight status? Was there a reason other than not taking a physical?*

(7) *Describe your communications with Colonel Killian about a transfer to Alabama in 1972.*

(8) *Did Colonel Killian or anyone else ever inform you that Colonel Killian was being pressured in any way about your status by a superior officer?*

Thornburgh was asking the threshold journalistic questions that had to be asked and answered before anyone could legitimately find fault with the broadcast. He was getting to the heart of the matter: Was our report *true*? He was putting these questions directly to the president, and he was doing it a month before his report was to be released.

Bartlett's response, more than a day later, was not surprising to me:

Sorry for the delay in getting back to you. I must say, I was somewhat surprised by the questions. I guess we viewed your work as more focused on what CBS did/did not do regarding their reporting, not the substance of their charges. The answers to your questions can be easily found in the public record so we would prefer to keep him out of participating in your report. Please call my office if you care to discuss further.

Totally shut down. The answers, of course, were not in the public record. We knew, because we'd looked. President Bush had danced and dodged whenever he was confronted with questions about his service, and Bartlett was the one who was usually sent in to protect him. In December 2004, Bartlett was not only letting Thornburgh know that he would not be getting answers from Bush to his questions, but he also made it clear that the White House didn't want him meddling with "inconsequential" matters—like whether the story that caused the whole firestorm was actually true.

Thornburgh's 254-page report, plus 700-page appendix, includes no mention of Thornburgh's request that the president answer the basic questions raised by the broadcast. It says nothing about the president's refusal to respond. After everyone had been interviewed, even Thornburgh knew that there were questions about Bush's service that still needed to be answered—questions that were important enough to ask a sitting president for written responses. It was clear, however, that dealing with the obvious journalistic principles at hand was never the goal of CBS News, or of Thornburgh's investigation. I concluded that their report, as published, incorrectly assumed that the story was not true, and then set out to assess blame.

My legal team would also learn about a key Thornburgh commission conclusion that was never mentioned in the report. Martin's team learned that Thornburgh's firm was quite aware that the vitriolic critiques of the Killian documents—the ones launched in the Republican blogosphere immediately after the broadcast—were bogus. Michael J. Missal, a K&L Gates partner of Thornburgh's who led the investigation, revealed this nugget at a seminar several years after the report was released. On March 17, 2008, Missal was a speaker at a Washington and Lee University symposium called Media, Law and the Courts. During his presentation, he made lengthy remarks about the work of the Thornburgh commission, including the following:

> It's ironic that the blogs were actually wrong. When they had their, their, uh, criticism, we actually did find typewriters that did have the superscript, did have proportional spacing and on the fonts, given that these are copies, it's really hard to say, but there were some typewriters that look like it could have a very similar font there. So the initial concerns didn't seem to hold up.

Ironic?

Based on what happened to my career and reputation, not to mention Mary Mapes's career and reputation, the word "ironic" is a grotesque mischaracterization. With this public statement, Missal was admitting that he and his law firm were fully aware that the "factual" underpinnings for the attacks on our Bush/Guard piece were not factual at all.

And that they knew it at the time they issued their report.

They understood full well that "factual" allegations made by the ultra-right-wing blogosphere—allegations that had been picked up wholesale by legitimate mainstream news organizations, including the *Washington Post*—could not be credited. At this same symposium, Missal described the work of K&L Gates as a fact-finding mission. *That's* "ironic."

"What we were trying to do," he told the audience, "is find out what the facts were, all the facts." Nevertheless, Missal, Thornburgh and K&L Gates failed to include many of the key facts they had discovered.

Our litigation efforts resulted in further progress in January 2008, when CBS was forced to cough up the report that investigator Erik Rigler had prepared, a report that also was nowhere to be found in the published Thornburgh report.

We already knew a lot about Mr. Rigler, whose sphere of expertise is the investigation of aircraft accidents. By any standard, he was an odd choice to delve into the authenticity of the Killian documents and the question of Bush's whereabouts during his stint in the National Guard. Not only did aircraft accidents have no bearing on the issue at hand, Rigler had been an investigator for the lucrative Texas Lottery Commission during Bush's time as governor of Texas. (Questions surrounding the Lottery Commission had been a key factor in derailing President Bush's nomination of Harriet Miers to the Supreme Court.)

When Rigler first began his investigation, Andrew Heyward had called Mary Mapes and directed her to assist Rigler in any way possible in his efforts to verify the Killian documents. At the time, Mary was still a CBS employee, and Andrew was still her boss. As ordered, Mary opened her files—and her home—to Rigler, and also to his wife, who functioned as his assistant and secretary. Judyth Rigler accompanied him on interviews. She took shorthand notes verbatim, then typed them up. Those records no longer exist. After her husband boiled the information down to a paragraph or two, he destroyed the verbatim transcript. Destroy original records? As an experienced investigator, Rigler surely knew better. This is hardly standard procedure for anyone who had been an FBI agent for more than two decades, as Rigler had, or who was accustomed to working with the Federal Aviation Administration or the National Transportation Safety Board.

In addition to looking into the authenticity of the Killian documents, Erik Rigler apparently had been given a secondary assignment: an investigation into Mary Mapes's personal life. As Joe Hagan put it in the *New York Observer*, "The fact that CBS had a private investigator looking into its own employee suggests that well before the panel issued any findings, network management had begun to shift its focus away from solving the mystery behind the documents, and toward placing blame for the decision to air the segment." As unsavory as this was, it was also oddly reassuring. It meant that the feeling I got in the immediate aftermath—the sense that no one but me at CBS was circling the wagons—was not just my imagination working overtime.

We learned about the attempt to dig up dirt on Mary through conversations that took place in the fall and winter of 2004 between Rigler and Mike Smith, the excellent researcher/investigator who had worked with us on the original Bush/Guard story. With the announcement that Richard Thornburgh, George H. W. Bush's former attorney general, was going to head the panel, Smith immediately smelled a rat. He suspected—rightly, as it turned out—that CBS might be looking to hang some of us out to dry. Mike Smith was the link to Bill Burkett, who had given us the Killian documents. (Burkett had become uncooperative with anyone from CBS itself, which was hardly surprising.) Because Smith had played such a key role in the story, he figured he might be among the fall guys. As a result, he taped all of his conversations with Rigler. Secretly.

He and Rigler spoke often. On October 27, 2004, Rigler confessed to Smith that he didn't really know whether he was working for CBS or for the supposedly independent Thornburgh panel. CBS, apparently, was never in doubt. Rigler put that question to CBS News senior vice president Linda Mason, who was assigned as liaison with Kirkpatrick & Lockhart, Thornburgh's law firm. She "chewed me out," Rigler complained to Smith. She then added, "You should never talk to those people!"

According to his taped conversations with Mike Smith, what Erik

Rigler was finding out was leading him to believe that the Killian documents were indeed genuine. Moreover, like all of us who had worked on the Bush/Guard piece, he became convinced that the underlying story of Bush's dereliction of duty was the truth. "It was so well known for years at Camp Mabry about Bush and his failure to serve in the Texas Air National Guard," Rigler told Smith. (Camp Mabry was where Lieutenant George Bush had been stationed.) "Most people just sort of looked at him as a draft dodger. They didn't hold him in very high regard at all. The story—and I'm talking to some people at Camp Mabry—the story about the files, the non-service, the memos, stuff like that, had floated around for years. For that reason, it makes you think it's likely true."

We already knew that the issues related to the Killian documents that had kicked up the most dust—the typeface and proportional spacing—were phony. We had manuals for the IBM typewriters in use by the military at the time in question. Now Erik Rigler, the investigator CBS had hired, was coming to the same conclusion we had—that the Killian documents were genuine.

It became clear, however, that the higher-ups at CBS corporate and its parent company Viacom didn't really want Rigler validating the Killian documents, certainly not before the election. On September 24, 2004, Viacom CEO Sumner Redstone had signaled his unequivocal support for George Bush's second term by saying that a Republican administration was better for Viacom than a Democratic one. On October 5, less than two weeks later, CBS president Leslie Moonves assured a Goldman Sachs media conference that CBS would not release the findings of the Thornburgh panel until after the votes had been counted. "Obviously," he said, "it should be done probably after the election is over, so that it doesn't affect what's going on."

In other words, CBS seemed to have placed its finger firmly on the Republican side of the scale. If Rigler had been able to authenticate the Killian documents that October, it would have been proof that the man who was now president of the United States had disobeyed a direct order from a superior officer to take a physical and was either AWOL or a deserter from his champagne unit for a year—a year when other young men were bleeding and dying in Vietnam. CBS would nevertheless have withheld that information from the American public until after the polls had closed.

But after the election, Erik Rigler was out of a job. There was no further need for his services. CBS terminated his contract as soon as it was clear that the Bush presidency would last another four years. Rigler himself had predicted as much. "I'm going to be unemployed after the election," he told Smith in late October. "Makes me wonder if this whole thing wasn't so CBS could tell Mary Mapes, 'Well, we tried.'"

When Judge Gammerman gave us Rigler's watered-down report in January 2008, James Quinn pooh-poohed the victory, suggesting that we would be disappointed by the contents. Perhaps he already suspected why. On December 8, 2005, Thomas Cowley, managing director of SafirRosetti, the security firm that had picked Rigler to conduct the investigation, had sent Erik Rigler's report to CBS News VP Linda Mason. Instead of passing that report on to Thornburgh, Mason supervised the preparation of an abbreviated and sanitized version to be delivered to the investigators.

So much for objectivity or, in Mike Missal's words, finding out "all the facts." "He [Rigler] was independent," Mason said, trying to (unsuccessfully) convince Mike Smith in late December. "Well, through me. If we had gotten information, I would have passed it on to the panel."

Except *that* didn't seem to happen. Even Mason's edited version of Rigler's findings was not part of the final Thornburgh report.

Erik Rigler himself summed it up best in another conversation with Mike Smith: "This is not a real investigation," he said.

And of course, Rigler was the only one actually tasked with finding out whether the documents were authentic. Everyone else associated with the Thornburgh investigation was very busy figuring out who within CBS News was guilty of putting a true story on the air.

Beyond access to Rigler's report, we wanted access to Rigler himself. In the courts, discovery is an unfolding process. First we got a little, and then we got more, and everything we got made our case stronger. In March, Judge Gammerman reaffirmed that discovery was to proceed, even as Quinn repeatedly introduced motions to dismiss, which the judge never cottoned to. In April 2008 we were given permission to subpoena Rigler for deposition. I was upbeat—finally it looked like we were on the brink of finding out what happened.

The judge did, however, narrow the scope of the suit. Martin had told me this was to be expected, since part of Judge Gammerman's job was to shrink the case before it went to trial. That same April, he tossed out four of the seven counts in the suit, including the count of fraud. Consequently, he also removed Sumner Redstone, Leslie Moonves and Andrew Heyward as individual defendants, saying that their actions had been committed in conjunction with their role as employees of CBS/ Viacom. I understood how that might get Heyward and Moonves off the hook, but Redstone? At Viacom, he was at the top of the heap. If he was acting in his capacity as an employee, who was he taking orders from?

The good news, however, was that the judge directed that the suit move forward on the three remaining counts and ordered depositions to begin. The defendants got the first at bat. I was to be deposed by Quinn, Spector, et al. Before the session, Martin and his team spent a lot of time with me, going over the details of the case and doing mock Q&A's of the issues that would likely come up. It was essential to have the facts "in my frontal lobes," as Marty put it.

The deposition took place at the Weil offices, and they spared no expense to document the proceedings. In addition to someone transcribing, there was also both audio and video recording equipment, everything short of aerial photography. During a deposition, the only people who are supposed to be in the room are the plaintiff and defendant and their legal representatives. When we arrived, there was of course the cool and collected Mr. Quinn, as well as Ms. Spector of the perpetually dyspeptic countenance, but there was also an added starter: Andrew Heyward.

I was surprised to see him, especially since he was no longer a named defendant and no longer a CBS employee. When Martin asked what he was doing there, we were told that he was a "consultant." My guess is that this was a command performance, a quid pro quo that was buried somewhere in the fine print of his $2 million bonus/severance package/ nondisclosure agreement.

Andrew looked daggers at me throughout the session, and an excellent job of it he did, too. If the goal was to unsettle me or make me uncomfortable, however, it failed as a strategy. I was sad for him that he was hauled in to be there, but his presence didn't distract me or make me angry. By then I'd been talking calmly at the red light on the camera for more than four decades—often with all hell breaking loose around me. I wasn't about to get rattled by stares from Andrew Heyward.

After we broke for lunch, Heyward did not return, but Quinn brought in yet another surprise guest star: Jeff Fager. First Heyward, then Fager. It was a stark reminder of how much had changed. These were men I had considered not just colleagues, but friends. I knew their wives and families. They knew my wife, Jean. We had socialized together. Sitting there in this very adversarial setting, that now seemed like a lifetime ago.

Martin asked the same question as he had in the morning session: "What is this person doing here?"

"This is Jeffrey Fager," Quinn said. "He is a corporate executive."

It was all I could do not to laugh out loud. At the time, Fager was still the executive producer of *60 Minutes*. If that made him a corporate executive, then I was the Dalai Lama. For as long as I'd worked at CBS, there had always been a firewall between CBS News and CBS corporate—a barrier so solid that the two entities were housed in separate buildings. And we in News Div were glad of it: By the code of CBS News, in which Jeff was ostensibly a true believer, calling someone a Black Rock corporate suit was about the worst thing you could say about a colleague.

It seemed to me that Jeff had just taken a giant step over to the dark side. It also seemed that he was not happy about it. If he had been freshly knighted as a corporate exec to get me rattled during the deposition, it appeared to have had the opposite effect. Jeff seemed far more ill at ease than I was. His internal battle between ambition and journalism, which I first noticed during Abu Ghraib, had not abated; instead, it had apparently gotten more intense. What was difficult then had now become anguished. Beyond the battle for his conscience as a journalist, however, Jeff wasn't nearly as good a starer as Andrew Heyward. His eyes didn't meet mine very often. This was not a role worthy of Jeff, and I'd like to think he knew it. (Today, Jeffrey Fager is chairman of CBS News. He retains his post as executive producer of *60 Minutes*.)

I was excited about starting the deposition process with my former colleagues, but Martin was philosophical about how much to expect from deposing those on the other side. He reminded me that the first rule of corporate litigation is damage control. Corporations understand that when a suit is filed, many of those who will be testifying are current and former employees. In the effort to have as much control over these potential witnesses as possible, it is common practice for corporations to provide free legal representation for those drawing either a paycheck or a pension. For an individual, this is a great boon, a relief from what otherwise might be a huge financial burden. For a corporation, it's just the cost of doing business. In most situations, it's probably a deductible expense. The company, of course, chooses lawyers sympathetic to its own cause, often from the same firm that represents the corporation itself. Under the circumstances, it becomes very difficult for an individual to do anything but toe the company line.

Because CBS provided attorneys for Moonves, Fager, Heyward and many others involved in the suit, the documents unearthed in discovery were key. In deposition, all of the CBS witnesses gave us the corporate version of "I'm sorry, Senator, I don't recall." It was as if they had taken a groupthink vow of amnesia: They wouldn't remember anything, or admit a single solitary fact unless we could jam it down their throats with a document that had their names on it. And sometimes not even then.

We deposed Leslie Moonves in September 2008. Unlike the rest of us mere mortals, however, Moonves got deposed in his own office. How come corporate executives get preferential treatment? Because, I was told, they have big businesses to run and they're very busy. That didn't sit well with me. Everyone is busy, including the schoolteacher, the single parent and the guy driving the hack who have to take unpaid days off.

"This is the way the courts operate. It's just the way it is," Martin told me.

"It's unfair and should be changed," I told him. "The theory of our system of justice is that everyone stands equal before the law."

"Let it go, Dan," Martin said. "This is not a hill worth dying for. Not now."

We went to Moonves's office. "Don't look for any great revelations," Martin warned me. "He'll be well briefed, and it's going to be really hard to get anything out of him. And remember—these sonofabitches *will* lie." In addition to the lawyers from Weil, there was also CBS corporate counsel present.

Moonves had obviously been very well prepared. The issue was raised of the agreement that had been reached with my agent, Richard Leibner, to extend my contract and to keep me on at *60 Minutes*, and the letter of intent that Moonves had signed to that effect. Moonves acknowledged that he had signed that document, but he maintained that it was not a contract and that he'd only signed it to get Leibner off his back. He said he never considered it binding and never had any intention of honoring it.

In other words, his signature meant nothing. Score one for *omertà*. I'm not going to accuse Leslie Moonves of lying, but I will accuse him of being so blatantly mistaken it would be hard to think that someone of his intelligence and experience would do that.

When it was over, Moonves came around the table toward me, bouncing and smiling, as if it had all been a great lark. He extended his hand. I shook it; I thought it was the gentlemanly thing to do. I didn't feel good about it, but I did it, even as I looked forward to him raising that very same hand at trial, being sworn in before Judge Gammerman, and trying to get away with repeating what he'd just said.

Martin had warned me to be prepared for smears in the press. His law firm had a team of people working to protect my reputation, but CBS was working equally hard to slam it. Instead of making me a villain, from the outset their strategy was to portray me as some sort of addlepated pensioner, a pathetic old fool hell-bent on ruining his legacy. Lead attorney James Quinn had condescendingly called the lawsuit one of those "sad cases where a person at the end of his career wants to go back after people he feels mistreated him."

Remarks like that from Quinn were to be expected, but I was surprised by the barbs flung by former colleagues. Morley Safer said I was suing because I enjoyed being a martyr. Jeff Fager told the *Washington Post* that I was "in some paranoid nightmare where everybody is out to get him. We're all witnessing the poor guy thrashing around, tormented…I can't for the life of me understand why he's doing this, how he could turn such a storied career into this train wreck."

In that climate, it clearly would have been self-destructive to anyone's career within CBS News to support me publicly. To former colleagues who kept their silence: my gratitude. And to those who called me on the QT to offer their tacit support: Thanks, I needed that. You know who you are.

A lot of my being painted as a doddering, deranged Don Quixote, tilting at imaginary windmills, evaporated when the flood of documents we won in discovery started coming to the surface. Judge Gammerman had made it clear that he wanted the case tried in the court, not in the press. As a result, we were barred from releasing any documents to the public, except those that had been filed in court.

Just so. Martin Gold, Gary Meyerhoff and Eddie Reich filed lots of motions, and in support of those motions, they attached documents. That put them into the public record. In November 2008, a document attached to one of their court filings got everyone's attention—Exhibit J.

Exhibit J was the short list of names that CBS executives had compiled in mid-September 2004. These were the nominees they had considered to head up the "independent, impartial" panel. Among others on the list were Tucker Carlson, Pat Buchanan, Matt Drudge, Bernard Goldberg, Lou Dobbs, Ann Coulter, Charles Krauthammer and Rush Limbaugh. Scrawled at the bottom was the name of one additional write-in candidate: Roger Ailes, head of Fox News.

Round up the unusual suspects.

All were longtime Bush supporters and sympathizers. There was nothing independent about them. There were also a few more reasonable candidates on the list, including former senator Warren Rudman (R-New Hampshire). According to a CBS in-house memo, Rudman was "mentioned by several GOP folks who feel he is above reproach, and he would be his own man."

Which is exactly what was wrong with him. Rudman was rejected because he would not, in the words of CBS News senior vice president Linda Mason, "mollify the Right."

The disturbing picture emerging from the documents won in discovery was that executives at the highest levels of CBS News, including both VP Linda Mason and president Andrew Heyward, seemed in a veritable tizzy, trying to "mollify the Right." After that stellar list of potential candidates was drawn up, Heyward and Mason vetted the names on it with Viacom's top Washington lobbyist, Carol Melton. As a lobbyist, Melton was in good stead with the Republicans, having funneled more than 60 percent of Viacom's political action committee contributions their way. She proceeded to run the nominees by her contacts within the Republican Party. From the feedback she got, this was how Richard Thornburgh came out the winner. Melton "did some other testing," Linda Mason's notes revealed. "T [Thornburgh] comes back with high marks from G.O.P."

I was absolutely horrified. In bringing suit, we had charged that CBS's actions were committed to appease angry Republicans and to advance the financial interests of Viacom. Now it was clear that CBS News was no longer simply part of Viacom. It had become the wholly owned subsidiary of the Bush administration.

This was not the CBS I knew. And it was not the Andrew Heyward I thought I knew. Heyward's faintheartedness and his desertion of his own staff—not to mention the abandonment of his own ethics—stood in sharp contrast with the behavior of Richard Salant, who had been president of CBS News when I was chief White House correspondent. All through Watergate, Salant never wavered. We never doubted that he had our backs, even though we knew that the pressure on him was intense. Richard Salant stood up for his journalists, not only to the Nixon administration, but to William S. Paley himself.

Salant was also president of News Div in 1971, when we aired *The*

Selling of the Pentagon. The documentary, which was accurate in the overall, actually had some errors and flaws—enough to bring us under sharp attack in the House of Representatives. Two powerful senior members of the House, Harley Staggers (D-West Virginia) and F. Edward Hébert (D-Louisiana), were the most upset. Hébert, chairman of the House Armed Services Committee, vilified our documentary as "un-American" and "Goebbels-like." Largely at his instigation, the Investigations Subcommittee of the House Commerce Committee, headed by Staggers, started looking into how CBS News had produced the documentary. They issued a blanket congressional subpoena demanding that we furnish "all film, work prints, outtakes, and sound-tape recordings, written scripts and/or transcripts" from the program.

For the broadcast media, this was equivalent to asking a print reporter to give up a source, and for upstanding journalists, that is simply not done. CBS Network president Frank Stanton—the Leslie Moonves of his day—pretty much told Staggers and Hébert to stick it where the sun don't shine. He gave them the finished version of the documentary, nothing more. They screeched and threatened, but Stanton remained resolute. To defend our First Amendment rights as journalists, the head of the network defied the subpoena, and in so doing risked a contempt of Congress citation and possible jail time.

Stanton and Salant. Moonves and Heyward. Sadly, they don't seem to make network executives like they used to, at least not at CBS.

Part of what was different now, of course, was that CBS was no longer a freestanding company. CBS had become a cog in the Greater Viacom Empire. CBS News may have been one of the best-known entities within that huge conglomerate, but in terms of commercial value, it ranked well below a host of Viacom's other assets. This had been true in the days of Stanton and Salant as well. CBS News was never the most profitable component of what was then known as the Tiffany Network—there were years when it wasn't profitable at all—but Bill Paley didn't care about that. He wasn't perfect when it came to news. He had his weak moments and made his mistakes. But he was as good an owner in this regard as there has ever been; I think the best. Not only was he a true believer in the idea that the news was a public service, he also understood that CBS News contributed to the bottom line in crucial but intangible ways. CBS News added value and prestige to the network by virtue of its excellence. In contemporary marketing lingo, when it came to efforts to build the brand, CBS News did a lot of the heavy lifting.

CBS News also satisfied an important legal requirement. Under the rules of the FCC at the time, every few years networks had to justify their broadcasting licenses. To be renewed, they had to show how their programming was in the public interest. CBS News was the network's ticket to fulfilling that function.

In the headlong rush to deregulation that began during the Reagan administration, however, that requirement was eliminated. In late 2004, in the deregulated Wild West of pro-business Washington, Viacom had a much larger agenda, which is to say that Sumner Redstone thought the company needed to get bigger and more profitable. The Viacom empire was already full of cash cows. In addition to CBS, Viacom also owned MTV, Showtime, Nickelodeon, TNN, BET, TV Land, UPN, Comedy Central, Infinity Broadcasting and VH1, as well as Simon & Schuster, King World Productions (which syndicated *Jeopardy!*, *Wheel of Fortune* and *The Oprah Winfrey Show*) and Paramount Pictures. Viacom was also accruing local television stations around the country.

In that lineup, CBS News was about as important as a nit on a gnat's nut. At the time, the lucrative permissions and licenses that Viacom was seeking were actually worth more than CBS News *in its entirety.* So, too, was the right to own increasing numbers of television stations, an issue that had been percolating in Congress during the two years before the Abu Ghraib and Bush/Guard broadcasts had aired.

An FCC rule known as the broadcast ownership cap restricted Viacom and other media behemoths from owning television stations that reached more than 35 percent of the country's households. The Republican-controlled FCC had raised the cap to 45 percent, the type of deregulation Sumner Redstone was endorsing. Democrats in the House and Senate were preparing legislation to push the cap back down to 35 percent. If that effort was successful and the cap was restored to 35 percent, Viacom would have had to start selling off television stations.

That would have made Mr. Redstone most unhappy. The battleground for this dispute was to be the House Energy and Commerce Committee, which had FCC oversight responsibility. At the time, the ranking Republican on that committee was Congressman Roy Blunt (R-Missouri), then the House majority whip.

Viacom hired the big Washington lobbying firm Cassidy & Associates to lobby Energy and Commerce. Who would lead the charge? Mr. Blunt's former chief of staff, Gregg Hartley. Hartley left Blunt's office, joined Cassidy & Associates and immediately started earning money by lobbying his former boss—Roy Blunt. That's politics, Washington style. Among the other associates at Cassidy is Andy Blunt, Roy Blunt's son. That, too, is politics, Washington style.

When the dust settled, the committee struck a deal to set the ownership cap at 39 percent, the exact percentage of households in Viacom's portfolio. Blunt and the Republicans in the House had helped Viacom keep its television stations.

On September 15, a week after our Bush/Guard broadcast, it was the same Congressman Blunt who had come out strongly attacking the story. He wrote a stinging letter to CBS News, specifically to president Andrew Heyward.

> *Dear Mr. Heyward:*
> *We are writing to express our dismay that CBS has become part of a campaign to deceive the public and defame the president . . . We urge CBS to retract its story, and to disclose the identities of the people who have used your network to deceive your viewers in the final weeks of a presidential election.*

On January 10, 2005, five days after the final Thornburgh-Boccardi report was made public and ten days before Bush's second inauguration, internal CBS documents show that Viacom lobbyist Carol Melton strongly urged Andrew Heyward to comply with Congressman Blunt's earlier request. Specifically, she wanted him to officially retract the Bush/Guard story. Appeasing Blunt was a priority, and not just because he was a major player on the Energy and Commerce Committee.

Although Blunt was House majority whip under Majority Leader Tom DeLay, Melton made it clear that Blunt was speaking for an even more powerful constituency—the White House. "Plainly the 'retraction' point per se seems to be a final shoe that some would like to see drop," she wrote to Heyward, "and have no doubt that Blunt is acting as the mouthpiece for this administration." Keep in mind that this is a corporate lobbyist pressuring the head of the News Division. That should never have been happening. And at my time at CBS, I never knew it to have happened before.

At Ms. Melton's deposition more than three years later, she did not deny it. "The White House was not engaging on this directly…Mr. Blunt was serving as the outside spokesperson, if you will, to express a point of view…for the Bush administration…That was his role."

Heyward did not want to issue a formal retraction on top of the "apology" I had already made. In an e-mail to Melton, Heyward acknowledged to her that the Bush/Guard story was a true story but added, "I would never say this publicly."

Wow. Way to stand up. This is the same guy who clearly was receptive to lobbyists giving President Bush, his surrogates and supporters the kind of pseudo-independent investigation they wanted, who cast his reporting team adrift and attempted to distance himself from the entire process.

It was Leslie Moonves who cast the deciding vote on the "retraction" issue. Howard Kurtz quoted Moonves in a January 11, 2005, *Washington Post* story. "Moonves said it is clear that CBS has retracted the story." That surely was not clear to me. It was not even clear to Andrew Heyward. I had apologized for including the Killian documents in the broadcast. We did not retract the story, nor should we have. But that was the way that Blunt and the White House wanted it, and Moonves chose to oblige.

In November 2004, two weeks after election night, lobbyist Melton had received a promotion from Sumner Redstone, becoming Viacom's executive vice president for government relations. In June 2005, about seven months later, she jumped ship to become a lobbyist for Time Warner. In October she named Tim Berry as her No. 2. Berry had been Tom DeLay's chief of staff, but DeLay was facing big-time legal trouble. When DeLay was indicted on September 28, he stepped down as majority leader. On an interim basis, that position went to...Roy Blunt. Blunt was thought to be the front-runner to win the position permanently but narrowly lost out to John Boehner the following summer.

Like DeLay, in 2005 Blunt had been named as one of the most corrupt members of congress by CREW, the Citizens for Responsibility and Ethics in Washington. Blunt was so honored again in 2006. What did he do that upset CREW? Like his predecessor, Blunt was tied to Jack Abramoff. He also attempted to push through special-interest legislation for Philip Morris at the behest of its lobbyist, Abigail Perlman (soon to become Abigail Blunt), neglecting to reveal that the two had a close personal relationship.

In 2003, Blunt had assisted his son Andy, at that time a lobbyist for FedEx and UPS, by inserting a provision into an emergency appropriations bill for the war in Iraq stipulating that military cargo must be carried by companies with no more than 25 percent foreign ownership. FedEx and UPS were seeking to thwart inroads into their business by a foreign-owned competitor. Both contributed heavily to the Blunt campaign in the years that followed.

Beyond that, however, Roy Blunt played a crucial role in what was known as the "K Street Project," a concerted effort to press DC lobbyists to wholeheartedly align themselves with the Republican agenda in order to gain access to influential officials. Blunt was a master at it. As described by Thomas Edsall in the *Washington Post* in May 2005, he was a Republican fund-raising machine. "Blunt has converted what had been an informal and ad hoc relationship between congressional leaders and the Washington corporate and trade community into a formal, institutionalized alliance," Edsall wrote. "Lobbyists are now an integral part of the Republican whip operation on par with the network of lawmakers who serve as assistant whips...[Blunt] became the House GOP's key liaison with the lobbyists who not only represent clients in virtually every member's district, but also direct the flow of individual and political action committee contributions from the 1,600 corporations and 1,200 trade associations with PACs."

The K Street Project was based on the principle of "reward your friends; punish your enemies." Viacom is nothing if not profit driven. The top priority of the company is to protect and expand its financial interests. If honest reporting threatens that in any way, it's going to come out second best. No wonder Viacom tried to bury the story—and the journalists involved. CBS News was messing up their agenda in Washington.

The bizarre connection between CBS and Roy Blunt did not end there. Today, Roy Blunt is no longer a congressman; he is now the junior senator from Missouri. Elected in 2010, he received campaign contributions from a wide range of businesses and individuals. Among those individuals was Leslie Moonves, who donated $2,400 to Friends of Roy Blunt and $5,000 to the Rely on Your Beliefs Fund (ROYB), Blunt's political action committee. Moonves also contributed $5,000 to the Missouri Republican State Committee. By contemporary campaign finance standards, this may strike some as chump change. What makes it unusual, however, is that prior to this time, other than a 2009 donation to the CBS Political Action Committee, Les Moonves had not made a political contribution in more than a decade. Stranger still, prior to the year 2000, all of his contributions were to Democrats. Perhaps getting Blunt into the Senate was the only way to get him off the Energy and Commerce Committee.

In July 2009, Judge Gammerman granted us access to more documents, including a lot of material from K&L Gates, which was the new name of Richard Thornburgh's law firm. (When the investigation, such as it was, was being conducted, his firm had been known as Kirkpatrick & Lockhart. In 2007, it merged with the Seattle-based law firm Preston Gates & Ellis—the "Gates" being William H. Gates Sr., father of Microsoft's Bill Gates.) When we sued, a lawyer from K&L Gates balked at our request for their documents, trying to plead attorney-client privilege. Judge Gammerman ruled against them.

The judge ordered the firm to surrender them within ten days. In addition to e-mail communications, memoranda, drafts of the report and notes, we had also asked for transcripts from the interviews K&L Gates had conducted during their investigation.

There weren't any.

K&L Gates claimed it had no transcripts, no audiotapes, zilch. Martin and I were in disbelief. Despite billing CBS more than $2.2 million for conducting the investigation and for follow-up work after delivery of the report, attorneys from the high-powered law firm headed up by the former attorney general of the United States, one of the largest firms in the country, claimed it kept no official records as they talked to witnesses.

Depositions of Thornburgh's partner Mike Missal and others revealed even more. K&L Gates did have lawyers take notes during the investigation's interviews, but Mr. Missal testified at his deposition that the note takers were instructed to *destroy* their interview notes. They were also instructed to destroy any drafts of the report that had existed. I found this even more peculiar than Rigler's destruction of verbatim transcripts. Why would lawyers destroy evidence?

Missal must have known this looked very bad, and he did not want the blame. He testified that he had been instructed to "not maintain any drafts" of the report by Linda Mason, at the time CBS's vice president for public affairs. Ms. Mason did not want the blame either. At her deposition, she testified, "I never gave that instruction." Well, someone did. CBS was seeking to remove its fingerprints from Thornburgh's "findings," and Missal and company had done so, even if no one would own up to who had given the order.

Judge Gammerman also restored our claim of fraud. At the same time, he told both sides that he was pushing to go to trial within four months.

Game on. I was elated. Gammerman was well known for moving things along. He didn't like things to drag in his courtroom, and the pretrial phase of this case had already gone on for almost two years. I was even happier two months later. On September 21, he approved several key depositions, including Dick Thornburgh, Sumner Redstone and even Dan Bartlett. That, I suspect, set off major alarm bells in

Black Rock and in Washington. Our next date before Judge Gammerman was set for December 22.

We never got that far. By this time there was already a consolidated appeal on file with the Appellate Division of the New York Supreme Court. In New York, unlike most other states in the country, it is not necessary to wait until the end of a case to file an appeal. Almost any decision made by the judge along the way can be kicked up to appellate court. In our case, this is what happened. Appeals of decisions by Judge Gammerman were made. Quinn appealed everything that had gone badly for them. We appealed what was unfavorable to us.

I attended the day the appeals justices heard the case in open court. Right from the start, it seemed to me that the justices treated Quinn almost deferentially. With Marty they appeared to be impatient and often dismissive. Watching as this conduct continued, my hopes began to sink. "We haven't got a chance," I thought.

Marty had the same assessment of the judges' demeanor but wasn't sure how much to read into it. "Well," he said, "they seem to have their minds made up, but with appeals courts, you never know."

As the session ended, I looked for a reason to be at least a little optimistic. "For one thing," I thought, "there is no way they can rule against what CBS had promised contractually about using me as a regular correspondent on *60 Minutes*, and what Moonves had promised me in person and in writing."

Wrong.

On September 29, about a week after Judge Gammerman indicated we were going to trial, the appellate court threw out the case. Completely.

My CBS contract had a "pay or play" provision; the appellate justices ruled that as long as CBS paid me according to my contract, which they had, I had absolutely no grounds to bring suit. "Contractually," wrote Judge James Catterson, who authored the unanimous opinion, "CBS was under no obligation to use Rather's services or to broadcast any program so long as it continued to pay him the applicable compensation." They stopped in its tracks the effort to let a jury decide anything in the case. They gave CBS a big victory. Marty called it one of the worst defeats he's ever had as a lawyer. The judges maintained that all that mattered was that I was paid. Not whether I ought to actually be on the air. Not whether they told me—or their viewers—the truth.

The five justices who heard the case were Luis Gonzalez, John Buckley, James Catterson, James McGuire and Dianne Renwick. All but Renwick had been appointed by former Republican governor George Pataki. There are twenty judges in the First Department of the Appellate Division. The process by which justices are assigned to cases is not transparent, but in theory it is random. In theory. What are the odds that these five, who among the twenty were by far the most likely to be sympathetic to CBS, turned out to be the ones who ended up hearing the case? Let's put it this way: If a pile of sand is dumped on a table, and when it lands, it happens to spell out "Nice try, Rather, but we can't risk this going to trial," that's random. In theory.

I was of course disappointed by what happened. Nevertheless, I have never second-guessed myself about the decision to go to court. It took a big whack out of my time, my psyche, and my bank balance, but even so, it was worth it. The suit accomplished much of what I set out to do. I filled in some of the key blanks in the Bush/Guard story and my role afterward. More important, the suit forced some of the really ugly truths about what CBS was doing behind the scenes out into the open. To find out that the president of CBS News had been dancing to the tune of a Washington corporate lobbyist was beyond anything I might have imagined. If you believe that politics and corporate influence are not heavily involved in the appointment of judges and how they rule, you're entitled. I believe they are. I also believe that they were factors in my case being stopped short of trial by jury.

Somewhere out there are a lot of people who know firsthand the truth of what we reported about what Bush did and didn't do in the military. But they remain silent. So far.

I know the suit pissed off a lot of people. It seems I've been doing that all my life, but journalism is not a business to get into if you have no stomach for making people angry. One of my reasons for writing this book is to show exactly what was at stake and what facts were gained by doing it. When you report something important for the public to know that somebody in power doesn't want out in the open, someone's bound to get mad. Perhaps my friend Bill Moyers put it best:

> *News is what people want to keep hidden.*
> *Everything else is publicity.*

CHAPTER 11

Reinventing Dan Rather

By the spring of 2006, I was out at CBS. It was not how I wanted to go out, not at all how I'd envisioned leaving the network, but by this time even my last, try-to-the-end hopes had been dashed. I was deeply disappointed but not bitter about having to leave. By any measure, I'd had a good run. As much as anything, I was in a fog.

When I was in the office in the final days and weeks, I was there physically, but I suspect my eyes were often glazed over, because my head was surely elsewhere. Various recollections of my time at CBS continually washed over me, like waves hitting a beach. Recordings from that jukebox in my mental museum replayed themselves at random. Someone had put a lot of quarters into that jukebox—44 years' worth, 24 of them in the anchor chair. What played was not just Rather's Greatest Hits. Some memories were good and some were not, but I had nothing to do with making the selections—these B-roll video clips from my past cued themselves up pretty much on their own.

As the end neared, I felt the stirrings of a fledgling identity crisis. I had tried so hard for so long to be the quintessential CBS News correspondent that it had become much of my identity. Maybe too much. "Dan Rather, CBS News" was more than just my sign-off tagline at the end of a broadcast. In my head, "Dan Rather" and "CBS News" had been welded together for so long that they had become fused—DanRatherCBSNews. *That* was my name.

If I wasn't that, who and what was I?

I went through my last day pretty much in a daze. After going out the door for the last time, I walked home through Central Park. That great, green oasis in the middle of Manhattan was restorative, as it so often is. As I walked, the fog in my head began to lift a bit; my senses perked up. I became alert to my surroundings—I stopped to smell the flowers and listen to the birds. As I did so, I was overwhelmed by a feeling of gratitude. "You are lucky and blessed, Dan. Don't forget it."

Close on the heels of gratitude came a self-administered pep talk. "You've been knocked down," said that persistent inner voice. "Don't stay down. You've always said you are a get-up fighter...Okay, now prove it." It might have felt more like the beginning of resilience if I'd been able to tell myself just how that might be done.

When I got home, Jean was all smiling and loving and full of positive energy. "Well," she said, "this day is the start of a new adventure." That wasn't how it felt to me—it still seemed much more like an ending, not a beginning. When I didn't immediately brighten up, she tried another approach. "Sit down," she said. "Let's have a glass of wine."

I knew the wine would be excellent—Jean likes wine and knows a lot about it—but I had something else in mind. "If you don't mind, I'd prefer a straight shot of bourbon."

"How could I mind?" she asked as she poured two jiggers from an old bottle of Wild Turkey into a glass.

For a few minutes, neither of us spoke much. Then, gently but firmly, Jean gave me a quiet talk about love, family and friends, about being a husband, father and grandfather; in short, about what's really important in life. "You were a helluva man before you ever got to CBS," she said, "and you're an even better one now."

Among all my blessings, she's at the top. As always, Jean knew exactly what to say and how to put the end of my time at CBS into perspective. After that I was no longer down, but I surely was at loose ends.

My friend and agent of 40 years, Richard Leibner, had tried to find

me another job. I made it plain to him that the compensation wasn't
the important thing; I had no expectation of drawing the kind of salary I'd had at CBS. Several other network news executives initially
expressed interest, but after discussing it with the higher-ups in management, they all had the same answer: "Dan, you're a lightning rod.
You are too hot to handle."

Once again, I was at a turning point in my career, as I had been
so long ago. Early on, it always seemed to be the case that guides and
mentors turned up out of the blue to help me. When I was a freshman
at Sam Houston State Teachers College, journalism professor Hugh
Cunningham had come along when I was floundering—and damned
near foundering—and he got there just when I needed him most. Cal
Jones at KHOU had taken me straight out of radio; when I started working for him, I was a guy who knew nothing about television. He taught
me everything he knew, which was plenty; under his guidance I became
an on-air reporter good enough to get hired by CBS in New York.

Now, decades later, my out-of-the-blue moment arrived courtesy of
George Clooney. I first met George when I profiled him for *60 Minutes II*. I realized immediately that he was a lot more than just the second coming of Cary Grant. Now he was to receive an award from the
Writers Guild for the movie *Good Night, and Good Luck*, and he had
invited me to Los Angeles to present it to him. Set in the 1950s, this
excellent film deals with the period at CBS when Edward R. Murrow
and Fred Friendly stood up to Joseph McCarthy. Clooney was deeply
involved in all aspects of the project. He not only portrayed Friendly to
David Strathairn's Murrow, he also wrote and directed.

George put me up in a first-rate hotel. At the gala, I sat with him and
his agent. They couldn't have been warmer or more genuine. Clooney
never said anything about CBS or the Bush/Guard broadcast or the
Thornburgh report, except for one offhand comment, said quietly as
he turned his head close to my ear. "So you got screwed," he whispered.
"Happens all the time in my business. Forget it."

Nothing more. Clooney really is as swell as everyone says he is. For
my money, even more so. This guy is grounded, "for real," as the cliché
goes. I've seen him a number of times since. Always the same. He wears

Hollywood stardom more lightly than anyone I've ever known, and I've known my share. After he introduced me to the audience, I received a standing ovation, which to me was greatly moving.

I was basking in the glow of this wonderful experience until reality set in on the plane back to New York. Somewhere over Colorado it hit me that I didn't have a job. I was staring at unemployment. For the first time in more than four decades, I would not have anyplace I had to be the next morning, and that thought was unsettling. I was barely 30 when I started at CBS. Now, even though I was damned near 75 years old, retirement never crossed my mind. I wasn't built for rocking chairs; there was no question that I'd rather wear out than rust out.

When I got home, a young *60 Minutes* producer named Neeraj Khemlani inquired about how the West Coast trip and my time with George Clooney had gone. Neeraj, whom I had not known very well for very long, had been helpful and understanding during my exile at *60 Minutes*. One of my few pleasant surprises while I was there was his support and encouragement. I found that to be in short supply during that difficult time, even from colleagues I had counted as friends, but here was a guy I barely knew who recognized what a tough situation I was in and was empathetic. Born in Queens and New York to the core, Neeraj was then in his late 20s. Among his other strengths, he knew all about high tech and the digital age. (Today, Neeraj Khemlani is an executive vice president at Hearst Entertainment and Syndication, specializing in digital media. I am confident that his career trajectory will continue upward.)

Beyond being whip smart, however, he was also wise beyond his years about many aspects of life at CBS, including how I was being sealed off—iced—at *60 Minutes*, and why. Quietly and discreetly he advised me that I needed to think outside the box about my future— outside the CBS box, that is. Although he admired my perseverance in my stated hope of surviving at CBS, Neeraj had always been steadfastly skeptical about my chances. That said, his attempts to offer me a reality check had been no more successful than anyone else's.

When I got back from Los Angeles, Neeraj asked me if someone by the name of Jeffrey Skoll had been at the awards ceremony. The name didn't ring a bell. Skoll, he explained, invests in and produces documentary and public-service programming and is at least an acquaintance and maybe a friend of Clooney's. I told him that he was not present that evening, but that it was my recollection that someone at the table had mentioned his name over dinner.

"You should call Clooney and ask his advice," Neeraj counseled, "and ask him about Skoll."

I took Neeraj's advice and called George. I didn't reach him but left a message that I was seeking advice. Even though I didn't mention Skoll in my message, Clooney's reply was a suggestion that Jeff Skoll might be a good person for me to contact.

To be honest, I'd never heard of Skoll before this sequence of events, but I was in great company—by his choice, he stays very private. Skoll had been eBay's first full-time employee and had designed its business plan—the road map that made it into an Internet powerhouse and a household word. He left the company with a personal bank account of about $2 billion and a commitment to philanthropy and social activism. Skoll went on to found Participant Media so that he could finance film projects that echo his beliefs. Participant Media had backed two Clooney hits, *Good Night, and Good Luck* and *Syriana*, as well as *An Inconvenient Truth*, *Charlie Wilson's War*, *The Cove* and many more.

Skoll was gracious when I called him. He agreed that I could come see him in Los Angeles. I flew out from New York and went to a small building in an unpretentious neighborhood, where he has a comfortable but modest office. No tycoon trappings for this guy. As I drew myself up to walk in, I took a deep breath and said to myself, "Well, this is a Hail Mary if there ever was one." Inside, he put me at ease right away. We talked for a while. He listened closely, then suggested that I talk with Mark Cuban, owner of HDNet and the Dallas Mavericks basketball team.

Mark had made his first billion within a decade of graduating from college. At the height of the dot-com boom, he took his first company, Broadcast.com, public before selling it in 1999 to Yahoo! Six months later, he bought the Mavericks and proceeded to transform the unsuccessful franchise into a playoff-caliber team and then into an NBA champion. Mark is famous—some might say notorious—for his devotion to the Mavs. That devotion includes openly criticizing referees who he believes have made bad calls against his players and calling out members of opposing teams who he thinks have been rough or unfair. His outspokenness has cost him; the league has levied more than $1.7 million in fines against him. (On his own, he voluntarily matches each penalty, dollar for dollar, with a charitable donation.)

A fixture at Mavericks home games, he often flies his Gulfstream to away games as well. You almost always know when he's in attendance, because he chooses to sit not in the skyboxes but among the fans, and as close to courtside as possible. In 2001, he launched HDNet, a TV station broadcasting exclusively in high definition format. Programming on the station covers a wide range of subjects, including adventure, travel, sports, music and news.

I had never met Mark. All I knew of him was what I'd seen watching Mavericks games, where, by his own description, he "lets the boy in me out." I did some quick homework about HDNet because I had barely heard of it and had never seen it before. We met at a Dallas seafood restaurant for lunch. He brought along his longtime friend and partner, Todd Wagner.

I was under the impression that this would be just a get-acquainted session. For the meeting, my job as I saw it was to put to rest the notion that I was a lightning rod for trouble. Given his history, perhaps I should have guessed that from Cuban's point of view, "lightning rod" was not derogatory. In fact, quite the opposite. "I *like* the fact that you are a lightning rod!" he told me. Barely three minutes later, he asked, "What do you want to do?"

I suddenly realized that this was a question I should have been prepared for. I wasn't. For a second or two I looked at him blankly, because I truly didn't know what to say. I ad-libbed and suggested that I could do a Charlie Rose–style talk show. "We can do that," he replied, then added, "What is it going to cost?"

I said I didn't know. That was the wrong answer. "What else?" he asked.

Ad-libbing again, I suggested, "I could get a morning show together, or a nightly news program."

"How much will those cost?" he asked again. Again, I had no idea.

"I want you to come to work for me," he declared. "Let's do something great together." Grabbing the nearest napkin, he said, "Here, I'll write it on this!"

I was appreciative—heaven knows, appreciative—but overwhelmed. I offered the thought that perhaps we were getting a bit ahead of ourselves. Mark didn't listen. He didn't even slow down. Once Mark Cuban makes a decision, roughly zero seconds elapse before he moves into implementation mode.

"Get me a list of the things you think you can do," he continued, "not necessarily in order of preference. Let's get a deal and get going," he said emphatically.

I left feeling immensely encouraged. At the meeting, there had been no mention of salary, which didn't bother me in the slightest. What mattered was what had always mattered—the news. Here was a prayer answered, a chance to get back into covering the news.

Some people call Mark impatient; I do not. Mark doesn't do small talk. Mark is intense, focused, decisive. To me, he's just a man who knows what he wants.

As it turned out, what he wanted was me. As he later told Jim Rendon in *Mother Jones*, "I thought news on TV sucked. It had become so corporate and ratings-driven that there was no journalism anymore. Dan Rather is a personal, guilty pleasure…That is the beauty of being an independent network. I program what I damn please. I thought this was such a great opportunity, not because I wanted to do a Fox or MSNBC type of thing. It was the exact opposite: I want Dan Rather being Dan Rather."

I went home and banged out a long e-mail (only to learn later that Mark *hates* long e-mails) that covered five ideas and a ballpark estimate of the cost of each (if the Astrodome is your ballpark). I had one more idea that I almost did not include, but I tacked it on at the last minute as No. 6 at the bottom. This idea was a way of getting back to what I loved the most—real investigative journalism. My No. 6 was my dream program—a combination of *60 Minutes*, *Nightline* and the classic Edward R. Murrow show *See It Now*.

I sent the e-mail to Mark Cuban at about 11:00 p.m. Eastern time. Within five minutes, he e-mailed me back saying, "I want No. 6. That's what I want to do." And of course, he wanted to know how much it would cost. I had a rough idea of what a segment of *60 Minutes* cost at CBS, so I put together a guesstimate and added that I thought it would take me seven or eight months to get it on the air.

Again, that was the wrong answer. I might as well have said eight years. It was now summer of 2006, and Mark wanted me on his air on HDNet in the fall—and by fall, he meant September, or October at the latest. "I am not sure that's possible," I told him over the phone.

"Make it possible," he replied simply. "Let's get a contract done. How soon can you be in Dallas to work out the details?"

I jumped on a plane immediately to go meet with Todd Wagner. Wagner runs HDFilms; Cuban runs HDNet, but because Wagner is an attorney, he does some contracts for Mark. The two men have been close friends since college. Like Mark, Todd exudes intelligence. He has, however, a different personal and business style. Todd is quieter, less exuberant, more cautious and private. It's a good fit—they complement each other. I found myself thinking, "It's no accident that these two guys have made billions together."

"Here's what we'll do," Todd said as we sat down in Dallas. "We'll work out a contract for each program, but we'll figure out your compensation separately." Working by phone with Phil Garvin, who runs HDNet for Cuban from the network's op-center in Denver, I had done some reconnoitering in preparation for creating a budget for the programs, but there were still a lot of variables. After Todd and I talked some and agreed on an approximate figure for the cost of each program, he dropped a conversational bombshell. "Mark wants to do a program every week, all year long," he said.

My jaw dropped. "Dream on, maniac," I said to myself. Only years of practice saved me from blurting out what I was thinking. I was certain, however, that this was way too much to undertake, especially for the first year. I had just left *60 Minutes*, a long-running, well-established program. With a large staff, a big budget and a major corporation behind it, *60 Minutes* does only about 26 to 30 original hours a year. They have a heavy schedule of reruns. We were about to become a begin-from-scratch start-up with a new network that was itself still a work in progress, and Mark wanted 52 original hours a year.

"Well," I said as I swallowed hard and managed a smile, "Mark obviously likes to dream big. So do I."

Todd and I settled on an initial contract with an estimated budget to produce 42 programs annually for three years. Included in the agreement was some wiggle room so that production budgets could vary from program to program. It wasn't only that we anticipated cost fluctuations depending on the needs of the story; we also had to build in a learning curve for me to figure out how to do this.

My new job was announced on July 11, 2006, when Mark Cuban and I faced the annual meeting of the Television Critics Association at the Ritz-Carlton in Pasadena. "We're thrilled that Dan is now part of HDNet," Mark told them. "Now that he is finally released from the ratings-driven and limited-depth confines of broadcast television, I am excited about the impact Dan can have on the future of news."

From my perspective, that was about the best thing he could have said. Despite our differences in experience and work background, Mark Cuban and I share a compelling vision about the importance of investigative journalism, both now and going forward. With his backing, my second act as a journalist began.

"As a team player," I promised, "I intend to give Mark and HDNet all of the hard work, loyalty and fearless, high-quality reporting possible." I meant it, but at the time we were still doing business on a handshake. When we had dinner together that evening, he told me that the lawyers were almost done finalizing the contracts and reiterated that he wanted the first program on the air by October at the latest. I told him I would try. It was a pleasant dinner, and it ended with him saying, "Go do it!"

"October at the latest…" Mark's words kept ringing in my ears. Without being sure I could do it, I signed the contract. We were off and running. The clock was ticking, and it already felt like I was way behind.

A few mornings later, I got up, read the paper, thought about the prospects and made some notes. The morning after that, I had begun to do the same thing when Jean asked me what I was doing. "I'm think-ing," I told her.

Yet another wrong answer. Jean looked me squarely in the eye. There was no avoiding her lasers. "The man told you to go do it," she said, "sooooo...*go do it!*"

"I don't know how," I confessed.

"Well, you need people, but before that you need office space," she said. "Why don't you call around to some friends who know a little about commercial real estate and get their advice?"

As it has been for more than half a century, Jean's wise, wifely kick in the pants was just what I needed. After talking with friends, I began looking for temporary quarters. I needed a beachhead to begin working, and finding a permanent location would take time. I was also warned that my interim address would be really important, and that it needed to be in prime real estate, like on Park Avenue. I put on my hat and walked from one building to the next on Park. By luck, I stumbled on a building that specialized in short-term office space. When I entered, the only person visible was a receptionist. I told her who I was and what I was looking for.

She looked at me skeptically, then pushed a button on her intercom. "Yeah, Harry. There's a guy here at the front desk. Tells me he's Dan Rather," she said, dripping cynicism with every Brooklynesque syllable. "Says he wants to look at aww-fice space."

Harry appeared from nowhere and showed me a space that looked good, or at least good enough. I checked in with friends to verify that the price was fair, and within two days, I signed a contract. HDNet headquarters in Dallas was pleased at how fast I was moving, but when I bragged to Jean about it, she had just one question: "When do the phones come in?"

Telephones? I hadn't thought of telephones. That's how naïve I was. The building took care of getting them, but Jean's prodding question was a reminder that I couldn't afford to be patting myself on the back when I really hadn't done anything yet.

At about the same time, I ran into Suzanne Meirowitz Nederlander on the street. Suzanne had been a colleague at CBS; she'd left the network to start a family, and we'd lost touch after that. As we caught up, I confessed to her that I was really struggling to get things rolling. She walked back to the office with me, took one disapproving look around and declared, "You need help."

It was true. I don't have any natural instincts to run a business or to start one up—quite the opposite. I was approaching everything piecemeal, and I was overwhelmed by the process. Suzanne sat down at one corner of the metal desk—the only desk in the place—and started organizing things. She began with a list of people I needed to hire and went on from there. Finally, there was a game plan.

I needed an executive producer. Wayne Nelson came immediately to mind. Wayne is an experienced producer—been there, done that, at least twice. I had worked with him at CBS; we'd been in all kinds of tight corners together. War zones, hurricanes, political campaigns. The list is long. When I offered him a job, he was on board right away. Within a week, he had started working on program ideas.

We then took on three new employees and got more phones, but it quickly became apparent that the office was just too small. Soon enough, it became ridiculous. We ran it like a Hong Kong hot-pillow joint. The chairs were timeshares—"You get the seat for the first six hours, but you'll be sitting on the floor after lunch, because someone else needs it then." People were elbow to elbow. With no place to go, our folks started spilling out into the hallway, and our overflow eventually became a problem for the other tenants. Suzanne finally found us permanent offices on 42nd Street, where we still are today. Once we moved into something we could call home, the chaos began to settle down.

Meanwhile, of course, we hadn't shot a single frame. When we did start shooting footage, it was at a breakneck pace to meet Mark's deadline. Eventually I called Mark to tell him that we could make his October deadline, but only if all of us were squeezed dry by the end of it. He gave us a month's dispensation. Our first segment was broadcast on November 14, 2006; entitled "Coming Home," it dealt with soldiers returning from Iraq and Afghanistan. We proudly put it on the air; nevertheless, we all knew there was not another finished segment behind it in the can. We still had a tremendous amount of work to do to get the next piece ready, and the one after that, and the one after that...

During that first year, I was the quintessential frequent flyer. I spent most of my life airborne, traveling from one story to another, one producer to another. One week I was on the road in Alaska, then in Florida and finally in Colorado. Wayne ran the office when he wasn't out in the field working with me. We had people coming and going, shooting stories, scripting stories, editing stories.

Everything was a work in progress, including the staff. In addition to everything else, Wayne also supervised the hiring. "I want people with a relentless work ethic and a driven pursuit of excellence," I told him. Beyond that, however, we were also looking for monks, nuns and/ or hermits. In the early going we needed people who in the short term didn't want/didn't need a personal life—someone who had retired, or who had no children. No one was going to get a lot of family time that summer and fall. Including me. I'd come back to the office for a half day to talk to the people Wayne thought I should hire, then take off again.

Looking back on that time, I marvel that we were able to get launched—I had not realized how much of a challenge it would be to build something new from a flat-footed start. I marvel even more that we managed to keep going. Christmas break was the first chance we had to catch our breath. By the time we got back in January 2007, I thought we were rolling pretty good, only to find out that other people in the business, people I respected, had decided we were barking mad.

I spoke with two producers I'd known for years at CBS. Both of them thought we were crazy. "Your show will be off the air in four or five months," one told me, "because by then you will have simply run your people into the ground."

"Dan, this is insane," the other chimed in. "You can't possibly produce programs of this length and at the quality you demand in this short a time."

In the words of George Bernard Shaw, "People who say it can't be done should not interrupt those who are doing it." That first season we were nominated for two Emmys. My former boss Bill Small, who had been the stalwart Washington bureau chief all through Watergate, at the time chaired the News and Documentary Committee for the Emmys. He didn't pick the winners, but he let me know that people viewing our segments had been telling him that our stuff could run with anyone's. That's what I thought as well, but it was great to hear it from an outside source.

We didn't win that year, even though I believe we deserved to. More important, we're still here ... and it's now five years and counting since that manic debut season. Over that time, we've been nominated for 16 Emmys and won three—so far. Our latest Emmy was awarded in September 2011. For the second consecutive year, *Dan Rather Reports* won the Emmy for Outstanding Business and Economic Reporting in a News Magazine. The honored segment was "The Mysterious Case of Kevin Xu," produced by Kelly Buzby. Kevin Xu is a businessman who conspired with others from his native China to traffic in counterfeit drugs. These were not just so-called lifestyle enhancement drugs such as Cialis and Viagra, but prescription pharmaceuticals used to treat serious conditions, including schizophrenia, stroke and cancer. The sting operation that took him down led to his arrest and conviction. He is currently in prison.

Mark Cuban was enthusiastic about the award. "What more can I say about *Dan Rather Reports*?" he exclaimed. "Week after week they cover in-depth stories with excellence, and the industry definitely takes notice. Two years in a row for this category is an amazing honor."

We try to pursue the stories no one else is covering, including complex stories that really need the hour we can give them. Some of the most impactful are discussed below.

"Lloyds TSB: Money Launderers for Iran"

One of the first stories I broke on HDNet concerned the bank Lloyds TSB, which has its roots in the United Kingdom. (Please note that Lloyds TSB is not to be confused in any way with the more well-known Lloyd's of London, the famed insurer of such celebrity body parts as Tina Turner's legs, Bruce Springsteen's vocal cords, and so on.) Lloyds TSB is a banking operation, and in the wake of the attack on the World Trade Center, it was involved in money laundering that facilitated Iran's ability to procure nuclear weapons and other dangerous materials.

On the black market, dollars are the only acceptable currency. Lloyds TSB would send perhaps $50 million in Iranian scrip to New York; it would be returned as dollars, with the understanding that no one would reveal where the money came from. Other banks have subsequently been identified as providing similar laundering services, but Lloyds TSB is probably the biggest.

Before Robert Morgenthau retired as Manhattan district attorney, he spoke to us about the money-laundering scheme that he had discovered. "Going back to 9/11 . . . New York is always going to be a prime target for terrorists. We've got to be on the alert here and make sure we're doing whatever it takes to make it difficult."

Morgenthau discovered a building on Fifth Avenue that was owned by Bank Melli, Iran's largest bank. More significantly, it is Iran's *national* bank; in other words, it is government owned. For about 12 years, the Iranians ran billions of dollars through Bank Melli and other financial institutions in order to have the currency to purchase weapons-grade nuclear materials on the black market. And Lloyds TSB was one of the biggest money launderers—much to the embarrassment of Britain's Parliament.

But the trail of money really leads to Dubai, where I talked with John Cassara, former CIA officer and Treasury investigator. "There are approximately 7,000 to 8,000 Iranian businesses in Dubai," Cassara told me. "Many of them are the proverbial import-export concerns or freight forwarding concerns. A lot of them, quite candidly, are front companies set up by the Iranian government in order to procure prohibited goods and technologies. And they are quite effective."

The production team on this segment included Wayne Nelson, executive producer, Elliot Kirschner, senior producer, and Andrew Glazer, producer. It won an Emmy—our first in this category at *Dan Rather Reports*—for Outstanding Business and Economic Reporting.

"Pornland, Oregon"

The most downloaded episode to date of *Dan Rather Reports* is a story that first caught producer Kim Balin's attention in an editorial she read in the *Oregonian*. The editorial dealt with sex trafficking in the state and included daunting statistics on the number of underage girls who were trapped in illegal prostitution rings. Kim was especially surprised by the prevalence of Caucasian middle-class girls who were involved in a supposedly clean, wholesome town like Portland.

Portland—City of Roses, bicycles, microbreweries, running shoes... We tend to think well of Portland. The idea that there might be widespread sex trafficking in children in this eco-friendly city seemed impossible, but our investigation confirmed what the editorial had found, and then some. We discovered 80-year-old men paying a premium to violate teenage girls. The girls were supplied by former drug gangs, who were getting into the business of child sex trafficking because it was so lucrative.

Balin was joined by producer Sianne Garlick and editor Laura Minnear in following the story of an 11-year-old girl who was manipulated by an older man pretending to be her boyfriend. He took her to dinner, showered her with presents and treated her like his true love. Meanwhile, he drove a wedge between the girl and her family, after which she left home and moved in with him. At his request, she had sex with his friends and then entered the violent life of full-time prostitution.

Ernie Allen, CEO of the National Center for Missing and Exploited Children, estimates that there are 100,000 to 300,000 girls—children— who are sexually exploited each year. A nationwide FBI sting operation netted the arrest of 99 pimps and the recovery of 69 underage prostitutes. The highest concentration of children recovered was in the Pacific Northwest. Portland remains one of the worst cities (it has more strip clubs than Las Vegas), but until this episode of *Dan Rather Reports*, there were only two officers assigned to the city's human trafficking detail. Now there are four—still not enough. The problem, however, now has a much higher profile in the city, which recently set up homeless shelters with beds specifically earmarked for victims of underage prostitution.

This episode won the Ida B. Wells Award for Bravery in Journalism.

"Plastic Planes"

On September 18, 2007, *Dan Rather Reports* took on Boeing, the biggest aircraft manufacturer in the United States, just as it was about to debut its new 787 Dreamliner, which has an innovative fuselage composed largely of plastic. Boeing had staked its financial future on the Dreamliner, and it looked like the bet was about to pay off. The lightweight twin-engine plane has a range of more than 8,000 miles, enough to fly passengers nonstop from New York to Tokyo. Despite a price of $185 million or more per aircraft, the orders were stacking up.

But there were allegations of significant problems, problems that the manufacturer was trying hard to ignore. We made contact with Vince Weldon, a loyal Boeing employee who had worked there for 46 years. Weldon had a sterling reputation within the company, having worked on the revolutionary wing design of the 727, the space shuttle orbiter and studies for NASA and the Air Force. Because of his strong background in composites, Weldon had been asked by Boeing to research the ways these lightweight materials could be used in the next generations of civilian and military aircraft.

Weldon knew all about the attributes of CFRP, or carbon fiber reinforced plastic. Because it is both lighter and stronger than the aluminum now used in aircraft fuselages, it would have decisive cost-per-mile advantages. While the Dreamliner was still in development, Boeing trumpeted the news that it would save the airlines 3 billion gallons of fuel over 20 years. Since the composites would have better fatigue resistance and less corrosion than aluminum, they also offered the possibility of a longer productive life for each aircraft.

Weldon is a conscientious engineer who believed that these economic advantages were offset by serious problems—safety issues that were being deliberately played down by company executives determined to rush the Dreamliner into service. Boeing's fast-track schedule called for just six months of flight testing, culminating in federal certification and aircraft delivery by May 2008.

Weldon was not alone; many other senior aerospace engineers at Boeing had reservations about the Dreamliner as well. All of the others, however, feared for their jobs if they went public. They needed a spokesman, a highly respected Boeing employee nearing retirement. Weldon stepped forward.

It soon became apparent that the job security fears of Weldon's colleagues were well founded. Weldon's supervisor did not react well when Weldon confronted him with his analysis of the safety issues of the 787. "You're dangerous," he told Weldon, "and you need to find another job." After Weldon contacted the FAA to express his concerns, he was quickly fired. He consequently applied for whistleblower status with the Occupational Safety and Health Administration (OSHA) but was denied.

The issues Weldon and the other engineers pointed out were serious and could have greatly affected the crashworthiness of the Dreamliner. The first is that composite is brittle. It breaks, as opposed to aluminum, which bends. This translates into a lack of toughness or resilience, in particular the inability to absorb shock on impact in the event of a crash landing. Weldon also pointed out that the smoke from burning composites is so toxic that the FAA had already banned its use inside aircraft that are currently in service.

We found these concerns and others to be credible, and we were troubled by Boeing's cavalier denial that any problems existed. Beyond that, we were alarmed by the FAA's lack of response to Weldon and by their cozy relationship to the aerospace industry, especially to Boeing. Marion Blakey, who is the president and chief executive officer of the Aerospace Industries Association, is also the top lobbyist for the AIA, of which Boeing is the largest member. Even more worrisome was that two of the top FAA officials in charge of certifying the 787 had ties to Boeing.

Our report shed light on what might otherwise have been swept under the rug. It triggered a reassessment of the certification process and caused Boeing to reluctantly acknowledge potential problems with the CFRP fuselage. In the aftermath, Boeing delayed delivery— seven times. Aircraft industry wags starting calling the Dreamliner the "7-Late-7." The first 787s were delivered to ANA in Japan and were added to their operating fleet in the fall of 2011. These were better, safer airliners because Boeing had finally taken more time before delivery.

This segment, produced by Margaret Ebrahim, was nominated for an Emmy for Outstanding Investigative Reporting of a Business News Story.

"Spiritually Bankrupt"

This 2010 episode of *Dan Rather Reports* dealt with the response of the Catholic Church to the many cases of abuse by priests. Initially I had very mixed feelings about this segment, because I have great respect for the church and its charitable work all over the globe. In this report, however, we discovered that many Catholic dioceses in the United States are using bankruptcy as a shield to evade paying the victims of their priests.

There is a quotation from Theodore Roosevelt that graces the website of the California law firm of Manly & Stewart: "Aggressive fighting for the right is the noblest sport the world affords." Attorney John Manly has represented hundreds of clergy abuse victims over the past 15 years and is at the epicenter of the fight to win judgments against the dioceses. He has been involved in litigation against the Archdiocese of Los Angeles, as well as the Dioceses of San Diego, San Bernardino, Monterey, Stockton, Sacramento, Juneau and Fairbanks.

A self-described "good Catholic," Manly is shocked by the way his church has conducted itself in the proceedings. "They operate in a way you would expect Bernard Madoff to operate, not how you would expect Christ to operate," he says. "When the church defends these cases, they don't defend it in a way that is consistent with their own theology and beliefs. They defend it in a way where the victim is under attack, the family is under attack. All of the values they say they believe in really go out the window."

Manly's Newport Beach offices are less than an hour north of the headquarters of the Diocese of San Diego, which has about a hundred parishes and one of the worst records in the country for clergy sexual abuse. After the scandals first came to light, the courts were deluged with lawsuits by victims who, in Manly's words, "had been too afraid, too ashamed, or discouraged by church officials to speak up as children."

In the aftermath, San Diego became the fifth diocese in the United States to file for bankruptcy protection. According to Manly, the San Diego diocese had about 160 claims, and he was astonished by the way the church dealt with the victims. The diocese first challenged the waiver of the statute of limitations and then deposed the victims. Immediately before the first trial was to begin, the diocese declared bankruptcy, which moved the proceedings into federal court.

"At the first hearing," Manly recalls, "it became very clear that they were minimizing their assets. The diocese owned several billion dollars' worth of real property, but they listed it in the bankruptcy schedules as being worth book value. In other words, they pretended that it was worth what they paid for it. Well, the diocese has been around since the 1800s, so there were buildings worth $5 million that they listed for $150,000, which is what they had paid for it originally."

As our researchers discovered, however, this was just the beginning. There were millions of dollars' worth of church properties that were simply missing from the official list of assets that the diocese had provided, including open land, parking lots and commercial buildings. One $65 million property in particular attracted the interest of Don McLean, who was interviewed for the program. He was serving on the creditors' committee, a group appointed by the court to keep those filing for bankruptcy honest in their claims. He had also been a ten-year-old altar boy when two priests molested him. "My major motivation was to get justice for that ten-year-old child inside of me. It was not about the money. Your childhood is stolen and part of you is gone. You can't replace that with money."

It would appear that the church is clamping down on the ability of victims like McLean to find closure. More and more dioceses are playing a shell game, hiding assets and moving money that could be used to reimburse survivors. They are seeking protection under the Vatican and under the international scope of the Roman Catholic Church—and they are finding it.

Some zealous defenders of the church have taken the position that lawsuits on behalf of clerical abuse victims are an excuse to destroy the Catholic Church on a worldwide basis. John Manly responds, "The problem with that argument is that this is not what they preach. I was taught differently as I was growing up in the church—and I had some very good priests as teachers. The church is not a building. It's not the Vatican. It's not a gold chalice. It is not an expensive piece of art. It is the faith. Nobody I know wants to kill the Catholic Church. Certainly, I do not. But there is an unwillingness and an arrogance to their defense. They are really not worried about the Church surviving. What they are worried about is protecting the hierarchical and patriarchal system that has imposed horrible evil on children. That's what they are trying to protect. And the pope has direct responsibility for this. He has been in charge for 25 years and is supposed to monitor priests. And he did not do a damn thing to protect kids. And that's a shame."

Produced by Andrew Glazer and coproduced by Steve Tyler, "Spiritually Bankrupt" earned an Emmy nomination for Outstanding Investigative Journalism in a News Magazine.

Lightning rod indeed. As these summaries amply demonstrate, we have taken on some very big and very controversial topics. Nevertheless, there has been no corporate hovering or meddling. When Mark asked me to join HDNet, he told me he'd give me complete creative and editorial control. Not only that, he put it in writing—it's in my contract. At first, I was worried that I didn't have much contact with him, but I have come to understand that if I don't hear from him, that's a good thing. I used to e-mail status reports to him once or twice a week; in general I got a response within two minutes, sometimes within half a minute. It was later brought to my attention that I shouldn't contact him unless there was something I was asking him to act upon, and then I should keep it short. Anything over a sentence or two is excessive.

One of the few times Mark initiated a phone call to me was when we did the Dreamliner segment. Not surprisingly, our story made Boeing very unhappy, and their response was to smear Vince Weldon, our source. They also contacted Mark and tried to apply pressure from above.

Big mistake.

"Investigative journalism means uncovering stuff that people are trying to keep hidden," I told him when he called. "Of course that makes them angry. Hard news needs owners who are willing to take the pressure and not back down."

"Got your back," he told me. Mark was a tiger on our behalf. In person, in print and on the Internet, he defended us vigorously, so vigorously I thought for a while that I was one of his Dallas Mavericks— which in some ways I suppose I am. He did so not just then, but whenever necessary thereafter. His staunch support stands in sharp contrast to the spineless, risk-averse management climate that prevailed at CBS since the network became a relatively small cog in a larger conglomerate.

I like to think we are doing Murrow's work, even though he had a bigger staff and a much larger organization. Today there are 22 people who work full-time for *Dan Rather Reports*, and I've hired every one of them. They have regular salaries, health care and benefits. We also have another dozen freelancers who work with us on a fairly regular basis.

I am the leader of this very small but mighty band of investigative journalists. I believe in the ten magic words: "If it is to be, it is up to me." We sink or swim based on the choices I make. The buck stops here and there is no safety net.

Executive producer Wayne Nelson is Captain Can-Do. He is a complete pro, and the relationship we have is one of complete and total trust. In addition to being willing and able to do whatever is required, he has a rare and valuable gift. Wayne has a tremendous sense of perspective, an ability to see the program as an entity, not just as the sum of its parts.

Elliot Kirschner is our senior producer. Like Wayne, Elliot has an impressive ability to visualize the entire hour of the broadcast. Acknowledged as one of the best young talents at CBS News, Elliot left a promising career there to come join us, and I was astonished to the point of amazement when he agreed to come aboard. He took a real chance, and I feel so fortunate to have him.

Wayne, Elliot and I constitute the command structure, as it were, supervising the work of our producers and of the rest of our staff. "Producer" is a term borrowed from the film business—in Hollywood, Jeffrey Skoll is a producer. In the news business, "producer" means something very different. Old school as I am, I tend to think of our producers as reporters. Most of the time I call them reporter-producers, and I don't think they mind. These people are my boots-on-the-ground journalists—my story hunters, story breakers and storytellers.

They are an extraordinarily dedicated group. Each of them chose us as much as we chose them, and every one of them has a backstory. Andrew Glazer, for example, is an experienced journalist who had been with the Associated Press for several years. When he heard about what we were doing, he called and said he wanted a job. We had an opening, but the fact that he was based in Los Angeles was a problem. Because we had no money to move him across the country, I initially turned him down.

He called back and said, "What if I move myself?" I was tempted but cautious. "Give me six months," he pleaded. "I'm sick of covering Kardashians. Who knew there were so many of them?" Andrew had a great passion for the work but no television experience.

Somewhere in the back of my brain, a bell rang faintly. Many years ago, someone had taken a chance on me when I had great passion but no television experience. With Cal Jones nodding his approval from on high, I offered Andrew the job and have never regretted it. We mentored and tutored Andrew about working in television, and he has become a fine investigative journalist.

Our staff is mostly young. I take the mentoring responsibility very seriously, even as it gives me great joy. I teach, but I am also taught by our younger people, who can use a computer in ways that make my head whirl. I struggle to keep up. What I give them in return is a perspective based on a lifetime in the news. We talk about sources. We talk frequently about how to do interviews. I think I'm a pretty good interviewer—I ought to be at this stage of the game.

Rather's Rules for Interviews

• Preparation is the key. The more you prepare, the better chance you have for a good interview.

• Listening is almost as important. Listen actively. Many times your best questions come from picking up on something the interview subject has said. Don't be a prisoner of your notebook, going down your list of questions.

• Prioritize your questions. I usually separate the interview into three parts: the key group of four to six questions that I must ask; another group of the same size that are secondary but nonetheless important; and a third set to ask if we get that far.

• Pay attention to nonverbal cues. Is someone avoiding eye contact, or fidgeting, or wringing their hands? How a response is given, as well as the subject's facial expression or body language, can be very telling.

• Understand the power of pauses. After asking a question, don't pop back with another one right on the heels of the initial response. The dead air may seem interminable, but you can always edit that out. On the other hand, I've heard a lot of interesting things that were blurted out by folks who got squirrelly in the silence.

I'm proud of what we've done here. We are doing good work, and it's getting better. I firmly believe that we are just about the best place to be for young investigative journalists. And I should emphasize that investigative journalists are becoming an endangered species, just when we need more of them than ever before. All of us here are living proof that reinvention and adaptability are alive and well—that it is more than possible to apply solid journalistic principles to new media, breaking stories even in a challenging economic environment.

When we first started, finding somebody who had seen the program was harder than finding an ivory-billed woodpecker. We now have more than 23 million subscribers. Our audience still may not match that of the networks—not yet, at least—but it's growing. And we are breaking stories that get picked up by other news organizations, including the major networks. At the networks, the choice of which news gets presented each night is increasingly made from the top down, not by journalists, but by executives. There are exceptions but in general that's the way it is now. Here our stories begin the old-fashioned way, with reporters who call in to tell us they're on to something. The news begins from the bottom up, with journalists who are out in the field.

And yes, we are still turning out 42 hour-long segments annually. How do I handle it? Mark Cuban taught me how by leading by example. Hire good people, then stand back and let them do their job—which is exactly how he treats me. I've hired a remarkable staff, and I know each of them personally. I care about them and know they care about me. More important, we all care about the mission. We depend on one another to get the job done. Working at HDNet is literally a whole new world to me, a world I could not have imagined in my darkest days at the end of my tenure—and my rope—at CBS.

Cuban. Skoll. Clooney. These men renewed and extended my career far beyond what I ever imagined when I left CBS, and at a level far above what I hoped was possible. When I left, I was thinking small. I dreamed of doing a few documentaries, or maybe being head of the journalism department at a prestigious university.

I am so grateful that these three guys came out of nowhere to launch me on a whole new career. That old phrase "the kindness of strangers" comes to mind. I confess that I've learned so much from each of them, which may surprise them. It surprised me as well. As you age and as you build experience, you tend to be less and less inclined to believe that you can learn—and learn big—from younger people. And the more you age, the truer it becomes—this is where that other old phrase, "set in his ways," comes in.

My interaction with these three remarkable men has been a genuine eye-opener and mind expander, not to mention a humbling experience. We so easily become complacent; it's just human nature. They have taught me that you have to fight to keep your mind open to new ideas and new ways of doing things, and that the fight to do that is never-ending. To stay sharp, boldness, creativity and determination are required. This is how they live their own lives.

By their example, they have taught me the difference between being privileged and being entitled. They take nothing for granted. To keep accomplishing, they know they have to work hard and keep striving. Although I've long carried that knowledge somewhere deep inside myself, they have prodded me to pull it up, place it front and center and put it into sharp focus.

None of them has to work. Each of these men has more than enough money to spend all his time sailing on the Aegean Sea or lazing around the south of France. None of them does that. Instead, their money, and the privilege that money has earned, fuels them to scale ever-greater heights. Not for more money, but to accomplish meaningful and important things.

When many people reach this level of accomplishment, they throttle back. These three use the opportunity to go full throttle forward, in many cases out into the vast unknown.

And they like it out there.

Cuban may not even *have* a throttle. If he does, I've never seen it. Mark is exuberant and intense and very public. Jeff Skoll is the opposite. Quiet and laid back, he works under the proverbial radar. George Clooney is some of each. All three share a desire to make their prosperity count for something, in effect to pay it forward. They are passionate about the causes they support.

For Clooney, this involves walking a particularly treacherous tightrope. He leverages not just his bank account but his celebrity in support of worthy causes. As a high-visibility public figure, he manages to use his fame to call attention to world issues without getting eaten alive in the process.

All three are extremely bright. I've spent a lifetime interviewing and interfacing with smart people, people a helluva lot smarter than I am, and these men are highly intelligent in the same particular kind of way. Each wants to break new ground, to do things that have never been done before. And they don't care much about what other people think, because they are secure in their own passion for what they want their lives to be.

This is especially true of Mark Cuban. More than anyone I've ever known, he really does not give a damn what other people think. Mark and I click. From my standpoint, it was that way right from the start. I'm not sure exactly why, but the thought frequently occurs to me that, although we grew up in far different times and places, and although we are well apart in age, there are certain similarities in our backstories. Like me, Mark was not born with a silver spoon. His father was an automobile upholsterer in Pittsburgh, and I am the son of a Texas ditchdigger and oilfield worker. Neither of us has an Ivy League pedigree. Both of us burn to accomplish, to live a life of meaning, a life that counts for something. Different eras, different paths, but kindred memories of scratching and fighting for every inch of accomplishment. The same understanding that nobody was going to hand you success, the same hope that empathetic strangers would give you a hand along the way.

Both of us grew up believing not just in the *value* of hard work, but in the *imperative* of hard work. With that as a preface, I am continually impressed with how hard Mark works. It isn't just that he puts in long hours. This guy is all-in, all-out, every day. Mark Cuban idles in overdrive.

Perhaps most important, Cuban and I share a common belief that Americans are not getting the news they need and deserve. Not by a long shot. This strong conviction is what has fueled our success with *Dan Rather Reports*. It is our shared passion and shared willingness to put it all on the line to make it happen.

I think I am now doing some of the best, most consistent work that I've ever done. At *Dan Rather Reports* we are building the body of excellent work I'd envisioned wistfully when I was sitting alone in my CBS office in the twilight of my time there. At the time, I feared I might never get the chance, but here I am at age 80, doing the kind of reporting that I've dreamed about since I was a boy—a one-hour program each week, 42 weeks a year, of real news, hard news with an emphasis on investigative reporting. There has never been a period where I have felt happier and more satisfied and more fulfilled in the work I'm doing. My learning curve is still going up—waaaay up. I am learning about budgets and about other managerial responsibilities; I am mentoring a handpicked young (mostly) staff who shares my commitment to investigative reporting. I feed off their enthusiasm, and they key off me in return. I feel a very strong sense of responsibility to all of them. I work hard to be worthy of their respect. More than any other place I've ever been, I can't come in here any day with less than my best game.

I have this eagerness to get on the story and stick with it and dig into it. It is sheer joy for me. Part of it is the opportunity to do what I want to do and to follow my own instincts about what's news and what isn't. To be completely, totally responsible for the result of those decisions is fresh and invigorating. This is what I got into journalism to do.

Being on HDNet is so different from being at CBS. I am constantly scrambling on a high wire, with literally no net. There are many, many days when it's like trying to change a fan belt on a moving Mercedes. I wear a lot of hats, and sometimes it looks like we've all escaped from an episode of *Saturday Night Live*. At *Dan Rather Reports*, it is just me and my small team against the world. I understand that we are unlikely to have as much impact as a large network news organization. The audience is far smaller. Fewer people are going to know what we are doing. But we know. *I* know. And I judge success or failure by my own standards, not by somebody else's.

This is a venture-capital-funded business model for delivering the news. Unlike corporate network news, which is profit driven and shareholder driven, it is borderline philanthropic. Moving forward, I believe there should be a bigger place for this kind of news organization.

I also think there inevitably will be. I'm optimistic enough to believe that in the future, there may be CEOs of large corporations, companies with a news component, who will once again see a news network as a public trust and delivery of the news as a public service. They will value high-quality news as a significant company asset that doesn't show up on a balance sheet. Till that day comes, my association with Mark Cuban is as close to an ideal model as I could have imagined.

For me personally, the sense of freedom and exhilaration and accomplishment I get from coming to work every day is unimaginable. This continues to be such an education and a growth experience, and it's unquestionably affected my mental and physical health for the better. Professionally, I've never been happier, and I'll keep working as long as I have my health, God's grace and Mark's support.

After I'd been working with him for a couple of years, I had a meeting with Mark to review where we were and where we wanted to go. As meetings always are with Mark, this one was brief. "Thank you for giving me this opportunity," I said as I was leaving. "Thank you for allowing me to do what I deeply want to do. You've given me so much, what can I do for you?"

Mark Cuban drilled me in the eyes and said, "Go piss people off."

Corporatization, Politicization and Trivialization of the News

I have written before about my adventures as a journalist. This book has built on those stories, but in writing this time, I became more aware than ever of the systemic changes to American freedom and democracy that have taken place during the past couple of decades. Powerful forces have overtaken America; we as individual citizens must try to understand and contend with them.

Much of my career has been dedicated to what we call "investigative reporting." In general, I find that phrase to be redundant: Any worthwhile reporting needs to be, on at least some level, investigative. It has been my greatest journalistic love from the beginning, and my passion for it has never left me. Although I'd wanted to be a reporter even as a child, I was in college when a single experience galvanized that dream into what I realized was my life's purpose. When I was all of 20 years old, I was the one-man band—the reporter, DJ, sportscaster and also the janitor—at KSAM, the low-wattage local radio station near Sam Houston State Teachers College in Huntsville, Texas.

It paid very little, but it was my first paying job in journalism. I reported the story of a fatal house fire in the African-American part of town. Several people had been trapped inside and lost their lives. At first, the deaths were ruled accidental. Then I received an anonymous tip at the radio station. A man phoned in to say that if I checked around a bit, I would find that it was a case of arson. I followed that lead and soon learned that at least one of the charred bodies had bullets in it. That made it murder.

In the beginning, I had only a piece of the story. When I sought to report what I had, the good and decent man who ran KSAM was alarmed. "A lot of powerful people are not going to like what you've found out, Dan," he warned. "And they're not gonna like *you* for having found it out. And if you report it, they will hate you."

This was startling stuff to hear at the age of 20, and to tell the truth I sort of looked at the floor and ran my hands around the brim of my hat as I listened. I loved and respected this man, and he had been terrific to me. To his everlasting credit, he never told me not to run the story. When I told him I felt we should report what we had, however, he went out of town for a few days. He left me alone to deal with the radio station, with my story and with its consequences. Running KSAM single-handed was the easy part. The challenge was dealing with the folks with the pitchforks. What he had told me about people not liking me, and worse, because of what I had reported was all too accurate. Not only did I have to answer some nasty phone calls, I also received visits from some angry townsfolk who showed up at the station—in person.

I'm not the hero of this story. Others, including some very good law-enforcement people, eventually broke the case open, revealing all of its horrid details. It turned out that a white man, a powerful and influential person in Huntsville, had shot the people in the house and set the fire to cover his crimes.

This was the experience that got me hooked on investigative journalism. I discovered that I had a passion for getting to the truth, or as close to the truth as I could get. In this case, mine was but a small, peripheral contribution, launched by an anonymous tip. Nevertheless, I followed up and helped move the investigation along. It was a powerful learning experience, one that I've carried with me ever since.

Among the things I learned was how hard it can be to dig out things that people, especially powerful people, don't want the public to know—

things that more often than not turn out to be things that your fellow citizens *need* to know. I also learned that my boss's warning was prophetic, not just for me in that situation, but for the future as well. When you do this kind of reporting, not everybody is going to love you or respect you for it. Do a good job and report the truth, and you're probably going to catch hell. The challenge is being willing to do it anyway.

The people with the pitchforks are still out there—those who are mad because a story is too inflammatory, or too controversial, or because it makes important people look bad. The catching hell part has happened to me many times over the years—during the civil rights movement, during the Vietnam War, covering Watergate and yes, reporting on Abu Ghraib and on President George W. Bush's failure to fulfill his military service obligations. This is where the gut check comes in—you have to ask yourself whether you are willing to accept the tumultuous aftermath that inevitably follows breaking an explosive story—and whether those above you are willing to support you as well. Sometimes you get backstopped by people of integrity—the Paleys and Salants of the world—and sometimes you get hung out to dry by the Redstones and the Moonveses.

I've told any number of young people this story, because it stands as a warning: Be careful when you start a career as an investigative reporter, because if you really get into it, it will become a passion. That's a good thing: Today more than ever, the United States needs journalists passionately committed to investigative reporting. A free press is one of the cornerstones of democracy—a press willing to report the stories that make powerful people angry.

Today, however, our free press—and with it the idea of an informed electorate—is in peril. The ascent of large multinational corporations has affected every aspect of American life. This includes the gathering and dissemination of news, particularly broadcast news. The networks have grown to be part of ever larger conglomerates. We've reached the point where six or fewer giant corporations control 80 percent or more of the true national distribution of news.

News has become big business, and much of it is owned by conglomerates. In the 1960s CBS owned only six television stations. Now the major networks each have more than 40. And they are seeking to have more than 60. The consolidation of media power in the hands of a few has contributed greatly to the change in our culture. There were more than 50 newspapers, TV stations or radio stations that were either national or superregional as recently as the late 1950s. In the 1960s it was 40. Now we are down to six or fewer. Media conglomerates want things out of Washington, and through their campaign contributions and lobbying efforts they usually get them. These huge enterprises, in which news becomes only a small portion of what they do, have extensive legislative and regulatory agendas in Washington.

Those agendas are very much threatened when investigative journalists uncover stories that are embarrassing—or worse—to lawmakers. The corporatization, politicization and trivialization of the news has inhibited the ability of the news to function as part of our system of checks and balances, as had been envisioned by the Founding Fathers. Even when reporters break important stories, there can be powerful forces at work to suppress them, or water them down, as was the case at CBS with Abu Ghraib. Too often, the top priority for large media companies is not the news, but the imperative to protect the interests of their parent companies and their advertisers. Burying or soft-pedaling a story is simply censorship masquerading as good business.

Media conglomerates also have a corporate mandate to increase shareholder value. Those objectives have colored and at times overridden journalistic choices about what news gets reported and how it is presented. When breaking news happens, regular programming is suspended—regular programming that is supported by advertising, and therefore makes money. This is not a new problem. Fred Friendly quit CBS in 1966 when the network opted to run old Lucille Ball comedies in preference to airing Senate hearings on the war in Vietnam.

The profit imperative also means that news has become conflated with entertainment. News is no longer what it was when I started: a public service. Today, few people talk about broadcast news in any other way than as a ratings getter and profit center. And as a network profit center, there is now every expectation that network news divisions will generate ratings and hence revenue, just like any drama or sitcom or sporting event—which is why the pope took a backseat to a tennis match, and why we now have four talking heads in a studio shouting at one another, instead of four overseas bureaus covering real news.

The contemporary picture is at least as grim in black and white as it is on television. Traditionally, newspapers have been the sources of hard news, but today they are thinner than they have ever been. Most of them have not been able to pull out of the economic death spiral of print media, nor have they been able to figure out how to reinvent themselves to make a profit online. In the quest for profitability, both newspapers and TV news outlets have participated in the corporatization of the news, the politicization of the news and the trivialization of the news. The once indelible line between editorial content and commercial content has become blurred and in some cases downright obliterated. Some newspapers have even turned to focus groups—asking citizens what news they *think* should be covered, as opposed to informing them what they *need to know*. When the front page is full of one piece of bad news after another, we shouldn't be surprised when focus groups ask for more stories on sports, or celebrities, or dog weddings.

Chris Hedges has written a riveting essay on the subject. Entitled "Gone with the Papers," he highlights what is at stake:

We are losing a peculiar culture and an ethic. This loss is impoverishing our civil discourse and leaving us less and less connected to the city, the nation, and the world around us. The death of newsprint represents the end of an era. And news gathering will not be replaced by the Internet. Journalism, at least on the large scale of old newsrooms, is no longer commercially viable. Reporting is time-consuming and labor-intensive. It requires going out and talking to people. It means doing this every day. It means looking constantly for sources, tips, leads, documents, informants, whistleblowers, new facts and information, untold stories and news. Reporters often spend days finding little or nothing of significance. The work can be tedious and is expensive...

The steady decline of the news business means we are plunging larger and larger parts of our society into dark holes and opening up greater opportunities for unchecked corruption, disinformation and the abuse of power...A democracy survives when its citizens have access to trustworthy and impartial sources of information, when it can discern lies from truth, and when civic discourse is grounded in verifiable fact.

The question becomes what to do about it—how to preserve what Alex S. Jones has called the Iron Core of News. In his excellent book *Losing the News*, Jones talks about the Iron Core as baseline journalism, exactly the kind of reporting that Chris Hedges was talking about, where someone actually goes out in the field, gathers the facts and reports the story. Jones also calls it "accountability news" because its function is to hold the powerful accountable—both in government and in daily life.

Too many folks get their news from TV and online sources that have become greatly distanced from the Core. These news outlets merely aggregate and repackage news from other sources, which is how some of them end up quoting one another or repeating the same inaccurate information. And, of course, there are some who exploit this echo chamber—those who cloak innuendo and falsehood in the guise of news by blowing stories out of proportion, or by inventing them out of whole cloth and then repeating them endlessly. In their hands, a devoutly held falsehood becomes a powerful political weapon, the modern-day descendant of Hitler's Big Lie.

For this and so many other reasons, more than ever we need unbiased reporters illuminating dark corners, whether far away in international conflicts or close to home in corruption-riddled state governments. In city after city, nobody is covering local government. There isn't nearly enough coverage of state legislatures. The watchdog role of the press has evaporated. This is a topic of major importance. We have to prevent the Core from shrinking any further and get it to the point where it can expand again with reporters in the field.

Oddly enough, one of the few glimmers of hope in this regard is at CBS News. After I was forced out, much chnaged there, and at first it was not for the better. Les Moonves, an entertainment guy, installed his ptotégé Sean McManus as News Div president. McManus, a sports guy, set about vigorously implementing Moonves's decision to break with the past. No more Murrow tradition. No more DNA of hard news.

Katie Couric was hired away from NBC to anchor a softer *Evening News*—you might even call it News Lite. Many from Couric's *Today* show team came with her. There ensued a purge of veteran *CBS Evening News* staffers, and indeed a dismantling throught the entire News Division. Foreign bureaus, staff and budgets were reduced (resulting in greatly diminished coverage of both the Iraq and Afghanistan wars); many of the best and most experienced people were either demoted or let go. A new CBS News was created. It didn't work. Viewership nosedived; morale reached an all-time low. After five years, they gave up on the idea.

U-turn time. McManus was moved back to his position as president of CBS Sports. Jeff Fager was made the new head of the News (with the title of chairman, not president). He took the assignment after apparently being assured that he could try returning CBS News to its hard-news origins—at least as far as the now shrunken News Division could be resuscitated.

And from what I can see, Fager is on the right track. He named Scott Pelley, a hard-charging reporter and a stellar *60 Minutes* and *60 Minutes II* correspondent, to replace Couric as anchor and managing editor of the *Evening News*. Pelley had worked with me and for me for many years, and I had repeatedly suggested him to management as a promising potential successor. I am happy to say that since ascending to the anchor chair, Pelley has done a superb job, both as an anchor and as a leader. He, Fager and what remains of the tradition-oriented core at CBS News are clearly renewing their dedication to Core journalism and real reporting.

I believe that the free press is essential to the balance of powers in our government. Our system of government was born of a love of freedom and a fear of power concentrated in the hands of one, such as a king, or a few, such as an aristocracy. We have few princes and earls today, but we surely have their modern-day equivalents in the very wealthy who seek to manage the news, make unsavory facts disappear and elect representatives who are in service to their own economic and social agendas.

The people who wrote the Constitution had foremost in their minds a system of checks and balances. They set up a system based on three branches of government—executive, legislative and judicial—that were supposed to counterbalance one another. To these three, the Founding Fathers added a fourth: a nongovernmental free press that was to be the voice of the people, to force government to be fair, reasonable and democratic.

In 1823 Thomas Jefferson put it succinctly: "The only security of all is in a free press." Alas, when you have a press that has become compliant to politicians, owned by corporations and staffed by people who only want to entertain and obey their corporate masters, the plan fails. The "free press" is no longer a check on power. It has instead become part of the power apparatus itself. And this is dangerous.

In search of a solution to this problem, perhaps we should each—as individual citizens—ask ourselves a group of questions that may lead to some form of action. The following important issues were first raised by journalism scholar Lewis W. Wolfson in his book, *The Untapped Power of the Press.*

- Do we still believe—to paraphrase Walter Lippmann—that it is the responsibility of the free press to find out what is going on below the surface and to tell people what it means, so that citizens can judge how well or how poorly their government and their leaders are serving them?

- Do we still believe that the press in its watchdog role should provide information for and should spur a sensible appraisal of government, a government's policies and appraisals of all government at all levels?

- Do we understand that no matter how ever-present the reporters are with their cameras and microphones and incessant questions, that government officials have tremendous—frequently overwhelming—power to manufacture their own reputations? And that it is a duty of a free press to present the reality of what a government official is *doing*, not just saying?

• Do we still believe that each American citizen is a stakeholder in this nation and it is to that public that every elected official is ultimately accountable?

• Do we still believe that every piece of paper produced by our government is the property of the people of the United States and should be accessible to the people—with the exception of national security matters and very little else?

• Do we still believe that journalists should be the people's surrogates in Washington and elsewhere?

• Do citizens believe that too many American journalists have become at best hesitant and reluctant and at worst frankly fearful and intimidated?

• Do we understand that a war rages daily in American journalism between seriousness and sensationalism?

• Do we believe that we, the people, need the power of a free press—battered and tarnished as it may be, damaged partly through the efforts of those who despise and fear it and partly through journalists' shortcomings and failures?

• Finally, do we understand that a free press is enshrined in the Constitution and the Bill of Rights as an intended and integral part of the democratic system of checks and balances?

I do not think that it is an exaggeration to say that the future of our nation—not only journalism, but the country itself—depends upon our answers and how we choose to act upon them. Some have suggested intervention by the federal government to strengthen the press. Some have suggested that a committee to study the problem be initiated by the Investigative Reporters and Editors organization.

Others have pointed to the work being done at the Nieman Foundation at Harvard University. The Nieman Foundation promotes watchdog journalism by helping reporters understand which questions to ask and of whom, so that those in power give the public the information it needs and is entitled to receive. They have also established the Nieman Journalism Lab to help find a way for investigative journalism to survive and thrive in the Internet age. No answers yet, of course, but it's good to know that great minds are searching for solutions.

That said, there is no time to be lost: The corporatization, politicization and trivialization of the press is a serious national problem that grows worse each week. More than anything else, this problem needs public scrutiny, awareness and spirited dialogue. As Supreme Court Justice Louis Brandeis put it, "Sunlight is the best disinfectant."

Acknowledgments

When professionals such as Digby and Kay Diehl help as much as they have with this book, it is not uncommon for authors to try to hide that help. Often the author succeeds. Let me be clear: This man-and-wife team were indispensable in helping me get this book down on paper and ready for publishing. It's definitely my book in every sense, but without their help it may never have come into being.

Working full time (and then some!) and traveling almost constantly for a weekly one-hour news program, I was floundering in my years-long effort to get this book finished. Digby and Kay rescued me and the project. They were incredibly hardworking, loyal and professional to the core.

My daughter, Robin, and son, Danjack, gave constant support and encouragement, especially any time my hopes for the book sagged. In the late stages, when deadline pressures seemed insurmountable, Robin's hands-on work was essential. Her patience in going over the manuscript line by line often exceeded my own.

My brother Don and my sister, Patricia Thompson, were supportive as always. Patricia was especially helpful in obtaining photos and other materials for the book.

Paul Fedorko, friend and literary agent extraordinaire, shepherded the project superbly start to finish.

I have had the enthusiastic support of Jamie Raab, senior vice president and publisher of Grand Central Publishing, from the outset. Rick Wolff, vice president/executive editor, has been the editor every author dreams of, a bottomless fount of encouragement and sound advice. They were aided and abetted by Meredith Haggerty, Mari Okuda, John Pelosi, Giraud Lorber, Jimmy Franco, Anne Twomey, Bob Castillo and countless others at Grand Central. Never have I been so happily published.

My dear friend, attorney Martin Gold of SNR Denton, helped me accurately recall any number of important details. So did friends David and Susan Buksbaum and Suzanne Meirowitz Nederlander. Mary Mapes, one of the most high-flying eagle producers, gave generously of her time and her expertise. I owe her another trip to Rosie's. I am also grateful to other former colleagues still at CBS News. I understand completely why they would prefer not to be mentioned by name.

Lisa DeVincent deserves a salute. She is not only an excellent transcriber but a longtime loyal supporter. It was Lisa who first heard the conversations that eventually became the raw material that formed this book and was excited about their potential.

Mike Hoover, a documentarian and expert on Afghanistan, contributed his expertise. I am also grateful to Eric Wybenga, a writer who helped me in years past. I am greatly indebted to Vita Paladino and her staff at the Howard Gotlieb Archival Research Center at Boston University. They were indispensable, helping me in so many ways.

I can't say enough about my team at *Dan Rather Reports* at HDNet. They have been granitelike in their understanding and support. Phil Kim, working in his spare time, kept us all coordinated. Cherisse Cruz backed up both him and me. To Wayne Nelson and Elliot Kirschner, and to Toby Wertheim, Terri Belli, Dana Roberson, Steve Tyler, Amanda Richie, Sianne Garlick, Jeremy Rocklin, Robin Stein, Kara MacMahon, Mark Laganga, Kelly Buzby, Meredith Ramsey, Andrew Glazer, Sari Aviv, Caroline Cooper, Tracy Wholf, Dan Madden, Laura Minnear, Kim Balin, Adam Teicholz, Holly Hladky, Jessica Courtemanche, Jimson Rodriguez, Chandra Simon, Adam Bolt, Henry Bautista, Jason Pawlak, David Forde, Colette Carey: Thank you. I can't think of a better reason to put on my pants and go to work each day.

Writing a book is a marathon, not a wind sprint, and no one gets across the finish line without a whole lot of help.

In the end, the recollections, opinions and conclusions written in this book are mine. I and I alone am responsible for the contents. Not everyone will agree with all of them; about some I may well be wrong. I'm not perfect nor is my work. But I've done the best I can. I have also given credit where credit is due. My apologies to anyone I might have overlooked.

Dan Rather
January 2012

Index